THE
WIDOW'S
GUIDE TO
DEAD
BASTARDS

THE WIDOW'S GUIDE TO DEAD BASTARDS

— A Memoir —

JESSICA WAITE

ATRIA BOOKS

New York   London   Toronto   Sydney   New Delhi

ATRIA
BOOKS

An Imprint of Simon & Schuster, LLC
1230 Avenue of the Americas
New York, NY 10020

First Atria Books hardcover edition June 2024

ATRIA BOOKS and colophon are trademarks of Simon & Schuster, LLC

Simon & Schuster: Celebrating 100 Years of Publishing in 2024

For information about special discounts for bulk purchases, please contact Simon & Schuster Special Sales at 1-866-506-1949 or business@simonandschuster.com.

The Simon & Schuster Speakers Bureau can bring authors to your live event. For more information or to book an event, contact the Simon & Schuster Speakers Bureau at 1-866-248-3049 or visit our website at www.simonspeakers.com.

Interior design by Jill Putorti

Manufactured in the United States of America

1 3 5 7 9 10 8 6 4 2

Library of Congress Cataloging-in-Publication Control Number: 2023053377

ISBN 978-1-6680-4485-8
ISBN 978-1-6680-4487-2 (ebook)

For Dash and Julianne

CONTENTS

Prologue: The Matrix of Porn   1

Four Missed Calls   5

"Sweetheart, Something Terrible Has Happened"   9

Turtle and Ducky   17

Remembrance Day   25

Highway to Helena   35

Mirror, Mirror   49

The Box in My Closet   61

FUSW Playlist   71

The Pact   83

M-O-N-E-Y   87

The Coin in the Crevice   103

Splintered Candy Canes   109

The Case of the Million Money Shots   115

Rebekah 2.0   121

Ho! Ho! Ho!   125

A Mated Pair   133

Lunch with Ty   137

Death by Remorse   145

Soul Mates are Bullshit   153

The Sean Show   159

Reversal of Fortune   171

"Signs"   177

Half Your Age + 7   181

Tinfoil Hat Club   185

Six Months of Kindness   191

Let It Be   199

Chicken Stick   203

Camp Widow   211

First Anniversary   217

He's Right Here   223

Grief Doesn't Give a Shit About Status   229

Endless Stories   233

Death Doulas   237

Cold Gin Jam   243

Yellow Rose   249

A Gift Outside of Time   257

Defragmenting with Declutterers   259

The Most Hurtful Lie   269

Escape Velocity   277

A Light in the Sky   283

Epilogue   293

In Defense of Grief   297

Cherry Gin Jam Recipe   305

PROLOGUE

The Matrix of Porn

December 2, 2015
Calgary, Alberta

I'm looking at nine vaginas at the same time. I mean, technically they're vulvas, but here on my computer screen I've got the full gynecological view, laid out in a three-by-three grid, like the Brady Bunch family.

These images have been stored on an external hard drive, a small silver box I found in the apartment where Sean, my husband of seventeen years, stayed when he worked in Denver. A USB cable was already attached, just begging to be plugged into Sean's laptop. I slid the connector into the slot, the password autofilled, and I clicked through to discover something I can only describe as a key—like the legend of a map—to the Matrix of Porn.

The "key" is a directory, a guide to the whereabouts of a dragon's hoard of flesh and bodily fluids and human action. Six computer hard drives *full* of still photos and videos, along with four other external hard drives, this one from Denver being the most current. As a solo human endeavor, the creation of this enormous catalog is impressive: picture a single ant building a subterranean network of shafts and tunnels big enough to support the whole colony, all by itself. Suffice it to say, this glimpse into the inner workings of my husband's mind has been a grim revelation.

I've been studying the cache to find out what Sean was into, and maybe to uncover the deeper reasons why I wasn't enough for him. (The latter answer came readily enough.) I could never be all that is contained in these pixels: every race, every size, every gender, every shape, every age—No. Not every age. Thank God, I've found no obvious child pornography, although some of the "barely legal" stuff is dubious. There are women older than me, with lumpier bodies and yellower teeth. I scoff at myself for trying wigs and that stupid, corseted getup. Magazines told me how to "keep him interested." Like that was my job. Like that was even possible. I have one vagina. I could never compete with nine.

Sean didn't create this grid. I can tell because it's the only grid I've found. I've delved deeply enough into his organizational system to recognize patterns. If Sean had been into grids, I'd have found "boob grids" and "ass grids" and "grids of grids," cross-referenced into the boob folder; the ass folder; the grid folder . . . indexed again into the "cute" or "attractive" folders if they met those subjective criteria for him. I marveled when I discovered that physical attractiveness wasn't a requirement for inclusion into the fold.

But someone, somewhere, decided that the dark-skinned girl with the juicy-looking labia would take center spot in the nine-vagina collage, with shaved girls across the top row, and two full bushes flanking the bottom corners. Was that person a hobbyist? Were they paid to create this image? Or is there an app for this now—some kind of pussy aggregator?

I remember four or five months ago, being in bed with Sean, maybe the last time we fooled around. He studied my naked body as though it were something new, novel to him despite our twenty years together.

"You're so beautiful," he said, tracing his fingers from my hip bone to the outside of my thigh. "Everything about you." He squeezed the bottom of my right heel into his cupped palm, then swung it gently outward, opening my legs. "Even your pussy is pretty. It's my favorite kind."

Kind. The word wriggled into my ear like a larval beetle. *There are kinds?* But then he was down there and—*OooOOookay*—I let the question slide.

Now I can see that, yeah, with a sample size in the tens of thousands, there are *kinds.* I can see how Sean's drive to categorize and classify things pervaded his life so much that his comment may have slipped out in a weak moment. Or maybe it was the highest compliment he could think to pay me just then. *The championship tier. A qualifying finalist. No, really, it's an honor just to be nominated.*

And then there's a glimmer of a chance that some part of him was feeling deeply connected and longed to bring me into his secret world. There were times, as I look back, when he hinted at some of his darker impulses. Maybe, *maybe*, he was testing to see if I could love and accept him the way he was. Then again, he could have been deciding where he'd place my pussy on this particular grid.

If I wanted to know, I should have asked Sean a month ago, when he was still alive, before the two-day business trip to Houston, where he collapsed in the airport and never returned.

That night, I was just so happy to be with Sean in a tender, erotic moment. Questioning him would have jeopardized not only what was happening between us right then, but also blown up my chances for more intimacy in the future. I was already doing everything I could to spark our sex life.

For the past several years, I'd been crying in the bathroom after sex, from the *release* of it. From how good it felt to be connected with Sean and how much more of that I wanted, while at the same time not wanting to be clingy or demanding. I tried never to cry *during*, but one time, tears leaked out and Sean noticed.

"Am I hurting you?" The catchlight in his eyes flickered with the candle's glow. I reached up and pressed my hand against the side of his cheek. Freshly shaved and baby smooth like the top of his head.

"No. I just love you so much."

I can see now, I was lying when I said Sean wasn't hurting me. When he touched my body, Sean's skin ignited desire lines and I burned with the shame of my loneliness, the humiliation of needing to feel cherished, touched, and held.

When I eventually confided my discoveries in two trusted friends, each of them said, "I'm just sorry you had to find out. . ."

They'd spare my suffering, if they could. But laced into their laments was pity for Sean, whose secrets threaten to topple his legacy. No one seems to see the source of my pain was never the detection; it was the water torture of having been chosen against and lied to and neglected. I'm embarrassed to admit that in our bed that night, I wanted Sean more than I wanted to know what *kind* meant.

FOUR MISSED CALLS

The soup is everything I'd hoped from a homestyle place like Guy's Café & Bakery in the mountain town of Cochrane, Alberta: translucent onion, garden peas, resolute carrot rounds, hearty golden stock. Earnest, nourishing goodness in a stoneware bowl. My hands have been cold since this morning, waiting with Dash, our nine-year-old son, for the school bus lights to pierce the purplish November morning. I cradle the stoneware, breathing in steamy chicken broth, warming my icy fingers, but the heat intensifies faster than I can—*ouch*. The bowl clatters onto the table. Soup sloshes over the edge.

I blow on my reddened fingertips. Across the table, my mom, Bonnie, and her friend are planning their golf trip for next summer. Their conversation doesn't involve me, but I don't want to be rude, so I peek at my phone under cover of the oak tabletop. The number 4, in a scarlet circle, glares up from the home screen. *Shit.* My stomach lurches. *Something must have happened to Dash. We're more than an hour's drive from his elementary school.*

But the four missed calls share a Houston area code. *Shouldn't Sean's flight be wheels up by now?*

I tap Mom's shoulder, in the black-and-white knitted sweater she borrowed from my closet this morning. She only ever packs summer clothes on her way through to warmer climes for the winter. "Sorry to interrupt. Someone from Texas is trying to reach me."

"Oh, good. They must have found Sean's jacket," Mom offers, having overheard me on the phone with Sean, just before we left Calgary for Cochrane.

A sigh of relief. *Yes.* The security manager of Sean's hotel, calling to arrange the return of his lost jacket. I button my coat as I slip outside to make the call.

Sean had phoned from the airport shuttle, tetchy that his leather jacket had gone missing from his hotel room. He'd wanted the security manager to question housekeeping about it, but the guy had refused. "Their loss policy guarantees the customer is gone before they investigate the claim," Sean fumed. "It's bullshit."

Odd that he gave the Marriott security guy my number. Sean must have anticipated being in airplane mode. I can already imagine the grin and the pat on the butt I'll get when I meet him at the airport. He spent a fortune on that black leather bomber. Wearing it with a scarf is one of his favorite things about autumn in Calgary, when the weather turns chilly, like today, November 4, 2015.

I step out in front of the café to listen to the voicemail. A woman, who identifies herself as the ER charge nurse at Memorial Hermann hospital, drawls, "Cawl me back right away. Ms. Wa-ite."

Oh, no. Sean's hurt. The Wi-Fi's not strong enough to scan headlines. *Mass shooting. Airport bomb.* I sit down on a pine bench near the entrance to the café and, with an unsteady hand, tap the number into my phone. The nurse says, "Ma'am, are you alone right now?" I say I'm with my mom.

The nurse asks if I have a pen. I'm going to need to write some things down. *But I'm not really with my mom, am I? Because I'm out here, and Mom's all the way inside the café, so actually I am alone and this nurse is very, very wrong.* She's emphasizing the Vincent, saying "Sean *Vincent* Wa-ite." I mean, she doesn't even know his name, so what she's saying can't be true, and how dare she call and say these lies and demand that I write down the case number, but the numbers are coming so I draw them onto my notepad and repeat them back to her. Then, the call is over.

I tuck my phone, notepad, and pen into the zippered pocket of my black leather purse. The slats of the wooden bench are hard and cold beneath me. I stare at the hood ornament on a red Dodge pickup in this strip-mall parking lot. The noon sun gleams off the ram's horns and makes my eyes twinge, but I don't reach for my sunglasses. I don't look away. I just stare.

When the roar in my head quiets, I stand and walk through the doors, back into the smell of soup and cinnamon and coffee, past the lunching ladies, to the table where my mom and her friend are just finishing up. My chicken soup must have cooled enough to eat, but I don't sit down.

"They said he died." A concerned frown behind my mom's glasses. She doesn't understand. I say the name to the pinched lines between my mom's brown eyes. "Sean." I put my hand on the back of a chair to steady myself. "They said Sean died. A heart attack, they think."

───────

Someone must have paid the bill because we're back in my van. I'm in the passenger seat. Mom pulls over to drop off her friend, and then we're on the highway back to Calgary. I watch the line between the shoulder and the road. I'm not crying.

"Sean was an organ donor. I have to talk to those people. They gave me a case number. I'm supposed to call them right away. . . ."

If Mom answers, I don't hear her. Thoughts are rushing; I blurt them out as the pavement rolls by.

"Why wouldn't they let me talk to the doctor? They said he never regained consciousness. Do you think the paramedics will talk to me? . . . .

"Sean's work people in Denver. I don't even know them there. I'll have to look up the number on the website. . . .

"How? *How?* He just had a full physical, ECG and everything. He was fine. Perfect health. . . .

"So, what, I'm a *widow* now? No. That's not right. I'm just a wife."

Bless my mom for keeping her eyes on the road and her hands on the wheel even when the sharp geyser of pain cuts its way up from my belly to my throat. Tears burst through, and I press my fingertips into my forehead as I choke out my dread, "Oh, God, Mom. How am I going to tell Dash?"

"SWEETHEART, SOMETHING TERRIBLE HAS HAPPENED"

I do not pick our son up from school. Each minute on the bus is one more minute that Dash's adventurous, fun-loving father is still alive for him.

Pacing between long slats of midafternoon sunlight on my living room floor, I make the first call, to the number the ER nurse provided. The medical examiner has no answers for me. She wants me to provide contact details for Sean's doctor. *Oh, no.* We got a letter from Sean's long-time family doc a few weeks ago, announcing his retirement and the closure of his office. That's a problem I'll have to deal with later. I call Sean's four brothers and his sister, and each of those conversations feels unreal, like I'm a bad actor reciting lines.

"Michael, we've lost Sean. He died."

"Riley, we've lost Sean. He died."

"Megan, we've lost Sean. He died."

"Darrel, we've lost Sean. He died."

"Ty. Oh, Ty—we've lost Sean. . . ."

I have to do better for our son. But what can I say, knowing I'm about to cleave our little boy's life in two? Nine years of noogies and belly-button checks, and now, what? Darkness is all I can imagine. I open my phone to our last family picture, a selfie Sean took with our enormous black-and-white rescue puppy, Panda, crawling over his lap. Dash grins toothily, his cheek pressed up to the side of Sean's bald head, wielding the green chucker stick that holds Woodward's full attention. I'm scooched in next to Woodward, our cream-colored goldendoodle, a swoosh of brown hair flying across my forehead, my smile wide and open-mouthed, basking in this close family huddle.

Dash was orphaned today. His real mother is gone. I'm just a damaged remnant that looks like her. I walk aimlessly around the house until four fifteen, then go to the kitchen, where my mom is at the table with her iPad and a cup of coffee. She's holding a pen between her fingers like a cigarette. She quit smoking a year ago and probably regrets it now.

I put on my coat and boots. "I'm taking him somewhere we never go."

Mom raises an eyebrow and tightens her lips together. "How far are you going?"

"Just a few blocks. It's okay. I can drive." The keys jingle in my hand.

"Not too far!" I hear her call as the door swings shut behind me.

———

The bus stop is less than a block away. I drive there and wait in the van. My old winter jacket has a loose button on the pocket and I rub the smooth plastic between my thumb and finger. I'm sick with raw cowardice, like a horrid predator lurking, working up the nerve to destroy a child's innocence.

The yellow school bus approaches. I get out and stand at the stop. Dash steps off the bus with his head down, pulling something out of his backpack. I motion to the driver not to pull away.

"Hop in the van, bud. We have to go somewhere."

I step onto the bus. "We've had a family emergency. Dash will be home for the rest of the week." The driver, Maureen, knows all the kids' names. She gives them treats and holiday cards. Maureen waits for me to pull out, then follows us as far as her route allows, a backup vehicle escorting us to the end of our street.

"Where are we going?" Dash asks.

"Not far. It won't take long."

"But where?" He sounds irritated, like he's going to push the issue. I speed up. The last thing I want is to snap at him.

"Just in the neighborhood. A few blocks away." A forced calm voice, almost singsong. I'm driving too fast now.

"I don't wanna go anywhere. I thought Dad was gonna be at the bus."

I steer us onto some street I never drive, where Dash doesn't walk or ride his bike or have any friends. I hope the tall trees and wide lawns of this suburban cul-de-sac can absorb the shock waves from the detonation I'm about to release. My stomach clenches and my legs feel lifeless, as if they've been hollowed out and packed with sand, so heavy I worry whether I can lift my foot off the gas pedal. I pull over to the curb. We both get out of the van.

Dash stands on the sidewalk in his private-school uniform: gray pants, powder-blue shirt, navy sweater. He must've run hard at recess; sweat has curled his shaggy blond hair around the ears. He's tall and lanky, but his cheeks are still just a little chubby. Nine years old and still our baby. I kneel and put my hand on his shoulder. His blue-gray eyes, the same color as his dad's, search mine, and his unsure smile makes his braces glint in the late-afternoon sun. Two weeks until the orthodontist takes them off. Sean will never see his son's new smile. Dash notices my tears and tilts his head.

"Sweetheart, something terrible has happened. Dad isn't coming home. He died in Houston today."

Dash turns away and screams. A primal, guttural cry of pain. I reach out to take him in my arms, but he shakes me off and runs a few steps away. He's screaming and crying, his balled fists flailing against the air.

I look around, panicked, hoping no neighbors come out, hoping no one calls the police. It looks like I'm hurting this child. And I am. I'm destroying him. Coming here was stupid.

I run up to Dash, wanting to take his hand, to lead him away from this terrible moment. He's clutching something so hard his knuckles are white. I put my hand out and he passes the object to me. It's a fossil cast of a *T. rex* claw, painted in blue, green, and gray. A treasure he couldn't wait to show Sean. I hold it and wrap my arms around his warm body. His shoulders shake into my chest.

"Your fossil is beautiful," I whisper. "Let's go home."

"Dad's really strong. I'm sure he survived but they just don't know how strong he is. . . ."

I don't answer. I just drive, coasting to keep my speed down, giving Dash time to sort out his thoughts.

"He usually goes on long trips, but this one was only two sleeps. That's why I was so excited he'd be back already. . . ."

"But we were going to finish *The Bully Boys* tonight. Who's going to read that with me now?"

My mom watches us come in through the garage door. Her face mirrors our stricken looks. She's prepared a plate of cheese and crackers and starts to peel back the plastic wrap, but I wave it off. No one wants to eat.

Dash goes to his bedroom and closes the door. Mom and I talk about which calls she's made and what needs to happen next. When the dogs pester for a walk, Mom takes them out. I knock on Dash's door and let myself in.

"Is this a good place for your fossil?" I slide the cast onto the glass shelf above Dash's dresser. The curved plaster groove conforms to my fingers like a rock-climbing hold.

I remember a sweltering Singapore afternoon, the second year we lived there, Sean waving down from the *Jurassic Park* climbing wall at Universal Studios. The red rock ridges were chockablock with dinosaur skulls, vertebrae, and rib cages, the handholds and footholds by which Sean had ascended about forty feet above the ground. "Dash! Look how high you were!" Sean twisted his torso away from the wall so his little blond six-year-old could see the dinosaur tooth he'd been holding when fear froze him to the spot. "You made it all the way to this pointy old chomper!"

Dash's upturned expression was surprised, then impressed—his missing front teeth made his grin even wider—but when that smile rounded into an O, I could tell he finally understood what we'd been cheering at him a few minutes earlier. He'd been *almost there.*

From the ground, the remaining distance looked negligible, and the path to the top was obvious. Dash watched intently as Sean scaled the remaining handholds and tapped his fist against the rocky outcropping that capped the wall, like Super Mario hitting a brick block.

The attendant belayed Sean to the ground. Dash rushed over while his dad unclipped the helmet and toweled off his sweaty head.

"Can I go again?" Dash's eyes darted between Sean and me.

We'd already had a hot, sticky peopleful day. The sky was thickening and whitening, heavy gray-edged clouds rolling in off the ocean. If the deluge started before we could get a taxi back to our apartment, we might be stranded for hours, waiting out the torrent. Maybe we could come back fresh in the morning? I looked over to see what Sean thought. He was tucking his wallet back into the pocket of his navy shorts. While I counted clouds, he'd already paid the attendant. The black-haired young man strapped Dash back into his safety gear. Sean joined me on a bench to watch.

Our little boy zipped up the wall, not halting for even an instant at the tooth-hold where he'd stalled his first time up.

"Look at him go, hon." Sean squeezed my hand, his voice choked with pride.

When Dash reached the top, a cooling breeze blew over us, carrying on it the sweeping refrain of John Williams's "Theme from *Jurassic Park.*" The music must have been playing all along, but I didn't notice until our triumphant son smiled down from the summit.

I was overcome with love. Together, Sean and I were destined to raise Dash into an excellent man. It had been me who'd perceived his terror, who'd guided him back down to earth. It was Sean who modeled the path forward, who granted Dash the instant chance to overwrite "almost" into victory. One parent to ground things, and one to reach for the sky.

I yank my fingers back from the fossil cast, quashing the memory before the understanding—*We've lost the sky*—can coalesce in my brain.

Dash's teddy bear, Honda, is wet in dark brown patches on the bed beside him. I lie down next to them. Sean used to sneak back into our hotel room on family holidays to arrange Honda in funny poses for Dash to discover: Honda playing cards; Honda doing a crossword puzzle; Honda tying Sean's shoelaces together. Now, Honda is a sponge, soaking up salty tears for the man who orchestrated his mischief.

Dash and I cry together for a long time. Eventually, he says, "Can we get Grandma and color?" So that's what we do. The three of us gather at the kitchen table, around the *Secret Garden* coloring book, for as long as we can, ignoring the incoming phone calls, taking a small reprieve before the doorbell starts ringing, too. Tracing my green pencil crayon along leaves and twisting vines, I tell myself I'll never have to be afraid again. I've already done the hardest thing I'll ever have to do.

Half an hour later, I duck into my bedroom to book a trip to Houston. I don't want to leave Dash, but Sean died all alone in a faraway place. Someone will have to navigate the bureaucracy and bring him home. The one stroke of luck in this nightmare: my mom is here. She can take care of Dash for a couple days while I attend to Sean. A Web search shows my best option as the same early-morning flight Sean took to Houston two days ago, which feels grim and poetic at the same time. I'm about to click RESERVE when another Texan calls. It's the organ-donation coordinator, and she has questions.

"No, not a drug user." This is the same kind of checklist I answer every time I give blood, so I know this is going to be a long conversation.

"Yes, he's traveled outside of the U.S." *Duh. I just told you he lives in Canada.* If I have to list all the foreign countries he's been to in the past few years, I'll never remember them all. I'm trying to think. I hear the doorbell and the dogs' trampling response. "No, never paid for sex with money or drugs." I strain to discern which of Sean's brothers is here, while the Texan reads her litany into my other ear. My answers are rushed, perfunctory, agreeing with everything until I hear "corneas."

"They'll put in prosthetics," she says.

Sean's beautiful blue-gray eyes. A roadside deer; scavenger birds plucking the juiciest bits. Bile rises and I want to call the whole thing off. I choke it back. *Respect Sean's wishes. Power through.* The woman mentions the doctor's report. "We're clear to use everything else, but we won't be able to use his heart valves."

"Oh, okay. Sorry." And then, mercy. We're done.

I curl into the fetal position on our bed, facing Sean's side. "I'm sorry, hon. I'm so sorry I gave away your eyes." I pull Sean's pillow in close to my chest.

Flying to Texas tomorrow is out of the question. I'd thought I could bring Sean home with me, but the organ-donation coordinator has made it clear how much red tape is involved. They won't release Sean until after the autopsy, which could be weeks away. Then there's Dash. His dad just flew to Houston and never returned; how will he feel if his mom takes off to the same destination in the morning? Beyond that, how can I walk into George Bush Intercontinental Airport—the place where Sean collapsed today, traveling all alone? How can I sit with Sean's lifeless, frozen body on a gurney, knowing underneath the sheet he's already carved into fragments? I can't look at his face, knowing there are doll's eyes in the orbits beneath his closed lids. The parts that made him my Sean are already divvied up. And because I can't face the stitched-up remainder version, I will never lay eyes on Sean again.

I sob for a few minutes. When the doorbell rings again, I get up, splash cold water onto my blotchy red face, and go out to join my family.

TURTLE AND DUCKY

The city's new LED streetlights are blinding to look at, but the bluish light they cast is weak, with shadowy gaps between the light posts. I'm in an underlit patch now, along a stretch of road near Heritage Park, and it's so, so dark. Though it's only nine thirty, there's no traffic, so it feels like the middle of the night. *This lonely road is my life now. Darkness all around, and a stoplight in front.*

A car pulls up in the left lane and taps the horn. A middle-aged woman motions frantically for me to roll down the window. I can't tell if she's annoyed, or if the blast of cold wind is scrunching up her face, like it is mine. "Turn on your headlights!"

Oh. I squint and feel around the indicator switch on my steering wheel. My lights usually come on automatically. Click. Things look just a little brighter, the rest of the way.

Jenn answers the door in a cozy fleece onesie with a blanket over her shoulders. They've got a fire crackling, and Ty, Sean's older brother, is at the dining table with his laptop open, still in his work clothes. I hand Jenn the flash drive of photos she needs to make Sean's video montage, and she takes it into the kitchen. "Kettle's on. You want something?"

"Anything decaf." I take a seat across from Ty. He pushes his reading glasses onto the top of his shaved head. The papers around him are inked with hand notations and I see he's working on his speech. Jenn brings me a decaf Earl Grey, then sits at the head of the table with her own mug. Mabel, their long-haired tabby, jumps into Jenn's lap.

Ty puts on his readers and clears his throat. His voice tremors in the first line of Sean's eulogy, but his momentum builds toward the closing section, a powerful question upon which the whole speech hinges: "Is there a God? I don't know. And I don't know if Sean knew either. But he does now. And I hope that somewhere, in the ethereal world of heaven, Sean is smiling, having finally acquired an eternal knowledge well before the rest of us."

When he finishes, I dab my eyes. "It's perfect, Ty." His speech has captured not only the man Sean was, but the essence of his relationships with other people. Ty's done us all proud. Jenn's in tears, too, and doesn't wipe them away, but pets Mabel in long strokes down her back. Ty choked up a tiny bit at the end. Now, he's relaxing back into his chair, taking a sip of coffee. His eyes are red rimmed and his five-o'clock shadow looks out of sync with the western-style dress shirt he's wearing. He's still running Cowboys Casino every day. I bet he's slept even less than I have in the five days since his brother died.

I'm a jerk for what I'm about to ask, but a lingering queasiness forces my hand. "Would you consider changing something?"

He looks dubious but hears me out. I'm worried the question "Is there a God?" will offend my sister's family, who are Apostolic Christians. Ty nods slowly, then scratches out the lines on his printed copy. His pen doesn't make the sound of a needle dragging across vinyl, but it might as well. He says he'll think about how to revise without losing impact. We both know that's not possible. If Ty defers, he'll deliver a watered-down tribute instead of a perfect one.

Sean's service is two days from now. Ty has depicted Sean's life so well, if I blow my speech, it won't matter. Still . . . I want to try. But how can I do justice to twenty glorious years with Sean? I think back to our early days, narrowing the choices, looking for something to say.

It's December 1995, and I'm living in Osaka, Japan. Strobe lights flash blue and white, bouncing off blue-black hair, long black hair, short black hair, bobbed black hair swaying and grooving in time to the DJ's mix of Scatman and J-pop. As I cut through the sea of dark heads, I catch the eye of my friend and fellow English teacher Kathryn (whose blond hair makes her as easy to spot as I am, standing a full head taller than everyone else on the dance floor). I point toward the door. Kathryn nods, knowing I'll be back, since it's only 2:30 a.m. and we're on an all-nighter, celebrating another friend's birthday. The trains won't start running again until 5:00 a.m.

The night was cool, and I could smell ramen broth wafting from a nearby street vendor. A couple of red-faced salarymen came out of a karaoke bar across the street, still singing, their black ties hanging loose from unbuttoned collars. They headed toward Shinsaibashi Bridge. I started off in the opposite direction. The nightclub's thumping bass was fading when I heard, "Jess, wait!"

I turned around. Sean waved and ran to catch up with me. "Can I join you?"

"Sure. It's so hot in there." I'd had a few drinks early in the evening but switched to water around midnight. I didn't feel tipsy, just tired.

"Yeah, I could use a break from the electronica."

We walked for a few blocks, chitchatting. Earlier that day I'd given our mutual employer, GEOS Language School, the required four months' notice of my intention to leave Japan.

When I told Sean, his tone became earnest. "Jess, I have a problem."

I stopped to face him. We were standing in front of a high-rise development with a postage-stamp-size children's playground wedged between two apartment blocks.

"Problem?" I gestured toward the playground. "Step into my office." I pointed to a ride-on duck for him to sit on. I sat down on the neighboring turtle, my weight supported by a coil spring at its base. My knees came up almost to my shoulders. I giggled. Sean watched me with a tender smile.

He said, "The problem is you."

The coil under my turtle creaked as I leaned back. My heels dug into the playground gravel. Sean and I had become good friends in the nine months we'd known each other, but not so much that my leaving should create a problem for him. I raised an eyebrow.

"Do you remember my welcome party at El Mustacho? The night we first met?"

"Sure." That Mexican restaurant was a favorite hangout for English teachers on the Keihan Line.

"You were wearing your glasses and a flowery dress. . . ."

Creak, creeeak. I rocked back and forth slowly on my turtle. I *was* wearing a floral-print dress that night. *Sean likes me.*

I'd suspected a crush months before, during Golden Week, the favorable accumulation of Japanese national holidays when many people travel abroad. Sean and I had met for a walk by the Yodo River, and he'd surprised me with a picnic lunch. He was like Mary Poppins pulling things out of his bag: a printed tablecloth; napkins; baguette; long, serrated bread knife; jar of mayo; jar of Dijon mustard; a whole tomato; sliced deli roast beef; pepper grinder; plates; glasses; and a bottle of Grolsch beer with a cork in it. Alarm bells had gone off in my head over how romantic it had seemed.

Sean went on about our first meeting. ". . . As soon as I saw your smile, I wanted to sit next to you. When you got up to go to the bathroom, I thought, 'Here's my chance,' but then I saw how tall you were and I was like, 'Welp.'" He threw his hands in the air and dusted them off on the way down.

I laughed. I'm six feet tall, about five inches taller than Sean. He was not so wrong in assessing his chances there.

"But, Jess, ever since we spent those five days in May together . . ."

He meant Golden Week, when Sean and I were the only other English speakers we knew in all of Japan. Packing for a two-year overseas teaching stint, we'd each filled precious suitcase space with compact discs. He had all the Beatles, I had all the Rolling Stones. At his apartment, we played Name That Tune and I tried to stump him with a World War II–era song, not noticing I'd nudged the karaoke tempo dial to its slowest setting. When I hit PLAY, a satanic-sounding voice spewed out the warning "Don't sit under the apple tree with anyone else but me." We cried with laughter. Our time together had been intensely fun until the picnic scared me off.

". . . I can't stop hoping. You're not like anyone else, Jess. Even tonight—"

"Tonight?"

"Waiting for the train. I heard you singing 'Cold Gin.' I don't know any girls who know that song."

Oh my God. He's confessing his feelings because I know some KISS lyrics. Creeeeeak.

"Anyway, Jess, I really like you. And now you're leaving Japan. I couldn't live with myself if I didn't . . . Will you go out with me?"

I was twenty-four years old. My would-be suitor was twenty-eight, balding, carrying a noticeable spare tire, and looking at me hopefully from atop a rocking duck.

Sean didn't get an answer that night, but his charisma and playful tenacity wore me down. Eventually, I agreed to go out with him, for four months only. When I left Japan, we'd be through. Long-distance telephone charges were crippling and I wasn't interested in trying to sustain a relationship across continents. What I didn't understand, then, was that even as he agreed to my short-term stipulation, Sean intended to prove himself and then never let me go.

Since the time clock of our relationship corresponded exactly with my remaining time in Japan, we made the most of every weekend. In March, we spent two days sightseeing in Kyoto, drinking sake under the cherry blossoms and visiting the wild monkeys in Arashiyama bamboo forest. As Sunday evening closed in, it was time for me to head home on the train. I climbed down the ladder from Sean's loft bed.

"Hold on. Don't forget this." Sean leaned down the ladder, offering me the cream-colored camisole I'd been wearing under my work clothes when I got to his place Friday night. My face went white as I realized I'd left an important chore undone.

Sean noticed. "What's wrong?"

I felt the color coming back into my cheeks. "No, it's nothing."

He coaxed it out of me: I was a laundry delinquent. Every item of clothing in my apartment was jammed in a wrinkled heap behind the doors of my futon cupboard. I'd left myself with nothing clean for work the next morning. I had a tiny washer on my apartment balcony, but the night had turned rainy and humid. Nothing would dry on the clothes-line overnight.

A sparkle appeared in Sean's eye. "We got this." He grabbed a full-size backpack and threw on his Boston Red Sox cap. "Let's go."

It was about 9:30 p.m. by the time we got to my apartment. Sean turned his back while I sorted through my garments. We stuffed his bag and mine with all the clothes. Sean knew of a twenty-four-hour laundro-mat a few blocks from the train station and led us there in the drizzling rain.

That late, there was no one else in the place. We fed clothes and coins into the machines and sat at a little table with a chipped laminate top, the barrels of the washing machines making rhythmic white noise. The inside windows were steamy, and the smell of detergent hung in the satu-rated air. Sean pulled out a deck of cards and riffle-shuffled, raising his eyebrows at me to suggest the game.

"Honeymoon Whist?"

Sean didn't know it, so I taught him. I remember the kibitzing, but not the details of our conversation, and just moments later, all the clothes were dry. Sean stood next to me, and we folded my warm cotton T-shirts into neat rectangles and Tetris-ed everything back into the packs. Instead of starting the week with my underwear inside out, I was all set. It was the best part of that weekend.

Faced with a looming mountain of someone else's laundry, a lot of guys would have said, "Well, I'd better let you get to it then," but Sean turned my screwup into a treasured memory. By the end of our allotted four months, I'd come to know him as a man who wouldn't duck out of the humdrum or messy parts of life. We were a match. We could be together if I'd release my hang-up about the man being taller. So, I did.

As a hockey-loving kid, Sean had watched the Edmonton Oilers dominate his hometown Flames, and once we'd established ourselves as a couple, Sean used to say we were like Gretzky and Kurri. One of us could send a pass up ice and *know* our partner would be there to meet it. We had the kind of synergy upon which a dynasty could be built. "There's no *Great One*," Sean said. "Only great chemistry."

None of these are stories I want to share at his funeral. They're too intimately mine; I'd never be able to articulate them without collapsing into sobs. Their embers—the joy Sean brought into daily life; the generosity with which he supported others—are already well-known. I've been clear with everyone who will speak at the service: We are communicating directly into the ears of a nine-year-old boy who has lost his father. We will not focus on the magnitude of what we have lost, but on the enoughness of Sean's life, and our ability to translate that into a path forward.

Now, if only I could figure out what I can possibly say.

REMEMBRANCE DAY

I tilt back in the swivel chair at Ronda's station, my hair dripping wet, smelling of grapefruit from the salon shampoo. I've been wearing a limp brown ponytail with varying degrees of side-straggle all week. Bless Ronda for washing my greasy mop without comment. It's the day of Sean's funeral, November 11, 2015.

Today Ronda's hair is pastel pink, darkening to violet at the ends. Her makeup is iridescent purple and shimmering pale pink. She's styled to live under a mushroom in an enchanted forest. I hope she can work some of her magic on me. This appointment is meant to give me an hour of quiet before the funeral car picks us up, but my phone pings, and I pull it out from beneath the black hairdresser's cape.

Scott, one of Sean's best friends, lets me know that colleagues have been arriving from out of town. Scott house-sat for us during our recent three-year Singapore stint, and though I'd hesitated to leave our dogs in the care of a fortysomething skateboarder (and Tony Hawk doppelgänger, with his tall, lanky build and short brown hair), Scott managed everything beautifully. He's helping coordinate things now, as people fly in from faraway places like Tokyo and London and Houston.

I text Ty. "OMG, Slavo's coming. I think that makes it a state funeral."

Slavo was a business mentor of Sean's. We secretly referred to him as Lord Vader, not because Slavo is evil, but because he strikes such a commanding presence, it's easy to imagine "The Imperial March" playing when he enters a room. On meeting Slavo in Singapore, Ty said, "If Sean sticks with that guy, he'll be driving the Death Star in no time."

I grab my purse off the hook beside Ronda's station and take out my notebook. I jot *Slavo: Ferrari cuff links* onto the list of Sean's personal items to pass along. Slavo introduced Sean to Formula One racing, and they attended the Singapore Grand Prix together a few times. Today is probably the last time I'll ever see Slavo. It's weird to consider how many permanent goodbyes might be said today, as the drawbridge to our old life creaks upward. *Don't think about it.* I close my eyes and relax into the warmth of the blow-dryer as Ronda brushes out my hair.

Sean measured his success as a manager by how well his team could function in his absence. By that metric, he'd have earned a performance bonus for the way "Team Waite" has pulled together his funeral. If I detach myself from the reason for the event, planning it has been almost easy. I follow Sean's modus operandi and every decision becomes clear.

Food, speeches, music: check, check, check. So many helpers, from the very first moment. The receptionist at Sean's Houston office got the first call when paramedics unlocked Sean's phone. She raced to the hospital, and though they wouldn't let her in to see him, she stayed in the waiting room. Sean died with a caring person standing by, not all alone, like I feared. But even with support from friends in Houston and loved ones in Calgary, we couldn't expedite the autopsy (still pending), which has delayed the cremation, which has meant scheduling the service without knowing whether Sean's earthly remains would be present.

"You'll be late for your own funeral," I'd ribbed Sean, many times, and now it's true. His urn won't arrive until some unspecified future date.

Still, Remembrance Day is the right day for the service. Sean's father, Jack, had been too young to serve in World War II, but when Jack's own father and brother went off to war, he tracked the battles via letters, newsreels, and radio reports. After the war, Jack read countless military history books and saw every war picture Hollywood produced. Sean grew up watching *Patton* and *The Great Escape*. He played solitaire with plane-spotter cards and played Axis & Allies with his brothers. When he grew old enough, Sean read all the same history books himself. He wore the poppy with humility and pride.

My hair is almost dry. I'll have to leave soon. My stomach flutters. *Why am I just sitting here instead of practicing my speech?* I flip my notebook to the dog-eared page and rehearse under the whir of the blowdryer. "Thank you, everyone, for coming today. I'm Jessica—"

The dryer clicks off and a hush lulls the whole salon. An echoey, disembodied voice from the ceiling says, "Hello, it's me."

Ronda and I exchange spooked-out glances in the mirror, then chuckle. It wasn't God. It wasn't Sean. It was the radio, playing a hot new single. Hearing that song for the first time, it's impossible to fathom, but no matter where I go in the year to come, Adele will be there, belting out greetings to her lost love on the other side.

Ronda holds up the mirror so I can see the back of my head. Long, smooth brown hair all in place. I'm as ready as I'll ever be.

At McInnis & Holloway funeral home, in the family holding area, we stand around, waiting for the service to begin. I greet aunts and uncles (who've driven eight hours from Weyburn to be here) with one arm locked straight out in front of me. "No hugging till after," I blurt into their wide-open arms. The bossy proclamation makes them laugh, breaking the tension. They understand. When everyone has arrived and the milling about becomes excruciating, I hide in a bathroom stall, counting backward from a hundred, losing track, starting again.

One step out of the washroom, I see Sean. The back of his shaved head. His shoulders are broad and handsome in a well-cut black suit. In a joyous reversal of being left at the altar, my man is here. Who will be the one to walk into the chapel and announce, "Sorry, everyone, funeral's off . . . but hooray!"

Before I can get to him, standing in a circle with his brothers, my knees buckle. I catch myself, one hand against the wall.

It's Ty, of course. Not Sean. My eyes have fooled my brain and dizzied my heart. I about-face back into the bathroom and stand with my hands against the cold edge of the sink. In the mirror, my face is as foreign as Ty's head was familiar. Faint freckles dot my nose. The slight cleft between my nostrils makes a shadow in the fluorescent light. What is this tiny fault line in my face? Am I two halves smooshed together? Or slowly being riven in two?

Mom appears behind me in the mirror, in her black silk shirt and long draping sweater. They're the clothes she was wearing when we left the house, so I know she's real. She puts her hand on my shoulder. "It's time."

Dash looks so grown-up in his child-size suit. He's wearing one of Sean's smaller ties, burgundy with thin gold and navy stripes. I kneel down and look him in the eye. "Let's stand up straight when we walk in." He nods.

I take Dash's hand. We hold our heads up and lead the procession into the chapel. I'm humbled by the hundreds packed into the room.

My tribute to Sean omits the ride-on ducky and focuses on a time soon afterward, still in Japan, when I got the news of my grandmother's passing. The family had assumed I wouldn't come from halfway around the world and opted to schedule her service right away. Sean knew how important my grandma was to me. "Get on a train to the airport right now," he said. "I'll solve the rest." Those were the days before online booking, when people used travel agents to navigate complex airline schedules. Sean's decisive action meant tickets awaited me at the counters in Osaka, in Los Angeles, and in Seattle, where I had to abandon my luggage and sprint to make the gate. I got to Weyburn, Saskatchewan, in the barest nick of time for Grandma Bell's funeral—and I only made it because Sean said, "Go."

On the flight back to Japan after Grandma's service, I realized it would be folly to squander my chance to build a life with such a stand-up guy. I told the congregation how Sean made a home for us wherever we went, and how, in private moments, the two of us expressed a grateful bafflement for a shared life that was better than either of us could have imagined.

Now, Ty's bringing us home with the final speech.

"While our parents raised us never to pick favorites, and with no deference to any of my other siblings"—Ty looks each of his brothers and his sister in the eyes, then looks toward the congregation—"Sean was my favorite."

Everyone laughs. Everyone gets it.

"Not my favorite brother. Just simply 'my favorite.' He is the single greatest person I have ever known, and I am *honored*"—Ty chokes up, only for an instant—"to talk to you about him today."

Ty is an excellent public speaker. The congregation is relaxed and laughing along with his stories of Sean's youthful exploits. Even I laugh a few times. When Ty gets to the part I'd been worried about, he uses inoffensive language, and although it neuters his meaning, the section still flows into his final question:

"And what becomes of the spirit of Sean Vincent Waite?"

I settle back against the padded chair and wrap my arm around Dash. He's done so well, even through the hardest parts, when (we'll find out later) his forceful sobs prompted a young father in the congregation to quit smoking, lest he cause his own children similar heartbreak. We're almost there. I drop my shoulders and let Ty's words wash over me.

"Almost two years ago, our mother, Pat, passed from this world. She was a very spiritual person: a Christian and a First Nations Elder and a complicated woman. At her service, Sean told a wonderful Blackfoot creation legend that would have made Pat so proud. He concluded with a telling observation about our mother that left the door open to Sean's own spirituality.

"Pat ended every phone conversation the same way . . . . 'Bye-bye for now,' she would say. And so it was that Sean bade his mother 'bye-bye for now.' He didn't know if their spirits would cross again, but he had faith that they would. He acted with hope. And, so shall I.

"Through Sean's own example and with eternal faith that goodness shall be rewarded, I must sadly say farewell to Team Waite's greatest player.

"Bye-bye for now, Sean.

"Bye-bye for now."

———

My shattered heart mends a little, hearing what people say about Sean after the service. The swell of support seems like it might be enough to carry Dash and me through the coming dark days. Back at the house afterward, longtime friends visit and swap stories. I sit down at the kitchen table with Kathryn, who was my next-door neighbor at "Shoko Mansion" in Hirakata, and three other good friends who all met teaching English in Japan, twenty years ago.

"Remember that first Christmas party at Sean's, when he gave stockings to everyone?" Kathryn asks. "I got a toy microphone."

"Cuz you always hogged the karaoke mic!" I half-expect the jibe to launch her into Bananarama's version of "Venus," but she can't perform her wavy-arm dance routine. Kathryn's nonfunctioning left arm is tucked into a discreet black sling, which she's coordinated with her chic black dress.

Seven months ago, Kathryn was making a left-hand turn when her Acura was crushed by a Winnipeg city bus. While her son in the back seat suffered only bruises, Kathryn was critically injured—partially paralyzed—and spent months in hospital and physical rehab. Kathryn flew here on her own from Winnipeg. Her very existence at my kitchen table is a miracle, but beyond that, her blond hair is coiffed and she's rocking a stylish pair of patent leather heels to complete her outfit.

"He made that big pot of chili, with chunks of steak in it, and home-made eggnog." Of course, foodie Kath remembers the menu. I remember wondering where Sean found all the ingredients to make everything at his Christmas party taste just like home.

"And then there was the time he de-mushroomed a whole can of soup for Jess," Laurel pipes in.

"Ah yes, chicken à la king in the courting phase." I laugh.

Slavo is standing by the fridge with his coat on. I go over to say good-bye. He gives his condolences and then looks into my eyes, measuring me. A tiny frown flickers between his eyebrows and he draws a breath. He's weighing whether to tell me something. If Lord Vader has wisdom to impart, I want to hear it. I put my hand on his wool sleeve. "What is it?"

"I know Sean was taking over as CEO of that Denver company," he says, businesslike. "But, my team is just now acquiring a big company in Calgary. I was going to tap Sean to lead it." His smile is bittersweet. "Perfect fit for him. Back home with your family. Too bad. Sean's future was so bright."

I can see why Slavo hesitated. He's handed me a ticket for the woulda-coulda-shoulda train, but this news feels like a gift. I nod. Slavo's trust and respect meant a lot to Sean. Knowing Slavo made a play for that company with Sean in mind tells me he earned it.

This news matters for another reason, but I don't tell Slavo why this vision of an alternative future means more than he could guess. I take the Ferrari cuff links out of my jacket pocket and press them into his hand. "Thank you, Slavo. For everything." I hug him at the front door.

The last friends finally leave around 1:30 a.m. Everyone in the house is asleep, and the bonfire in the backyard has burned down to coals. My eyes feel like they belong among the ashes, and four glasses of wine haven't dulled the ache in my back. I trudge up the wooden steps on my deck, ignoring a couple of red Solo cups on the ledge.

Funny, coming in drunk from a bonfire in the backyard. If this were a typical summer barbecue, I'd wake up the next morning to a spotless yard and kitchen. Sean would have put away the lawn chairs, bagged the garbage and recycling and carried it all to the alley, loaded the dishes, and wiped the counters down. Sean was the shoemaker *and* the elves, but there won't be any magical cleanup tonight. Whoever wakes first will find a hell of a mess, and it will take the bunch of us to do what Sean would have done invisibly, all alone.

I strip off my black pants and blazer. I wore a dress to the funeral and didn't take off my control-top pantyhose when I changed into my pants suit. No wonder my back hurts. Dark red lines run along my midsection where the seam of the tights has been cutting into my torso. I scratch the indented skin, fall into bed, and pull the covers up to my chin. A box of Kleenex is on my nightstand. I sit back up and lay tissues over the pillowcase so that if I cry in the night, I won't have to move.

Bone weary as I am, sleep won't come. When I close my eyes, details of the service replay in my mind. I see Dash's grade-four classmates in their formal uniforms, solemn in their sweet-faced solidarity. I hear Scott, at the podium, his throat so constricted he sounded like Kermit the frog, his Adam's apple bobbing over his white collar, "Dash, buddy, if I talked all day and I talked all night, I still wouldn't fully express how proud your dad is of you, how important you are to him. Your sweet, beautiful heart, which he spoke of often, and in those terms . . . ." Dash wailed so hard, even his in-breaths sounded like moans.

I get up to check on Dash. When I tucked him into bed, I saw he'd written *I mis you Dad* in teal marker on the whiteboard over his bed. *Oh, my little lovebug.* Spelling was the only life skill Sean didn't rock. When he handwrote anything, from a grocery list to a birthday card, he'd throw up his hands and say, Forrest Gump–style, "I'm not a smart man."

I peek into Dash's room. He's curled up on his side, the light from the hallway casting a half-moon over his sleeping face. Honda is tucked into the crook of his neck. He looks cherubic and I hope his dreams are carefree and innocent. I turn my eyes to the message on the whiteboard and see he's added a red letter *s*. *I miss you Dad.*

Back in bed, my cheek wrinkled against the tissue-lined pillow, I consider Slavo's offer of a fantastic job for Sean in Calgary. What would that have meant for us? Sean's commute to Denver was an incredible strain on our entire family, but would he have been willing to jump ship so soon after taking the lead at his new company?

It doesn't matter now, but knowing we had options gives me hope. If Sean had lived, there's a chance things could have worked out better than I was expecting for our family. The pace of our lives might finally have slowed down enough for Sean and me to have some overdue conversations, face some real facts. I haven't been able to shake what happened three months ago, on our road trip to Denver, right after Dash's birthday. Since then, I'd been evaluating options and preparing in secret for a possible change. If Sean had lived six more weeks, he'd have come home for Christmas and I would have presented him with the least appealing gift imaginable: an ultimatum.

HIGHWAY TO HELENA

N o peeing on the lava traps!" I warned the dogs, but they'd heard the gate latch and were already bounding away from the mounds of red and orange tissue on the back lawn. I came around the side of the house to see two wagging tails, and two tongues licking the top of Sean's bald head. His black carry-on was beside him. No need to unpack. He'd flown home from Denver just for Dash's Indiana Jones–themed birthday party, and we'd be driving right back to Colorado, first thing the next morning. Sean saw me, jumped up, and saluted, "Reporting for duty. I'm here to build the Temple of Doom."

I laughed. Sean wrapped me in a bear hug and kissed me on the lips. "I missed you."

"Me, too. Wait till—"

"But guess what, Jess?" Sean was buzzing with energy, but his face looked haggard, with deep bags under his eyes. "The condo's painted." He sounded breathless. "I stayed up all night and almost missed my flight, but I got it finished for you guys. You're gonna love it!" He gave me a huge smile.

"You painted the condo?" The plan was for me to do that. I had five whole days to spend in Denver while Sean was working. I forced my mouth into a surprised smile. Clearly, he wanted me to be impressed.

"Yeah. Now you can just get out and enjoy Denver. You and Dash will have so much fun exploring the riverfront. It's gonna be awesome."

"Wow. Thanks, hon. You're amazing. I can't believe you did that."

"Yep. And now it's Indy time. When's the party again? And what's on the to-do list?"

I gave Sean a rundown of the plan. Kids would arrive around 2:00 p.m. and his role didn't come until later, after the kids had found the treasure. Then, I'd funnel them along the side of the house, chased by a giant boulder (my gray fitness ball), and he'd pop out, disguised as Belloq, and rob them.

"If you're heading to the garage, would you hide those toy snakes under the workbench?"

"I'm on it."

An hour later, I was in the kitchen, filling a hinged plastic monkey head with red gelatin and crushed pineapple. I'd never put this much effort into Dash's birthday before. I took pride in not being a parent whose kids had such elaborate and Pinterest-y parties that nothing in their adult life would ever compare. But we'd just moved back from Singapore and Dash had spent much of third grade making new friends at school. With only a handful of kids available for a summer party, I wanted to make this one memorable. Sean came in with a smear of gray dirt on his head, his jeans were dusty, and part of a decayed leaf clung by its stem to the cotton knit of his polo shirt. I picked it off and dropped it in the compost.

"Monkey brains?" The chunky red mush looked too convincing to taste test.

"Mmmm, disgusting."

"No, really, do you want some? It's just strawberry Jell-O."

"Nope. Haven't had carbs since Monday. I'm feeling great. Come check this out."

Sean led me into the garage and closed the door behind me. The windowless space was lit only by two tiki torches, glowing red. Sean had rigged them with LED flashlights wrapped with red cellophane, so they gave off just enough light to show the entrance to a cave. I took a torch and crawled inside, wincing as my bare knees crunched on the gritty, cold concrete. I could hear my heart beating. My red tiki light glinted off a strand of gold beads, guarded by a human skull. The path twisted around as I entered the deepest part of the cavern, where battery-powered candles flickered to reveal a pit of snakes. I'd bought those damned rubber snakes at the thrift store, but in the eerie light they were slithering, eyes glinting. One might have hissed.

I didn't have room to turn around, so I crawled backward, faster than I'd have believed myself capable, and hollered to Sean, "Okay! Turn on the lights!"

Sean grinned as he watched me emerge. He explained how he'd built the structure out of ladders, poles, and tarps, and how the labyrinth ended in a wire dog crate, "for that claustrophobic feeling."

"Claustrophobic?" I said airily. "Maybe for some." The cave was going to blow the kids' minds. I held up my hand and Sean gave me a high five.

Around one thirty, Dash came home from the friend's house he'd been visiting while I got the party ready. He spotted Sean and ran into a wide-armed hug. "Dad!"

"Happy birthday, bud-bud!" Sean squeezed his newly minted nine-year-old tight and lifted him off the ground. "You'll be taller than me soon, little man. Shoulda got you a shaving kit." He rubbed Dash's smooth cheek. "Yep, stubbly. We'll swap your present out for a razor."

"No!" Dash laughed. "Can I climb the tree out front and wait for my friends?"

"You want your first shave in a tree? Well, it'll be tricky, but okay!" Sean chased the giggling Dash to the front door. When he came back, I offered Sean a pepperoni stick, one of his favorite snacks.

"Nah, I had some almonds on the plane. Not hungry at all."

He'd stayed up all night painting the condo and almost missed his flight. There was no way he made time for breakfast. All he'd had to eat in the last sixteen or seventeen hours was a pack of almonds? This worried me.

"I invited the Greenes to barbecue tonight," Sean said, looking at his phone.

The Greenes were the kind of close friends we could hang out with in the short, messy space between birthday party and road trip. Most of our life seemed to hang in the messy spaces, these days.

"Their kids will love that fort in the garage." So would their dad, Jeremy, one of Sean's preferred people with whom to nerd out over board games and sci-fi movies. "Wait. Are you trying to show off your snake cave to Jeremy?"

Sean laughed, then sidled up to me, flirty. "Snake? Cave?"

The doorbell rang, and the party was on. Many shrieks later, after the kids had been snaked, bouldered, robbed, caked, and picked up by their parents, Dash watched his new *Merlin* DVD while Sean and I cleaned up the house and yard. In the twenty minutes before the Greenes came over, Sean had just enough time to grab a quick siesta in the hammock, his Indiana Jones hat over his face, shading him from the late-afternoon sun.

———

At five thirty the next morning, my alarm went off. We'd stayed up later than was wise, building an outdoor fire and having gin and tonics with the Greenes, while the kids roasted marshmallows and the dogs basked in all the attention. I rolled over to tell Sean he could keep sleeping. I'd take care of the packing and prep to get us on the road. Sean wasn't there.

Rubbing my eyes, I pulled on some travel duds and went to make coffee for Sean. The kitchen was spotless, and through the window I saw the backyard was also immaculate, the ashes even swept out of the fireplace. I packed the leftover barbecued burgers and veggies into a cooler, keto-friendly food for the road. I was packing the dog food and dishes when Woodward and Panda rounded the corner into the kitchen, panting from a hard run.

"I need that bowl," Sean snapped.

I looked down at the floor, at a chip in the tile in front of the dishwasher. He could use any bowl for dog water; it didn't need to be the one I'd just packed. I felt an inkling of alarm, but thought if we could get into the van without a blowup, he'd nap on the road, get into a better mood. I handed over the bowl and left Sean to water the dogs.

Dash was still asleep, Honda curled under his chin, and I roused him with a gentle hand on his shoulder, hoping he'd stay sleepy enough to snooze away the first couple hours.

Once the van was loaded, I offered to drive the first shift. As we headed south on Deerfoot, I said, "Thanks for cleaning up the yard and everything."

"Mm-hmm."

"Did you get any sleep at all?"

"No time."

I gestured to the blue travel mug in the cupholder. "This coffee's for you."

"I get Starbucks in Lethbridge."

He said it like I was an idiot for not knowing his routine. He said it like Fuck. Off.

My preference would have been to turn on the radio, but I deferred. Keep things quiet. Let the wheels hum an asphalt lullaby.

"Did you lock the back garage door?"

So much for quiet.

I'd set the alarm and checked the locks on all the doors to the house, but not the door to the garage. "I assumed you locked it when you cleaned up."

"That's right. *I* cleaned up. And you went away for a week without even checking all the doors." Something was happening to Sean as he tried to provoke me. His voice was resonating in a slightly lower register. His face wasn't exactly contorted, but the muscles were slack across his cheeks and around his eyes. He looked like a different person. And the vibe he was giving off—if there had been milk in the coffee mug, it would have curdled.

I didn't want to fight. Dash was dozing in the back and we were twenty minutes into a seventeen-hour road trip. Sean could be moody at times, but this was extreme. If we were to have any chance of halting the careening spiral of his mood, he needed food and sleep, pronto. Otherwise, something bad was about to happen. I took a deep breath and said nothing.

"I cleaned up. I loaded the car. I do *everything* for you."

That wasn't true. Just last night he'd thanked me for all my hard work getting the birthday party and this trip ready to go, and for taking care of Dash on my own for the last two weeks. He thanked me, genuinely, every time he went away—which was often. If Dash only aged on days when he saw Sean, he would have just turned five years old, not nine.

"Sean, I appreciate everything you do for us. I got up at five thirty this morning to help. I packed this food for you. Why don't you eat something?"

"Don't try to manage me." He spat the words through gritted teeth.

Holy fuck. I turned on the GPS, knowing he'd take over if I started to program our destination. The last thing I actually wanted was to know how many minutes were left in this car ride. The diversion worked, and we went back to driving in silence.

In Lethbridge, Sean got coffee but no food. He switched to the driver's seat so he could show his NEXUS pass at the border. I leaned my head against the window and pretended to sleep, but kept my eyes open a crack so I could peek at the rugged Montana scenery through the watery filter of my eyelashes. *Goddammit. We should be belting out songs from the playlist I made, or listening to Bill Bryson's* A Short History of Nearly Everything. *Our road trips are fun. What a waste.*

After a scenic rest stop in Montana, Sean refused my offer to drive. Back on the highway, I pulled out my phone and started tapping notes, listing places I wanted to check out on our next trip, when Sean would be back to his normal self.

"I know what you're doing." Sean's voice was full of contempt, like I was an idiot if I thought I was fooling him.

My eyes widened, but I didn't look up from my phone. *Does he think I'm J. Edgar Hoover, keeping notes on him?* "What exactly is it you think I'm doing?"

He didn't answer. In my peripheral vision I could see his frown. Slit eyes glaring at the highway ahead. Hours passed. Khrushchev and Kennedy locked in a moving vehicle.

By Helena, I couldn't stand the tension in the car anymore. We had enough daylight to carry on for a few more hours, but I said, "Can we stop here? I always build to Helena in Ticket to Ride, might as well see the place." I offered up the board game reference to lighten the mood, and to remind Sean of who he was. Who we were.

We found a dog-friendly hotel. The place was clean and welcoming. Once we'd settled into the room, I ventured, "Let's grab dinner and hit the pool after."

"Not hungry."

Dash and I walked to a nearby Tex-Mex place. When we finished our fajitas, I ordered a green salad topped with steak and sliced tomatoes. I put it in the minifridge when we returned to the room. Sean was watching the sports highlights on TV.

Dash darted past me, swim trunks in hand, into the bathroom to change. I took my swimsuit behind the partition wall and crouched down to undress there, so Sean wouldn't see me naked. My softest parts might not withstand his hostile gaze.

Dash came out smiling, ready to rip, in his shark-print trunks and matching swim shirt. "Your family will be at the pool if you care to join them," I said, cursing the sound of my flip-flops for undermining my haughty exit.

The over-chlorinated water seemed just right to bleach away the ugly vibe of the day. Dash and I splashed around. We were the only people in the pool so I took a chance: "Otters holding hands?"

When he was little, Dash used to swim up to me on his back and take my hand. I'd kick up my feet and become the mama otter. At nine, he was surely past the game, but, bless his heart, he rolled onto his back and floated next to me. I was buoyant with my little otter for half a minute, then Dash swam away. Some other kids came in with toys to dive for, and he joined their game.

The hotel room was empty when we returned. We showered off the chlorine and got into pj's. I felt better and hoped what the swim had done for me, the long dog walk was doing for Sean. As Dash brushed his teeth, I put Honda on his pillow and pulled *Harry Potter and the Chamber of Secrets* out of his backpack. *A nice tuck-in, a good night's sleep, a new day tomorrow.*

I tidied up the room and stowed Dash's backpack under the desk, next to the wastebasket. There, in the garbage, sat the unopened steak salad.

My back molars gnashed as I took in the still-sealed carton. The only reason to chuck that salad was to spite me. Worse, Sean apparently had no interest in leveling out. His body had to be tired, had to be hungry, but he wasn't feeling it, and any gesture toward solving those problems was an affront to his autonomy.

Dash and I read a chapter, and I stayed next to him in bed until he fell asleep. As I lay wondering how Sean would be upon his return, I thought about how much of my life I spent waiting for Sean. Waiting for him to get home from work, waiting for him to return from business trips, waiting for him to be in the right mood to talk about . . . anything. Since I married Sean, even my name was Waite.

Click. I heard the door unlock and the jingling collars of the dogs coming in. My eyes were closed and I tried to fake sleep, but Panda came straight to me and nuzzled his wet snout in my face. I reached my hand out to pet him.

Sean sneered, "You're sleeping with Dash?"

Well, I am now. "Oh, I guess I dozed off here so maybe I'll just stay."

I yawned, trying to seem drowsy even though my nervous system was hyperalert. "You can watch TV if you want, it won't bother me."

"Why am I even here?" Sean growled. Fair question. I'd been wondering the same thing myself. He muttered something else from the other side of the room, but my earplugs filtered out the venom, filtered out the meaning. Dash was mercifully asleep. I could feel his chest rising and falling beside me. I tried to match my breathing with his, a full-body cradlesong helping me through the night.

Around 6:00 a.m. Woodward barked. I looked around the room. Sean's bed wasn't rumpled. His laptop was open on the coffee table, and I could hear him running water in the bathroom. It was impossible to know if he'd slept at all.

We packed quickly. I grabbed fruit and muffins from the continental breakfast table on our way out. Sean got only coffee. He was into his third day without eating or sleeping. But what if this had started in Denver? It was unsettling to realize I had no idea where the deep end of this mood swing actually began. Sean's health had been compromised by extreme mood swings before. Five years earlier, a bad spell had almost ended our marriage. I was wary and watchful as we made our way out of the hotel.

Sean took the driver's seat and our GPS picked up where we'd left off the previous day. All was quiet until Sean said, "We're on the wrong road. We've missed a turn somewhere."

Uh-oh. Our minivan was nine years old, and we'd never updated the navigation system. When I turned on that map, I'd never intended to actually rely on it. We were still in Helena, passing through an industrial area. "Okay. Let's pull over and figure it out."

Sean kept driving. I waited a few blocks for him to pull over or correct our course, but he kept going. I suggested pulling over again. Nope.

When I said it a third time, Sean shouted, *"Pull over where?"*

"Anywhere!"

He cranked the wheel hard to the right. We thumped over a curb. The dogs yelped and snarled in the back, tumbling over each other.

"Jeezus, you're going to kill the dogs!"

"I'm going to fucking kill *you*!" Sean slammed the van to a halt, throwing the dogs into another frenzy. I tried to stop the coffee mug from tipping out of the cupholder. Hot black coffee spilled onto the floor mat and dripped from my fingers as I righted the cup. Sean's words reverberated in my mind. I wasn't in physical danger, I was sure of that, but Sean had meant the hatred in those words. I could feel their dark ugliness. I wiped my hands on my capris and turned to confront him.

Sean was gone.

He'd bolted, leaving the driver's door wide open as he sprinted across the parking lot. For a short-legged guy, Sean was a shockingly fast runner, and there's no way I could have chased him down, even if I'd wanted to.

I turned to Dash in the back seat. His eyes were Disney-character big. He let out a weak giggle and said, "Nervous laughter."

"It's okay, sweetheart." I patted his hand, letting my fingers rest against his forearm. "Dad won't hurt me. He just said that, but he doesn't mean it." Dash nodded, still unsettled. "Let's take Woodward and Panda out for a pee."

The dogs were anxious to be sprung from their too-close quarters. Woodward strained on the leash, pulling me toward a tree, where I found the van's keys glinting in the gravel at its roots. Sean must have flung them when he took off running. I picked the keys up and felt the pull of their power. I could lead my charges back to the van, start the ignition, and drive away. The getaway urge was almost overwhelming. But Dash's voice would be strong, too, protesting against leaving his dad behind. And I could picture my future embarrassment, dissecting the desertion on a marriage counselor's couch. I put the keys in my pocket.

We walked to a shady corner of what I now saw was an auto-body-shop parking lot. It was Sunday and the place was closed. Having privacy was a mercy while we trespassed, awaiting the conclusion of our domestic dispute, or whatever this was. The dogs lay down, panting. I gave Dash my phone so he could play Cut the Rope.

Eventually Sean made his way back. I saw him coming and loaded everyone into the car, put the windows down all the way. *No, windows up in case there's yelling or another death threat.* I started the ignition, cranked the air-conditioning on full blast. "Sweetie, come and get me if it starts to get hot in here, okay?"

Dash nodded and went back to his game.

I crossed the parking lot to meet Sean in the shade. He told me he was going on to Denver without us. *Oh, yeah? How?* I knew better than to ask. My voice was measured: "Think carefully about what you're doing."

"I know what I'm doing." Sean wasn't confused in any obvious way. "I'm leaving my family." He seemed rational and in control, yet he wasn't really Sean. His voice, his body language, everything about him was off by a few degrees.

If we'd been in Calgary instead of a parking lot in Helena, Montana, maybe things would have turned out differently. I'd have recruited help from the family and tried to get Sean into the Rockyview Hospital. Maybe he'd have benefited from treatment. Maybe he'd have lived past November.

But we were lost, outside our home country, and there was no one to help. No one to look after Dash or the dogs. No trusted physician to refer us. Even if Helena had a psych ward I could find, Sean was talking about leaving us. I couldn't persuade him to eat a bloody salad, let alone commit himself into psychiatric care. I'd have to take him in against his will, and he was presenting as completely lucid. The person at the intake desk would see me as a desperate, spurned lover, not a concerned partner upon whom it was finally dawning that her husband might be having some kind of nervous breakdown.

"We get to Denver. Dash and I drop you off, then we turn around and go home." My syntax was deliberate. I spoke to Sean the way he spoke when proposing a plan. He nodded and put his hand out for the keys. I shook my head and got behind the wheel.

The vast Montana grasslands blurred in my peripheral vision, and the lines on the asphalt looked bleary. My face muscles were relaxed and my breathing was normal, but water poured from my face. I didn't wipe it away. Still driving along the highway, I was afraid to move.

Something terrifying was happening inside my chest. My heart was being dipped into molten metal that chilled and solidified on contact. With every beat, layer after layer of armor coated my cardiac muscles, making them more and more constricted. Shrunken and shrinking. Cold and colder.

I remembered a gut-wrenching scene in the movie *Blue Valentine*. Ryan Gosling and Michelle Williams enacting, with exquisite precision, the moment their marriage died. *This is it. Our* Blue Valentine *moment.* I loved Sean, but nothing would be the same for us after this. He'd abandoned us in an auto-body parking lot. He'd threatened to kill me in front of Dash. Maybe my heart was steeling itself against the future.

Five years ago, in a less dramatic episode than this one, Sean said he was leaving us. My most pressing worry back then wasn't how to save the marriage, or what would become of Dash and me. It was who would act as a grounding influence for Sean. He struggled with bipolar and OCD tendencies. We talked about it sometimes, usually in the aftermath of a blowup, but Sean didn't have the familiar long cycles that might have helped us recognize a need for medical intervention. In 2010, I didn't know about rapid-cycling mania and depression (mixed bipolar), so I thought Sean was managing, most of the time. Beyond that, we'd each visited loved ones in the psych ward, and neither of us was clamoring for a more in-depth experience there. We handled things in-house. I'd emailed Scott and confided that Sean wasn't well.

Scott was surprised. In all the time they'd spent together, the only thing he'd gleaned about Sean's mental health was that you could mess with him by turning the pen and pencil on his desk a few degrees off perpendicular. Other than that, Scott considered Sean a Master of the Universe, omni-capable and always in charge. I don't know how seriously Scott took my request, but I asked him to look out for Sean, to whatever extent their friendship allowed.

My steeled heart told me this time was different. No one's grounding influence would be enough to keep things from disintegrating. Sean had spent the past couple months lining the nest of a condo in Denver. A perfect bachelor pad for him. He had a U.S. visa, but Dash and I did not. If Sean was ready to fly, his landing pad was prepared, and I'd be left holding the bag in Calgary, which, for practical purposes, I was doing already.

Things had been untenable even before this current crisis. While our three years in Singapore had seemed almost charmed, Sean's work pace had been grueling and landed him in the hospital more than once, with exhaustion and diverticulitis inflamed by continual air travel. The company let him go—just weeks after awarding him as a top performer—as soon as we moved back to Calgary. Sean saw the termination coming, a political housecleaning after Sean's boss lost a horse race for leadership of their division.

I was happy for Sean to have time off to recuperate, but because our contractor hadn't completed the final renovations we'd paid to have done while we were overseas, we were forced to live in an active construction zone. For Sean, who was razzed by having his pen nudged a few degrees off-center, the discombobulation was emotionally taxing. He fought through and found a new job right away, succeeding the founder of a technology company, splitting his work time between Australia and Denver, while keeping a family in Calgary.

The stress of a job loss; or an international move; or a chaotic home renovation; or taking over a midsize corporation . . . each would have been hard enough on its own. Cumulatively, it was far too much for one human to bear. Sean told me he'd deleted all our family photos from his phone because he missed us so much, he couldn't see our faces without breaking into tears. It had become too embarrassing for him, crying on airplanes.

He cried at home, too, and flew into rages over the smallest trigger. Recently, after one of his rants, I'd said, "If Dash ever treats me the way you do, I will have failed as a mother." None of us could continue with things the way they were.

As we cruised down the Montana highway, I glanced at Sean in the passenger seat, typing feverishly into his phone. He sensed me watching and looked up. "You're crying," he said kindly. "Do you want me to drive, hon?"

"I'm driving," I said, monotone. "I'll talk to you when we get to Wyoming."

By the time we pulled over at a rest stop, Sean was visibly calmer and conciliatory. He wasn't leaving us anymore. It was as if blowing the lid off the pressure cooker had fixed things for him. Or maybe he'd tapped into the secret reserve of functionality he relied on to get through his workdays. I don't know. He felt better, so he went on as if everything were better. But it wasn't better for me, because the metal slug in my chest was still there, tight and painful with every beat of my heart. The ultimatum had already formed in my mind.

Christmas, I thought. *I have five months to get my ducks in a row.* At the end of December, Sean would be home for two whole weeks and we'd finally have time for a serious conversation. I'd present the options: you get real help with your mental health, or I'm out.

MIRROR, MIRROR

Sean sat, shoulders slumped, in a white undershirt and boxers at the end of the bed. He'd put on one dress sock while the other hung from his pinched fingers like an empty black banana peel. I patted his shoulder on my way past, "Morning, hon."

This was 2010, five years before the scene in the parking lot in Helena, Montana, and one year before we moved to Singapore.

If Sean replied, I didn't hear. I'd already left the makeshift bedroom we'd set up in our unfinished basement, and I was hobbling up the stairs to get four-year-old Dash ready for preschool. It usually took about forty-five minutes to get him fed, dressed, and walked to the community center at the end of our street, but I was moving at half speed. We'd been tackling renovations for four years straight. It had ground us both down. My back was out so badly, I walked with a limp. Sean was dressing himself in stop-motion animation. More stopped than animated.

When I got home again after dropping off Dash, I went downstairs to start the laundry and was startled to see Sean, partially silhouetted in the light of a bedside lamp, still in his underwear, still slumped, the black sock still dangling in his hand. Lifelessly still.

My heart plummeted. I focused on the wrinkles across the back of his undershirt, looking for proof he was breathing. My lower back twinged as I ran toward him. "Are you okay?"

I knelt in front of Sean. His eyes were faraway, almost catatonic. "Sean, do you need help?"

It was only a moment, but it felt like interstellar time and galactic distance until he came back. "What? No! I'm just daydreaming."

"You've been putting your sock on for, like, an hour."

"I'm just tired."

No doubt he was exhausted. Sean's career had been taking off in recent months. At the office, he was putting together strategic-partner deals, presenting to senior management, and mentoring junior employees. He left the house by 5:30 a.m. so he could work his twelve-hour day and still be home for dinner with Dash and me. After he'd read the bedtime story and tucked Dash into bed, Sean worked a couple hours toward finishing whatever room we were renovating—currently our bedroom—hence the basement campout.

That night I made a baked-chicken dish Sean really liked. When we were done eating, I put my hand on his hand. "What was that, this morning?"

He let out a full-body sigh. "Something's wrong with me. You just made one of my favorite dinners, but it tasted like nothing." He'd scraped most of his portion into the compost bin. "Everything on the plate looked gray. It's like I've gone backwards in the *Wizard of Oz* . . . out of Technicolor and into black and white."

We talked for a while and came to terms: I'd find a contractor to finish our bedroom, then the renos would come to a hard stop. Unless things got worse, Sean would keep performing his job. The higher-ups at the company were considering him for a promotion, and Sean wanted to avoid any possibility of rumors, so I promised not to tell anyone he wasn't well. We also promised to each get medical help: I'd see a sports medicine doc for my back. He'd see a psychiatrist. Tears pooled in Sean's eyes at the end of our conversation, reflecting the first rays of hope after a long dark night.

————————

The day he met with the psychiatrist, Sean came home visibly relieved. He relayed the details as he changed out of his work clothes into a T-shirt and shorts. "The doctor was great! As soon as I began describing my symptoms, he knew just what to ask me about."

"Like what?" I sat down on the end of our bed, so he could get past me to hang up his suit jacket.

"Racing thoughts, feeling frustrated when other people are slow to get to a conclusion that's obvious to me . . ."

"Did you tell him you can't sleep without listening to radio shows all night?"

"Yeah. He said it's all normal for the kind of person I am."

I don't know what my face did, but inside, I balked. Even though I was happy Sean felt understood and less alone, and even though many kinds of operating systems can run a human brain, I failed to see how a person could work so hard and sustain constant sensory input twenty-four hours a day. Never quiet, never still. "Normal" or not, it was agitating for Sean. He could never rest. I could see its toll in the throbbing veins of his temples.

"So, did he give you a prescription? Or a follow-up appointment?"

"Nope." Sean smiled and waved his hands in the baseball signal for "safe." "I'm all good."

The business-as-usual part of him had converted a bunt into a home run. I felt so abandoned I wanted to shove the *DSM-5* up the doctor's ass. How could anyone make an accurate assessment in a fifty-minute hour, without ever talking to the person's family? As if there could be any certainty Sean had disclosed the full truth. As if whatever was afflicting Sean was fully contained within him. Granted, he didn't seem catatonic anymore, but he was still exhausted and joyless most of the time. His bad moods were polluting our home like a moose carcass rotting in a shallow pond.

The medical intervention for my back would sideline me from mom duty for about a week. Sean came home from the office with what seemed like the perfect solution: his coworker Rebekah had a live-in nanny who could look after Dash. Rebekah's daughter was also four, and Rebekah had a six-year-old son. Sean would drop Dash off at her house in the mornings and they'd carpool to work together. Rebekah had invited us for dinner that weekend, so everyone could meet.

———

Rebekah and her husband, Brett, lived in a new subdivision at the edge of the city. I held a box of cupcakes on my lap while Sean drove us there. When he veered off the freeway onto the correct exit, I noticed he hadn't programmed the GPS—something he did even for trips to our neighborhood Safeway, because the technology was new and he loved using it. Unaided, Sean steered through the sea of triple garages and nouveau-gingerbread trim and parked in front of a large two-story house, near a developer-made lake.

"Have you been here before?"

"What? Oh, yeah." Sean rubbed at the end of his nose. "Rebekah has dropped me off from work a couple times. Last time I had the van, I returned the favor."

On days when I didn't pick him up with our shared vehicle, Sean rode his bike or took transit home from downtown. He hadn't mentioned catching a lift with anyone. He walked around the front of the van and opened the passenger door for me, then took the box of cupcakes. I stood up and adjusted my coat, trying to look less crooked and gimpy as we made our way up the walk.

Rebekah greeted us at the door with a straight white smile. She was casually dressed but meticulous in appearance, wearing a slim necklace and a bare makeup look that could have been airbrushed on. She reminded me of a morning-show host, big bright eyes beckoning the attention of a bleary audience. In their foyer, her daughter peeked at Dash around the tapered leg of her mom's designer jeans. Rebekah's son rolled in with a flashing toy. The three kids hit it off, and Dash was led away to check out their rooms.

After dinner, the nanny took the kids downstairs to play in the basement. Rebekah got up to make espresso from a fancy machine on a granite side-counter dedicated to coffee accoutrements.

"Apprentice barista?" Sean asked, going over to look at the appliance.

I stayed at the table and chatted with Brett. He was a smart and personable guy who'd been a semipro hockey player in his youth. We knew some people in common. I told him about my basketball coach in Weyburn, who shared a temperament with his legendary goon of a brother, hockey star Tiger Williams (who holds the NHL penalty-minute record to this day).

Brett was broad shouldered and good-looking in an everyman way, the perfect high-end sales guy. As we spoke, I remembered something Sean had told me a few weeks earlier. Brett had been involved in a bad business deal, putting their family finances in jeopardy. At the time Sean mentioned it, I didn't know who Brett or Rebekah were, and Sean had been vague on the details . . . they'd lost a nest egg or had to take a second mortgage, something like that. According to Sean, Rebekah's salary was barely keeping them afloat. It was none of my affair, and I felt sheepish having this intimate knowledge resurface as Brett and I bantered about sports.

It was none of Sean's business either. *Why had Rebekah confessed something so personal?* Sean was Rebekah's manager. *Had she been angling for a raise?*

"So, are you going to coach your kids' teams?" I asked Brett, trying to steer my mind back into our conversation.

The espresso machine made a loud hum, and over the noise of it, I heard Rebekah tittering. I turned around and saw Sean making a play for the big silver dial on the coffee maker's control panel. Rebekah blocked him with her petite frame. He nudged her out of the way with a gentle but exaggerated hip check. Her face was coy, a duck-lipped pout. She crossed her arms over her formfitting black T-shirt and giggled, tossing her long dark hair. Sean adjusted the knob and grinned at her in triumph.

There he was: the shiny, playful partner I'd been missing for months; the man I'd been trying to resuscitate, to transfuse with my own joy. He still existed.

It was me—stiff-backed and sore on a hard wooden chair—who didn't exist. I felt as invisible as the fragrance of freshly ground coffee.

Brett was still talking about the Little League system. *How is he not noticing this open flirtation? Maybe Rebekah is like this all the time?* Brett's lack of reaction gave me nothing against which to calibrate Sean's whiplash-inducing change in demeanor.

Sean came around with lattes for everyone, and Rebekah followed with a plateful of colorful cupcakes. I'd bought those cupcakes from Crave gourmet bakery. Brett was sitting at his own dining table. Yet, somehow, Sean and Rebekah had become our hosts. My mental Merriam-Webster's went berserk.

host *verb* (1)
- to assemble in an army usually for a *hostile* purpose

host *noun* (2)
- biology: the larger, stronger, or dominant member of a *symbiotic* pair

Moist dark crumbs scattered onto the plate as I separated the cupcake from its crinkled paper. I bit through thick, sticky peanut-butter icing, and the jolt of buttery sweetness overrode my brain waves before they collided into the miasma of hot feelings in my belly.

"Mmmm. Looks delicious." Rebekah stood at the end of the table. I nodded, my mouth still full of the fudgy mass.

"Wish I could partake." She smoothed her hand down the contour of her hip, along the seam of her tailored jeans. "But I'm watching my sugar."

―――――

The next night after dinner, Sean said, "I checked in with Rebekah. The nanny and kids are all on board. We're good to go." He smiled. "Also, she said you were very pretty." He nodded, as if seconding the opinion. As if it were a compliment.

Pretty. Not friendly; not kind; not well-intended-but-off-the-mark with sugary confections. *Pretty.* I heard it as a subtle volley against a romantic rival. Pretty, sure, but who was the fairest of them all?

Until that dinner, the question of Sean's fidelity hadn't crossed my mind. Not because either of us was morally impeccable, but because Sean seemed to be burning out and simply lacked the energy. Their display in front of the coffee maker had opened the door to my suspicions, and this attempted flattery crystallized the threat.

"So kind of her, but I talked to Angie today and she said they'd take Dash. That would be best, don't you think? Such good friends already, and Dash can still walk to preschool." My friend Angie had swooped in like Wonder Woman.

Sean seemed nonplussed but didn't argue the change in plans. When we went to bed that night, he fell asleep right away. I was still drifting off when a light flashed, bright enough I could perceive it from behind my closed lids. Sean's phone stood upright on the charger, still glowing with a text message from Rebekah: "Goodnight."

I shook Sean's shoulder.

"Hmmm?" He rolled toward me and opened his eyes.

"Are you having an affair with Rebekah?"

"Huh?" He propped himself up onto his elbows. "What? Jesus, no. Why would you even—"

I flipped on the light so I could study his reaction, then passed him his phone. Over Sean's shoulder, I watched him enter his passcode, 1139, the house number of his childhood home. The message popped open. His face was neutral.

"Goodnight. . . .Yes, steamy. I can see how you got affair from that." He set the phone face down on the headboard ledge.

"Don't give me that. You don't just send someone a goodnight text at midnight. That's intimate. And last night you two were totally into each other at the espresso machine."

"Okay, yeah." Sean rubbed his eyes. "I know what you're talking about, but you've got it wrong, hon. I love *you*. You're my chother." He looked groggy, but earnest, calling back a sweet thing our little niece used to say: *You're my chother because we love each chother.*

My heart was still racing. I looked at his phone, tempted to flip it over in case any more messages came in. I pointed at it instead. "Well then, what the hell?"

Sean sighed. "The last few months have been hard, right?"

I raised one eyebrow. *Go on.*

"So, I was fed up with life in general, and Scott was struggling, too"— I nodded, knowing Scott and Carmen were separating—"and Rebekah was devastated over Brett's tanked investment. The three of us went for a beer after work one night and just sort of . . . bonded over everything. Our kids are all the same age, we're all on the fast track at work. We're close friends, almost a support group."

Hmmmm. If this is true, I'm relieved Sean is getting support from some-where, given that abomination of a psychiatrist appointment.

As I thought about it, I could see what he was saying. It explained his knowledge of Rebekah's family finances, and also how Sean had been privy to details about Scott's marriage breakup. Sean had been raving about how amicable Scott and Carmen were through the separation. He deemed it "the best divorce ever," in a weirdly proud way.

"Okay, but that doesn't explain why Rebekah's wishing you good-night."

Sean looked at the clock. "We were working on a project together until about half an hour ago. She thought I was still up. It was like saying goodbye to a coworker on your way out of the office."

I didn't like it. But it did compute.

Things went on, more or less as they had been, for a few more weeks. I had the sense of treading water. Sean continued to invest in his friendships with Scott and Rebekah, but he was more open, and I was invited to join them socially. Scott had developed a stand-up comedy act and was advancing in Yuk Yuk's Funniest New Comic contest. We went out a couple nights to see his set, and everyone laughed a lot. The nightmarish fog seemed to be lifting, even as the dark days of winter dragged on.

Then, Sean's godmother died. She'd never been married and had no siblings or children of her own. Sean and I had been helping her, in her old age and infirmity, and it was Sean who was called to view her body prior to cremation. I offered to go with him, but he wanted to do it alone.

He came home ashen and sat across from me on our sectional sofa. "I'm leaving you." Sean's face was barren and sagging, like he'd lost the musculature to shape expression.

The blood rushed out of my hands and I sat there, cold. "Why?"

"I'm not happy. I haven't been for a while. Things aren't getting better."

"And you think it's because of me?" My stomach was churning, but I kept my voice level.

"It's not you, exactly." Each phrase took effort, as though he had to give himself the Heimlich just to get the words out. "It's just . . . my life feels like constant drudgery."

Oh, for fuck's sake. His life was legitimate drudgery, but it's not like joint custody and maintaining two households with half the resources was going to be a *relief* from hard work. No one in Sean's family was divorced, but I'd grown up in a broken home and knew he was choosing a harder road. But then I saw it: Sean's romanticized interpretation of Scott and Carmen's split. Best divorce ever. Scott standing tall on the comedy stage, commanding the room, making everyone laugh. Scott winning, round after round. It did look appealing, from the audience side.

"Look, I can't stop you from leaving, and I won't try. If you don't choose me, then I don't want to be with you, either. But this won't work like you think. You can't outrun yourself."

He frowned and nodded. It didn't matter. He was stationed at the north pole and all roads led south. He was out.

"Is there someone else?" I was asking about Rebekah, but didn't want to say her name.

"No." He shook his weary head. "I shouldn't be with anyone right now."

I silently agreed. Maybe it would actually be best for me, too, to have this break. We looked sadly into each other's eyes, consolidating the goodness in the fifteen years we'd spent building a life together, before pressing the self-destruct button. All the tension dropped from his face. He said, "I don't have the energy to train a new person."

Those words hit me right in the solar plexus. I also took them as a backhanded acknowledgment: Sean knew he was difficult to live with. I was a damn good wife to him, whether I'd been *trained* that way or not.

We moved into separate bedrooms. Without telling him, I saw a lawyer. Sean probably did the same. Before we told Dash or executed the logistics of the split, we had a single session with a marriage counselor. I don't remember how we found her, but she was a seasoned therapist, nearing retirement age, who'd seen pretty much everything that can happen in a relationship. Toward the end of the session she said, "I don't normally disclose to clients what I'm about to tell you: I'm not fundamentally opposed to divorce. Sometimes it's best for everyone. Sometimes it's best for one party. Either way, those couples are better off parting ways. I don't see that for the two of you. There's so much love here. There's something worth saving."

I don't know if her words made a difference or exactly how things shifted over the next three months, but by springtime, Sean felt better and wanted to reconcile. I had never wanted the divorce, so I agreed.

Eight months after that, Sean's company offered him a three-year stint in Singapore. We recognized the tremendous professional and travel opportunity, but it was scary—for both of us—to consider the move. *What if we leave our entire support system then hit another bad spell, like the one we've just been through?* At the same time, we needed a fresh start.

Putting 8,185 miles between us and whatever the hell happened, or was about to happen, between Sean and Rebekah was copacetic with me. Scott was available to house-sit and care for our dogs, who wouldn't cope well with the long flights and tropical heat. Dash was about to start kindergarten, and keeping our home would let us spend summers in Calgary, maintaining close friendships, picking up where we left off after Dash finished grade two. As the plan took shape, Sean asked only one thing of me: "Promise you'll tell me if I'm ever falling into a funk like that again."

I held his hands and shook my head no.

"I love you, Sean, and I would if I could. But you won't believe me when you're in that state. I can't be your brain police. The only thing I can do is take you to a doctor."

THE BOX IN MY CLOSET

There's a box in my closet.

Yesterday, when I got home from the hair salon, just ahead of Sean's funeral, my front door swung into the box with a thud. As I heaved it aside, I noticed the customs label:

Shipped from: Houston, TX.

Contents: Personal effects of deceased person.

The funeral car had been due to pick us up in thirty minutes, so I pushed the box down the hallway, into my bedroom, and into my closet. The closet door doesn't close all the way now.

A lot of people are still in my house. Mom's staying here, along with my sister, Catherine, brother-in-law, Darren, my fifteen-year-old niece, Hannah, and eleven-year-old nephew, Isaac. I'm glad the younger cousins are here, hanging out in the basement with Dash. Friends and other family members are coming and going. Sean's sister, Megan, came by to take the flowers to a nursing home. So many flowers. I don't know how Megan fits them all into her van. By late afternoon things are tidy, and most of the commotion has died down. I go to my bedroom for a nap, but I can't relax—because my closet door is open.

The sharp corner of a ruler cuts cleanly through the packing tape, and I lift the box flaps. A white trash bag sits on top. Sean's belt buckle pokes against the flimsy plastic, creating ripples of strain. Inside must be the clothes he was wearing. I set the white bag aside, revealing Sean's black computer bag and carry-on. I take Sean's wallet out of his computer bag, and a money clip with US$600 in folded bills. That's more cash than I would ever carry, but Sean's dad had used a money clip, too, and Sean liked to be like Jack.

I pull the cards out from the wallet slots: debit, RBC Visa, Citibank Mastercard, and another Visa I don't recognize. Maybe it's a company card, but it's only in Sean's name. There's a business card for the Marriott security manager, the guy who wouldn't confront housekeeping about Sean's leather jacket; and a loyalty card from the 420 Apothecary in Denver. I look more closely: it's a Frequent Bud Buyer card with seven of ten stamps already filled. My stomach sinks. That's a *lot* of weed consumed in the few weeks Sean spent in Denver.

Not long ago, standing in our living room, I asked Sean if he'd tried smoking legal cannabis in Colorado. He looked me right in the eyes and said, "No." A definitive, unflinching no.

Why lie? I only asked because legalizing marijuana was a political issue in Canada and I wondered how things would change once pot was decriminalized. I knew Sean occasionally smoked with friends and didn't think it was a big deal, now that we were back from Singapore, where a drug conviction could have resulted in deportation or the death penalty.

Oh my God. If Sean lied to me, did he lie on his life insurance application? My hands are trembling. I've barely eaten all week, but I feel like I might vomit. Sean's new employment contract hadn't included any life insurance benefits, so he'd filled out the application paperwork and had the physical exam, but no policy has come in the mail. I used to work for an insurance company. There will be a lot of scrutiny on a claim like this. If there's an opportunity to deny, they'll take it.

What's shaking me up is not just the likelihood that our financial future is now in jeopardy over something as stupid as Sean smoking a joint . . . okay, many joints. That would be bad enough on its own, but there's also the ease with which the lie was lobbed in my direction. My natural inclination was to catch it. The pool of dread in my stomach deepens.

I don't want to bring this revelation to the kitchen table for discussion. I can equally imagine Darren, my sister's husband, dismissing the whole thing: "For Pete's sake, can't a hardworking fella blow off a little steam?" Or inflating it into a full-scale condemnation: "How could Sean be so selfish? I expected better of him."

Why risk tarnishing Sean's reputation and painting him as a drug abuser in the eyes of my family? Until I figure out what this means, I'd rather keep it quiet . . . but if I have to carry this alone, I'm not going to make it. My mom and sister are at the kitchen table having happy hour.

"Mom, will you come with me to get the mail?" Mom's pursed lips strain against the oddness of the invitation. The mailbox is across the street, barely far enough to be worth getting your coat on, even though it's dark and freezing outside.

"Sure." She sets her glass next to the mountain of paperwork she's been organizing all week. Medical records and utility bill transfers and legal documents and lists of people to send thank-yous for flowers and food and gifts of money. I spent last week preparing for the service. This week we're going to have to tackle all that paper. I crumple inside just thinking about it.

Outside in the crisp night, I tell mom about the weed card, and the lie, and my worry about the insurance claim. Her face mirrors my concern, and my shoulders drop a little when I see that she's *getting* why this feels like such a big deal to me, and why I'm so afraid. "There's something else."

"Go on." I can see Mom's breath as she answers and I talk quickly because I know she hates to be cold.

"The day before Sean died, I tried to buy a croissant at a little bakery downtown. It was three dollars, but my debit card was declined for insufficient funds. I called Sean, and he transferred money into our checking account." I lean in closer and lower my voice, even though there's no one else in sight. "But there's twenty-five-hundred-dollar overdraft protection on that account, so not having access to three dollars means we were way in the hole. And I just charged over twelve grand on Sean's funeral." I look down at the sidewalk where a white ring of frost has formed around a small puddle. "Mom, what if I'm broke?"

Mom puts both her hands on my shoulders. "Look at me, honey bunny."

The streetlight shines off her short silver hair, freshly curled into the wavy style she prefers. Years of sunshine and smoking have worn deep creases into her face, like pre-folds in origami paper, making it easy for her to form her usual expressions. Right now, though, her skin looks soft as an angel's robes.

"You're going to be okay. We were broke your whole childhood. Don't you remember?"

I let out something between a scoff and a laugh. "Yeah, I remember."

Mom's brown eyes are soft, but her jaw is set. "I'll go to the bank tomorrow and arrange to loan you enough money to keep you afloat while we get things sorted out."

I melt with relief. Not just because my immediate financial pressure is gone, but because my mom has reminded me of who I am. Someone who knows how to live below the poverty line; someone who knows how to live without a man in the house; someone resourceful and capable of providing for herself—albeit with some big-time help in the interim. I wrap my arms around Mom's waist and she wraps hers around my shoulders. It's the reverse of how we normally hug. I'm taller than my mom, but right now she feels so much bigger than me. Her body is soft and warm. I don't feel cold at all.

———

I retreat back into my bedroom to finish going through Sean's belongings. I lay out the clothes he was wearing on his side of the bed. The clothes from his suitcase go in a laundry basket. In the mesh pocket of his shaving kit, I catch a glint of gold. I unzip the pocket, remove his migraine medication, and there tucked into the corner is Sean's wedding ring. *It's here!*

The morning Sean was due to be cremated, I'd panic-called Houston's Brookside crematorium, pacing my bedroom floor as I waited to be connected with the woman who'd been handling my case. Her name was Jessica, too. Before she could even finish her hello, I blurted, "Jessica! Please don't burn Sean's wedding ring!"

She put me on hold and went to check. His body hadn't gone into the cremation retort yet, but "His wedding ring was not among his inventoried items."

My forehead pressed itself against the bedroom wall, creating a third point of balance for my unsteady feet. I thanked Jessica and said goodbye, but didn't hang up. I held the receiver and imagined a crowd of onlookers in the Houston airport, gathered around a collapsed lone business traveler. Among them, one opportunist checked the unconscious man's pulse. There was no pulse. The ring slid easily off the dying man's hand and into the living palm. I'd heard of this happening. I couldn't believe it had happened to us.

I press the gold band against my heart, then slide Sean's ring onto my thumb, where it fits perfectly. We had the bands custom-made: melting down gold from the wedding ring my dad gave my mom, and engraving Japanese kanji characters for our names around the outside. Our Canadian goldsmith carved them as best he could, but the characters aren't perfect. Japanese friends who've tried to read the inscription have smiled sympathetically and shaken their heads. The symbols were only meaningful to us. A pidgin language for two.

I used to imagine if anything ever happened to Sean, I'd wear both our rings on my left hand like this, one on my ring finger and one on my thumb, with a gold chain joining them across the palm. Now, that doesn't seem practical. The chain will catch on everything. I'll have to imagine some other way of joining them together, but I don't have the energy tonight.

In bed, I'm under the duvet while Sean's empty white dress shirt and jeans lie beside me on his side of the bed, a vanished mannequin. I considered bringing them under the covers with me. It's hard to know what will lend comfort and what will hurt—that line is thin and constantly shifting. Presumably, there's a path to healthy grief expression and a path to Norman Bates. Tonight, those paths seem separated only by the thickness of my down blanket.

I stare at the curve of Sean's shirt collar. I stare at the color of the wall, bleached khaki, like sand on a cold winter beach. I stare at the birch shelf of Sean's nightstand. I stare at everything at once. The paperback Sean had been reading comes into sharper focus: *The Norman Conquest* by Marc Morris. *The Norman Bates Conquest. Hahaha.* I can tell I'm punchy by my own stupid joke. *Go to sleep.*

The Norman Conquest. One of Sean's dreams had been for his career to take us to London for a few years. Based there, he could have steeped in British history, using weekends and holidays to visit important historical sites. At the top of his wish list was a walking tour of the Battle of Hastings, where William the Conqueror led the Norman invasion in 1066. I wonder how far Sean read into his book, and what he would have said if someone had told him he wouldn't live to finish it.

Maybe I'll finish it for him. I sit up and flip through the pages. They're full of details I can't concentrate on right now. I put it back and unplug Sean's iPad from the charger. The battery's full, but the lock screen blocks me. I type his usual passcode, the house number of his childhood home. 1139. PASSWORD FAIL. Sigh. It probably doesn't matter if I have to wipe the memory and reset this device, but I don't want to. *What if there's some clue on there about what happened to Sean? Or a partly written message he didn't get to send me?*

I type in 1066, the year of the Norman invasion. The screen opens. *Wow.*

Ping, ping, ping, ping. It sounds like a slot machine paying out, notifications popping up on Sean's calendar. *Ping, ping, ping . . . My God, he's missed so many appointments already.* I look at his schedule for November 4, the day he died. A phone meeting in the morning. Time blocked off for travel. His flight confirmation details. Oddly, no in-person meetings in Houston that morning. Things would have been so much easier if he'd come home one night sooner. If he had to die, he'd have wanted to be in Calgary.

I look through the photos on Sean's iPad. They're almost all of airplanes. Some are from Wings Over the Rockies Museum, others are pictures he took himself: silver wings extending into azure sky, into sunsets, clouds below. There's the odd screenshot, whiteboards with meeting notes. Nothing on that camera roll would make Sean cry on an airplane.

Looking at planes has lulled me to drowsiness. I turn off the iPad and lie back in bed. Tomorrow's to-do list: tackle the paperwork. *I should write the hospital's phone number beside my bed so I can call the medical examiner as soon as I wake up.* I open Sean's iPad to search Houston hospitals. I type in *H-O-* and the field self-populates: "Houston escorts."

My mouth falls open, and I scramble to turn on the lights and grab my glasses. I'm barely breathing. The browser history starts with Houston escorts and drills down. First, by "Galleria" (the area of the city where he was staying); then by type of service; then by price. Then girl, by girl, by girl. This isn't browsing behavior. It's shopping.

The last girl is a large-breasted brunette, whose profile says she's twenty-five. After her, the browser history lists porn site after porn site.

My breath has stopped. I launch myself into the bathroom, splash cold water on my face, then sink to the floor, clutching the nubby cotton bath mat in my fists, and trying to get some air into my lungs. My chest hurts so much, I might be having a heart attack myself. As soon as breath comes, I'm sobbing, writhing, and trying to keep quiet because this room shares a wall with Dash's bedroom. *The shower.*

Under the jet of hot water, I take shallow, jagged breaths and cough them back out. Sitting on the pebbled shower floor, I shake and moan until the water runs cold down my spine.

Back in bed, covers pulled up to my neck, I go through the search history more slowly, looking for any way I could be misinterpreting. There's no evidence to support a mistake in my perception; the wedding ring, tucked away handily at the top of his carry-on; the seemingly unnecessary extra night in the hotel; and the most damning evidence of all, his missing leather bomber. The Marriott security manager was savvy to shield housekeeping from a false allegation, especially if the prime suspect—and her cleavage—had walked past security cameras in the hotel lobby.

Did my husband spend his last night on earth with a prostitute?

I don't know. I wasn't there. But I didn't read all those Nancy Drew books for nothing.

I can neither tell anyone about this nor keep it inside. I search with my own computer until I find a counselor available for an urgent appointment first thing in the morning, which is only four hours from now.

How long has this been going on? I flash to a weird conversation Sean and I had last year, when we were getting ready to move home after three years in Singapore. I mentioned Orchard Towers and Sean gave me a baffled look.

"Y'know, *Orchard Towers*? Four floors of whores? Even its Wikipedia entry calls it that."

Sean, face overly perplexed: "Oh, is it? I had no idea."

That was like living in Amsterdam for three years and not knowing there was a red-light district. I'd chalked Sean's daftness up to fatigue, but what if he was laying cover?

During our time in Singapore, Sean and I lamented the horrifying ways women from neighboring countries were exploited, both as domestic helpers and as sex workers. One of Sean's more despicable colleagues talked openly about his penchant for what he called LBFMs, "little brown fuck machines." Sean hated that guy and spoke of him with contempt, but had Sean's disdain belied some fear of missing out?

Orchard Towers was a twenty-minute walk from our apartment. Beautiful young women worked there. A guy could help them earn a few extra bucks to send back to their families, couldn't he? Tip overgenerously? Make himself into a minor hero for a night? I cringe over the easy leap in logic that could lead an otherwise indignant, righteous man to the unlimited human buffet at Orchard Towers.

My imagination runs amok. Every business trip Sean ever took is an international sexcapade, too spicy for Larry Flynt. Thai lady boys. Nubile Indian girls with tantric talents. Long-legged Muscovite models contort themselves in, around, and on top of Sean in my perverse waking nightmare.

In the morning, I get Dash onto the school bus, say goodbye to my sister's family, and tell my mom I have an urgent appointment. The psychologist's office is in Currie Barracks, twenty minutes from my home. She's got a nice floor lamp and a Persian wool rug over the concrete floor, but the room still feels cold. I sit on the couch and we go over the consent form. By the time that's done, and I've blurted out the most basic outline of my situation, the session is more than half over. I cut to the chase: "What if there's more to find out? I'm afraid I'm only scratching the surface."

She takes visual stock of me. I hate imagining what she must see: a beyond-desperate housewife turned widow, almost hyperventilating, in dog-hair-covered yoga pants. I sit still and breathe deeply through my nose, trying to look calmer than I feel. She says, "I won't be prescriptive or tell you what you should do—"

I frown and look down at my salt-stained black winter boots. Her professional guidelines call for her to be nondirective with clients, of course. I have a psychology degree myself, so I know the jig. But I'm spending $180 of about-to-be-borrowed funds on this session. I won't be able to ask my friends for guidance because I'm not bloody well telling them about this. I could really stand to have a bone thrown my way.

"But"—she leans toward me and softens her voice—"I would ask you to remember that you've been through a lot of trauma in a very short time, and we can never unsee things once we've seen them."

I hear that. The sex show from Sean's iPad is still playing like a projector behind my eyes. I nod. It makes sense to give myself a break.

I say, "I know sexual promiscuity and drug abuse are textbook signs of bipolar mania. Sean was never diagnosed, but we both grew up in families with mental illness. His mom was hospitalized several times and on lithium for years."

The psychologist makes a note on her file. "So, he never saw a psychiatrist?"

"No, he did see one, five years ago. But he must have snowed the doctor because he came away without a treatment plan."

She nods. "That's actually pretty common. Was Sean quite intelligent?"

"Brilliant." My eyes well with a different sort of tears. "And witty as hell." *Jesus, why am I singing his praises. Shut up.* I take a Kleenex from the box on the table.

"So, what do you want to do next, now that you know all this?"

"Well . . . " I lean back against the leather couch and look up toward the ceiling, "If this was someone else with bipolar, I wouldn't even judge them. I would know they were acting out their symptoms, and it wasn't personal. But Sean was lying to me—*big* lies—every single day. It feels like everything he ever said to me must have been a lie." My face feels hot. I cover it with my cold hands to stop myself from breaking down, but it doesn't work. "I mean . . . did he ever even love me?"

She waits for my emotions to run through, then stays silent, so I feel like I have to say more.

"I guess if I could have something to hope for, I'd wish to bring *my* Sean—the good one—back to life in my mind so I could forgive him. But how?"

She nods. It's a big question, and not one she'd attempt to answer. How does a devastated spouse forgive a dead one?

FUSW PLAYLIST

Back home after my counseling session, it's early afternoon, Mom and I sit at the kitchen table pushing paper. Our only conversation is around setting up errands for later in the week. Around three o'clock, I walk the dogs. Under the overcast sky, the landscape is a monochromatic blur of gray, white, and dirty brown. The sun is already low by the time I get home. I lie down for a quick nap while Mom preps supper, making sure to be up by four thirty when Dash gets home from school. *This schedule could work.* As long as my mom's here to help, I can function during the day, have a little rest, get through dinner, and sort my emotions out at night.

Dash's daily pattern seems to be shaping up in much the same way as mine, but he doesn't get the nap. He looks so pale and drained. At tuck-in time he's under the covers, his head propped up on a bright blue pillow with a skiing raccoon on it. He says, "I'm the only one in my class who doesn't have a dad." He's fiddling with Honda's fur, which is matted in places, and thin under the arm. I hope the stuffing doesn't start coming out. Honda first showed up in Dash's car seat, a promo gift from the salesman when we bought our minivan. I don't know if this little bear was built to be so intensely loved. "Jaden's parents got a divorce," Dash goes on, "but he still sees his dad on the weekends."

"Y'know what, Dash?" I sit up to face him, stroking his soft blond hair across his forehead. "It's hard to be the only one in your class without a dad. It was almost the same for me because I didn't live with my dad or see him on the weekends. That started when I was ten, so just a little older than you."

"Did your dad die?"

"No, but he was really, really sick. He didn't want us to see him like that, so he stayed away and we missed him."

"I miss Dad, too."

"I know sweetie, so do I." *But he's lucky he's not coming home tonight, the lying asshole.* I struggle to force my anger back down. Dash needs something from me right now. I think about what I hated most about being the only kid in my class without a dad: feeling so abnormal.

"Dash"—I put my hand on top of his hand on top of Honda—"you're the only one in your class who doesn't have a dad right now, but every single kid in your class . . . all their dads are going to die. I hope it's not for a long time, but when their dads die, then they'll know how you feel right now. And you'll know how they feel because you've already been through it."

"Yeah." Dash nods, blue eyes sincere. "And when their dads die, I'm not going to say they're *lying*."

Oh, my heart. "Did someone say that to you?"

He nods.

Immediately upon Dash's return to school we saw Mr. Clark, the school counselor. His support, along with that of Dash's teachers and classmates, has been amazing, but every day there's recess and lunch and a whole schoolyard of kids who don't know Dash and couldn't possibly understand. I can't even imagine.

"Do you need a place to have quiet time?"

"Nah. Mr. Clark has puzzles in his office and I can go do them whenever I want, but I don't want to. I just want to stay with my class."

Dash wants me to stay with him until he falls asleep. My body's exhausted and would love to curl in with him for the night, let each of our heartbeats soothe the other to sleep, but my mind is racing, racing, racing.

". . . the ceiling was made of Glowstone . . ." He's talking about his *Minecraft* world. My own thoughts hiss and explode, like the Creepers in his video game. I want to bolt from this room, and the strength of my desire to escape fills me with shame. I'm not fit for the task of mothering. I stay until he's almost ready to nod off, then kiss him on the forehead. "Good night, sweetheart."

As I change into my housecoat, Sean's clothes are still laid out on his side of the bed from yesterday. His wedding ring is on the nightstand beside the lamp. Just sitting there, inert and meaningless, like it must have sat all the other times he took it off. The lofty forgiveness I spoke about this morning gets sucked into the vortex of that empty gold band.

"You're a fucking liar and a cheat!" I yell-whisper at Sean's side of the room, so as not to disturb my son. "I'm divorcing you, right now!" I take off my wedding band and fling it across the room. It bounces off the wall with a dull thud and rolls under the bed.

"You can get your shit out of here." I throw the clothes from the bed into a laundry basket. In his top dresser drawer, battalions of socks are folded Marie Kondo–style in neat rows. I grab them in bunches and fling them into the basket. Expensive dress socks with fun designs, plain black work socks, white cotton sports socks, fly into a messy heap.

"I get the house. I get Dash. You get nothing. Not even your stupid sushi socks!" A woolen array of nigiri sushi dangles from atop the basket, which is now heaping over.

Jesus, that was just one drawer. Uncompressed, the socks are like a snake that's exploded out of a tube. Sean was a genius at organizing things and he maximized every square millimeter of storage in this room. There's way more stuff in here than I can manage on my own, and every single garment is an accessory after the fact. It's smothering me. I won't be able to stay in here until it's gone.

There was an ad for a professional organizer in the Willow Ridge community newsletter last month. I take the basket of socks to the laundry room. When I come back upstairs, I find the organizer's number and call her. She's had a cancellation and can come tomorrow. Perfect.

———

In the morning, as soon as the stores open, my mom runs to the liquor store to get packing boxes. She unloads them in the garage and heads out for a well-deserved day to herself. My mom lives in the quiet village of Kenosee Lake, Saskatchewan, a ten-hour drive from Calgary. She was just visiting, on her way through to Mazatlán, when Sean died. Mom's been here for eleven stressful days and will stay for two more weeks, or until things have leveled out.

Karen, the organizer, shows up looking fresh and efficient with boxes of her own, reusable totes that we cram full of Sean's clothes and other belongings. I keep one navy fleece pullover with the Queen's University crest, one T-shirt, and, to save money down the road, a few pairs of shoes that Dash can wear in a year or two. Karen takes the rest away in her SUV by midafternoon.

The dogs are itching for a walk, but I'm feeling spent. I take a few minutes and put together an iTunes playlist to help keep my feet moving. I call the playlist FUSW, as in Fuck You Sean Waite. I populate it with angry songs, vengeful songs, sad songs, hopeful songs, and rousing anthems. I don't know it yet, but I will listen to this playlist every day for the next two years. The music will be as faithful a companion as the two dogs who'll romp alongside me as I put one foot in front of the other.

There will be days when I step up because Sara Bareilles wants to see me be brave. Days when I believe Beyoncé, that Sean must not know 'bout me. Other days, like today, I'll feel like I'm nothing, and P!NK will ask me pretty, pretty please not to feel that way. *I dunno, Pink, my case is looking pretty solid.*

Woodward, Panda, and I have walked over to "the bowl," an off-leash park we visit almost every day. The park slopes down on all four sides, with a flat, grassy span about the size of a football field at the bottom. This dreary afternoon, the entire expanse is ours. I chuck Woodward's orange ball and he takes off after it. Panda follows, but gets distracted by a smell in the dried brown grass.

I remember a sunny afternoon here, just six weeks ago, when the grass was still green. Panda, at eight months old, had never seen autumn before. He'd chase one falling yellow leaf, only to have his attention captured by another, wagging his tail in all directions, dizzy with the wonder of it. Dash gathered up an armful of leaves and tossed them into the air. Panda jumped and twisted his giant, pliable black-and-white body, trying to catch all the leaves at once. Dash was belly laughing. I pivoted toward Sean, standing a few feet up the hillside, to make sure he didn't miss the beautiful moment. My head turned just in time to catch his wafting words:

"The best thing that could happen to you is if I died."

His soft voice hit me like a spray of buckshot. I searched Sean's face, scanning for some context, a punch line I'd missed. He just looked tired.

What does that mean? I was about to ask, but Dash hollered, "Panda!"

A jackrabbit raced across the bowl, Panda galloping behind, heading up the slope toward the road. Sean sprinted across the field to catch our puppy before he ran into danger.

I'll never know if Sean intended me to hear those words, but they mean something different now. That day, I discounted their quiet urgency and life rushed on as usual. Now, I imagine he'd been filling out the life insurance application and it brought his mortality front of mind. I think the innocent, tender scene of Dash and Panda playing in the autumn leaves didn't reconcile with everything he was hiding.

The betrayed part of me wants to freak out on Sean's head. "This? *This* is the best thing that could happen to me? Being broke and broken and left to raise our child *by myself*!" It feels like such a cop-out, to just wish himself out of the world.

But another part of me recognizes the sacrifice Sean was willing to make. He knew he was hurting us and wanted to stop. He wanted us to have a good life and didn't think that was possible with him still in it. It gives me the same feeling I had at the end of *Saving Private Ryan*, when Captain Miller, who'd led his detachment through occupied territory and sniper fire, found the young soldier they'd all risked their lives to rescue. He told Private Ryan, "Earn this."

———

Mom's at the table with an almost-happy-hour rye and ginger when I get back from the dog park. I'd love to have a drink with her, but since I developed Hashimoto's thyroiditis a couple years ago, I've lost the ability to metabolize alcohol. Even one glass of wine wakes me at 3:00 a.m., and being alone with my late-night thoughts is bad enough when it occurs naturally.

I pour myself a glass of water and sit down with Mom. She clips the tags off a blouse with a pair of nail scissors.

"Scored big-time on the clearance rack." Mom holds up a sleeveless, black-and-white crisscross top. "This was seventy percent off."

"Maybe I should check out the sale. Got loads of room in my closet now."

Mom hears something in my tone. "You know"—she swirls her ice cubes—"a person might be in a big hurry to clean out someone's closet if that person was angry about something."

I want to laugh at how unnatural she sounds. My mom doesn't speak in terms of "a person." She's choosing her words, trying to be gentle. My mom was the only person I knew who didn't like Sean. She'd seen him bark at me, in 1997, and never trusted him after that. I've told her about the drugs and the money, but I haven't told her everything because part of me hates to confirm her negative opinion.

My forehead wrinkles and the corners of my mouth turn down, giving away everything I'm trying to hold back. I press my palms into my eye sockets. My hair falls in a loose shield around my face. I say, "It's bad."

Mom sighs. She's quiet for a bit, then says, "Do you remember when we left your dad?"

I look up slowly, holding my breath.

My mom does not talk about the past. All my life, when something upsetting has happened, I've seen her do the same thing. She presses her lips together; a glare of concentration comes over her face; she blinks a few times; she keeps going. Her vault is tighter than Fort Knox and for deposits only.

We left my dad in 1981, when I'd just turned ten and my sister, Catherine, was almost nine, the same age Dash is now. It happened abruptly, over the course of twenty-four hours. My memory reel is short and choppy:

Grandma Bell is here. "Hi, Grandma!" What a nice surprise to see our Weyburn Grandma all the way out here on Vancouver Island.

Catherine and I stand awkwardly by the empty monkey bars at Drinkwater Elementary in Duncan, British Columbia. We've been given a few minutes in the schoolyard to say goodbye, but it's too early and none of our friends are here.

Dad wears a dark blue hospital gown. He has a beard, but not the nice, soft kind. Dad cries. Afterward, in the car on the way to the airport, Mom asks if we told him we loved him. Catherine says, "He knows."

Catherine and I sit in the rear-facing back seat of our grandparents' wood-paneled station wagon. Grandpa Bell has picked us up at the airport in Regina. As he drives us home to Weyburn, we watch the wide horizon of prairie expand, boundaryless, through the rear window. The road we've already traveled rolls out, endlessly, in front of us.

I peek now through my hair shield at Mom, avoiding any quick movement for fear the vault will slam shut and lock her decades-old secrets inside. "Yeah?"

"Your dad had stocked up on booze and locked himself in the basement bathroom for four days. He barricaded himself in. Said he'd kill himself if I got help."

"What?" I sit up, push the hair out of my face, and look right at

Mom. That bathroom had a dark brown wood-veneer door, a toilet, a sink, and a narrow vanity. "Wasn't that bathroom tiny?"

"Yes. It wasn't very big. He started out the first day in the laundry room, but when the beer ran out, he moved into the bathroom with the hard stuff." Mom takes a sip of her rye.

Oh my God. Poor Dad. I once heard a researcher call alcohol "an agent of cognitive narrowing." That description illuminated large swaths of my life, and nothing has brought it to bear more than this. My dad's boozy thoughts drove him into smaller and smaller spaces, both in his mind and in the physical world. Dad died of an alcohol overdose seventeen years later, but it could just as easily have happened back then, when he was only thirty-five.

I say, "I kind of remember not being allowed to go downstairs. The TV was down there and we didn't get to watch anything that week."

"Yes. I told you girls your dad was very sick and he was in the basement and you weren't allowed down there. I went down a few times a day to check on him and bring food, but he wouldn't eat anything." Mom's face pales as she puts herself back in that time. She goes quiet.

For me, this conversation is happening on multiple levels, like a game of 3D chess.

Ten-year-old me remembers being in bed and hearing thudding noises from the basement in the night. Mumbling in a Dad-like voice that made no sense. Knowing not to ask Mom because her stress level was already maxed out. I wrote "Get Well Soon" on a paper airplane and tried to swoop it past the landing so it would reach my dad. *Poor Mom. I can't imagine her life that week, getting us to school, showing up to work so she didn't lose her job. Hoping she'd come home to find Dad sobered up. What must it have been like, to race home and discover he'd gotten worse?*

The mom in me is appalled at the parenting decisions. *Don't go downstairs? That's a solution?* "Why didn't you call the doctor?"

Mom's shoulders clench. "I did." She grips her glass. "I called every day, but Tom's doctor wouldn't see me. I finally called my mom to fly out. When your grandma got there, she took one look at your dad, put me in the car, and we drove to the doctor's office"—Mom straightens in her chair—"and do you know what that doctor did? He patted me *on the head* and said, 'Now, Bonnie, if I called for an ambulance every time someone's husband had a little too much to drink . . .'"

Even now, three decades later, the condescension in the doctor's voice activates something in my mom. If a white-haired lady in bifocals could turn into the Incredible Hulk, the seams of her blouse would be splitting open right now. "So, Grandma stepped in front of me, and she made herself *big*, and she pointed her finger right at him and said, 'The man is dying. You will get him an ambulance. Right. This. Minute.'"

"So, you guys saved Dad's life," I say, bursting with pride over badass Grandma Bell.

Mom shrugs. "I guess. We decided it was best for you and your sister to go back to Weyburn with your grandparents while your dad went to rehab."

Whoa. Part of me thinks I should feel even worse, throwing new fuel onto the dumpster fire. But I don't. I feel *better* because my mom's not judging Sean or suggesting what I might have done differently. My mom knows what it means to love someone who's struggling, to try to hold your family together, how things can get way out of hand.

As Dash matures, I'll think back to Mom's disclosure and use it as a guidepost for opening up with him. Way down the road, I'll wonder . . . Did my mom choose her moment to open the vault? Or did my full-tilt overwhelm, my belly roiling with suppressed rage, invoke the precise combination of feelings my mom had felt all those years before, allowing us to crack the code together?

———

Ty comes straight from work the next evening, in his cowboy business attire. As general manager of Cowboys Casino he wears boots, jeans, and a cowboy hat to work every day, not just during Stampede, when lots of people dress that way. Ty doesn't know this, but I summoned him because, in the night, I smashed the shit out of a ceramic popcorn bowl Sean had designed with the iconography of our favorite board games. Sean spent a week's vacation painting that bowl. His creative triumph was the centerpiece of our games table. Swinging it overhead and slamming it to smithereens on the concrete floor turned out to be a Band-Aid on a shark bite. A gesture in the right direction, but not nearly sufficient. Better to get Sean's other treasures out of harm's way, just in case. Downstairs, I lead Ty to the unfinished mechanical room where Sean kept bits and bobs from his family history, and where he often worked on his computer at night.

"Wow," Ty says, looking around. "There's a lot of stuff in here. What's in all these bins?"

"We are fully stocked against the Home Depot Apocalypse." I gesture to the floor-to-ceiling shelving and Rubbermaid tubs stacked along three of the four walls. "And the great Tamiya model shortage the world's been dreading." There are more categories of stuff in these bins than I let on, but Ty gets the picture.

We box up the things he's taking, and before we head back upstairs, I ask him to take a seat at his parents' old dining table, which is now in our rec room. "Coffee?" He shakes his head. I'm sure he's thinking about getting back across town in rush hour and hoping to get home for dinner with Jenn and Emma. I get to the point. "Are you still able to come with me to Denver to clean out Sean's apartment before the end of the month?"

He nods.

"Okay." I take a deep breath. "Then I have to fill you in on a few things. I don't know what we're going to find down there."

I tell him what I've discovered so far, drug abuse, infidelity, hidden debt. He takes in the information solemnly, his shoulders level with the plaid lines of his button-down shirt. At the casino, Ty sees the most compulsive and impulsive sides of human nature play out, night after night. Nothing about this story should shock or surprise him. But I'm talking about Sean. His little brother. His favorite. Ty's spent his share of time at a poker table, but his face gives away traces of what he's feeling: love for Sean; distress at the pain these revelations are causing me; shame that's baked into the whole tawdry thing.

When I'm done telling him everything I've discovered, Ty nods. "Well . . . he paid the price."

"What do you mean?"

"I mean, he's dead." Ty shrugs his shoulders and turns his palm up. *Duh*.

I bristle. "Uh, yeah, he's dead and doesn't have to face a single"—the pitch of my voice is getting shrill. I swallow—"consequence of his actions." I point at Ty. "We're the ones left to clean up the mess. Me and you. But mostly me." *Hmph. So there*. I glare.

"Okay." He nods. He's been managing people his whole career. He's using his ledge-talk-down voice. "I hear you. So then, what's next? We gotta keep moving."

"I guess it's just shoveling out this shit pile till Christmas. Come January, I'll figure out my job, if we move, sell the house, and, and, and . . ." I sigh. Ty's got dark circles under his eyes and a shadow of stubble on his face. It's past dinnertime. I need to let him go.

"Ty, do you think Sean loved me?" I didn't mean to ask. The words leaked out of my trembling bottom lip.

"You know he did, Jess." Instant. Certain.

"I thought I knew it, but I have to tell you, all this"—I wave my hand in a sweeping movement, indicating everything—"*this* doesn't feel like love."

Ty looks into me. I feel more pathetic than I ever have before, but he's not treating me with pity. I can see in his red-rimmed eyes that he's as brokenhearted as I am. Words aren't medicine for the way I'm feeling, but he offers his best shot. "You have to keep reminding yourself, Jess. With bipolar, two things can be true at the same time."

THE PACT

I t's a little icy at the top," Sean said, reaching back to clasp my hand, steadying me over the last step up the dirt trail under the railway bridge. Our golden retriever, Arrow, overdue for his bedtime walk, was already barreling down the other side. His flexi leash pulled Sean toward the Bow River and we ran down the hill in a chain.

Sean and I had been at the midnight premiere of *Harry Potter and the Sorcerer's Stone*. For Sean's thirty-fourth birthday, I'd stood in line to get tickets to the special screening. Now it was almost 3:00 a.m., and with no one else around and no traffic noise in the distance, all we could hear was the rushing water and our footsteps.

We walked the stretch of bike path just around the corner from our townhome in Inglewood. The path was treed on both sides, following the curve of the Bow, just downstream from its confluence with the Elbow River. The lights of downtown Calgary looked just steps away. My pulse quickened with the vibrancy of being in the heart of the city and the wild of nature at the same time.

Whoosh. The flicker of a shadow overhead. The slightest ripple in the air. I tracked swift movement, skimming above us, stopping in a pine tree a few yards ahead. Wide-spanning to almost invisible in an instant.

"It's an owl," Sean whispered.

Whoa. The fibers of my scarf tickled against my neck. I stared at the spot where the owl had landed, trying to force myself to see it as clearly as it could see us. All I could make out was a compact grayish form, settled and motionless on a pine bough.

I touched Sean's sleeve and whispered, "Hedwig," although this wasn't a snowy owl, like the one who companions Harry Potter in the movie. Arrow tugged toward the tree where the owl had landed. He was a year old and always eager to meet a new friend, even one that could blind him with its talons. Sean retracted the leash and kept Arrow in close, still watching the owl. After a few minutes of silent communion, Sean and Arrow began to walk again, and I fell into step with them.

Whoosh. The owl didn't pass over our heads this time, but sailed to another stand of trees in a silent, graceful arc. It landed on an outstretched branch about thirty feet ahead of us.

"Did you see that?"

Sean nodded without looking at me. His eyes were fixed on the bird.

We stopped again when we reached the owl's landing spot, and this time Arrow sat unaware.

"We should train it to send letters for us," I joked in a hushed tone. Owls flooding the Dursley house with invitation letters to Hogwarts had been a standout moment in the film.

"Owls are messengers for the dead." The gravitas in Sean's voice surprised me.

"What do you mean?"

"Owls are wise, right? And they can see in the dark."

"Sure."

"Well, they know the way between the realms. They go between the world of the living and the world of the dead."

Around the time Sean was born, his mom had begun doing advocacy work with some of the First Nations communities around Calgary. As a boy, Sean went with her to powwows on the Tsuut'ina, Stoney Nakoda, and Siksika reserves. Eventually, Pat was adopted by the Blood Band of the Piikani Nation within the Blackfoot Confederacy and eventually became a chief. I wondered if Sean had absorbed this idea about owls from legends he'd heard as a child. His mother's Blackfoot name meant Small Young Owl Woman.

I looked back at the owl, suddenly self-conscious, like it had heard my chatter and thought I was a silly girl who'd demean a supernatural being with simple human errands. I started walking again. Arrow and Sean caught up with me.

Whoosh. The owl crossed us for a third time and landed on a tree near a lamppost on the corner of our street. It was a great horned owl, ears lifted, tufts of wispy gray feathers softening the edges of its "horns." Its deep yellow eyes were trained on us, and the broad triangle of its forehead was edged with white feathers that looked like stern, frowning eyebrows. Those ancient amber eyes told me, yes, I was foolish; but, no, the likes of me could not possibly demean it. After a long moment, the owl swiveled its head away from us and turned its attention toward the river.

"Sean, what do you think happens when we die?"

We spent the rest of the walk home evaluating the usual suspects: heaven and hell, reincarnation, eternal nothingness. We were still talking about it after we'd undressed and snuggled ourselves under the soft, dark blue duvet on our bed. This wasn't the first time we'd stayed up talking until the early hours of the morning. Arrow was curled up and snoring at the foot of our bed. Sean was lying on his side with his head propped up on one hand.

"Let's make a pact." His eyes were bright despite the late hour. "Whoever dies first comes back on their birthday, to prove it to the other one."

I laughed. It was so like him to strategize like this, to make a game out of the mystery of death. "How? I'm not sure I'll know how to just apparate somewhere."

"Okay." His gears were going. "What do you mainly think of when it comes to paranormal stuff?"

"I don't know." My mind scrolled back for an encapsulating image. "Like, *Poltergeist* I guess. The little girl in front of the snowy TV screen."

"Me, too. People always say that. It doesn't matter if they're talking about ghosts or aliens or whatever, people always talk about the electricity wonking out."

"I see your hours of listening to Art Bell are paying off." Sean liked to fall asleep listening to old-time radio shows from the 1930s and '40s. The late-night program that followed was Art Bell's *Coast to Coast AM*, an unscreened call-in show that often featured paranormal topics.

"For real, though. It makes sense: if we have a soul, and if it carries some sort of energetic current, then moving through electrical lines would be the easiest way to communicate."

"Okay, so whoever dies first comes back as electricity, to prove it to the other person on their birthday. Not in a scary way. The *nice* poltergeist."

"Deal." He sat up and extended his hand.

I sat up, too, and we shook on it. From the handshake, Sean pulled me in close and wrapped his arms around me, our bare chests pressed together. We sealed our pact with a deep kiss.

M-O-N-E-Y

Bills have been coming in. I've been ignoring them for twelve days, but I'm meeting with the bank tomorrow, so avoidance time is over. Each envelope acquaints me more fully with the monthly cost of livin' la vida widow. *Good grief. Our cell phones cost over $250 per month.* I barely use mine. Easy cutback there.

The next envelope is addressed to Sean directly and has been forwarded from his office. It's a high-limit card with over $35,000 owed. *Holy shit.* The bottom drops out of my stomach. I check the statement to see if there have been any transactions since Sean's death. Nothing since November 4. Everything looks legit. *Errr, kinda legit.* Some of those hotel bills seem pretty high. If they're business expenses, maybe I can claim them back. There are about $4,000 in hotel charges. I email the hotels and ask for itemized receipts.

My mom comes upstairs with her hair wet from the shower. I hold the credit card statement up by the corner, way out from my body like a stinking diaper.

"What is it today?" She slows down on her way to the coffee maker to peer at the page. "I can't read it without my glasses, but it looks like a big one."

"It's pretty big." I sigh.

"Do you want me to come to the bank with you, for moral support?"

I sure do. Mom's leaving in two weeks, the first of December, so I'll take all the help I can get in the meantime. I push my chair back from the kitchen table and look up at the ceiling. Four pot lights shine down onto the piles of paper on the table. I remember Sean working in the attic, cutting the holes to install them. He'd also cut a hole big enough to install a speaker, and he popped his head down from the attic through the hole in the ceiling. Dash was two then, and he and his four-year-old cousin Isaac went wild with laughter, playing hide-and-seek with Sean's upside-down head in the ceiling. Then I remember, it's Sean's birthday and we made a deal.

The rest of the day, I alternate between staring into the light bulbs and chastising myself for keeping up my end of the bargain. In the afternoon, I sneak out to Crave cupcake shop to buy Sean's favorite: chocolate cake with peanut butter icing. I do this for Dash, to keep his dad's memory and traditions alive. After supper, I put a candle in a cupcake and light it for Dash to blow out. We don't sing "Happy Birthday," but we talk about how fun Sean made birthday parties and how cool the snake-pit maze in the garage was when Dash turned nine.

By bedtime, it's clear: no light show is forthcoming. Sean's not going to blink out "I'm sorry" in Morse code. Messages from family and friends remembering Sean's forty-eighth birthday have pinged in all day. Individually, the messages help me feel less alone as I share a brief exchange with people who care. Cumulatively, they force me to feel the weight of our loss. At bedtime, Sean used to bring me a hot pack for my feet, kiss me goodnight, and tell me how much he loved me. When he was away, we'd talk at bedtime, and afterward he'd still text, "Sweet dreams, my love. I miss you." So many texts today, but no goodnight from Sean before I go to sleep. I feel more alone than I ever have.

Bad news at the bank. The line of credit we'd secured for an emergency has a big balance owing, and the mortgage insurance we believed we'd purchased was held up by a technical error. The policy never went into force. The only way we could have noticed was by picking up on a small premium *not* being deducted from our pre-authorized monthly payments. Neither of us was looking that closely. My adviser at RBC said she'd try to help, but I don't see any recourse.

My head hangs and my shoulders are stooped as Mom and I exit the bank. A neon sign flashes from a pub in the strip mall, and I consider steering mom inside to get plastered and win some video-slot money to pay the bills. Instead, we trudge through the dirty snow to the van.

I start the ignition and turn the defroster to full, letting the van warm up. "Have you seen *Kung Fu Panda*?"

Mom shrugs. "If I did, I don't remember."

"There's this soft flabby panda, just living his life, and one day he stumbles into a training hall for kung fu masters. It's full of brutal obstacles, giant clubs with spikes sticking out. . . ." It starts to snow. I click on the windshield wipers, but they squeak against the too-dry glass so I turn them off again. "The panda gets knocked down and lit on fire. Every time he stands up, the next horrible thing gets him"—the pitch of my voice rises—"then the next, and the next." Tears are choking me off. I look right at Mom. "Should I just stay down?"

"Sweetheart." Mom's matter-of-fact tone tells me she's unmoved by the trials of animated pandas. "When we get home, you can lie down for the rest of the day. But tomorrow, you're getting up and. . . ." She checks the little datebook from her purse and reads aloud, "meeting your friend, Carmen."

Carmen has her laptop plugged in before I've even had a chance to offer her something to drink. She and Scott reconciled the second year we were in Singapore. Carmen, Scott, and their daughter, Ashley, lived here in the house together. Carmen looks right at home as she pulls folders from her bag. "I did two plans for you. One if the life insurance pays, and the other if not."

"Let me put the kettle on. You like peppermint tea, right?"

"Sure, that's great." Carmen leans in to enter her password. She's lovely even in the dull, bluish light of her computer. Her long light brown hair frames the delicate features of her face. To me, Carmen is like a porcelain doll crossed with a wolverine, sleek and fearless.

She was eating lunch in a sandwich shop once when a paunchy middle-aged patron said to the girl in a headscarf, working behind the counter, "Why don't you go back where you came from." Carmen got up from the table and went at the guy. "Why don't *you* go back where *you* came from?" The guy took a step backward as Carmen approached. "That's right. No one wants you here. Get the fuck out until you can treat people with respect."

If Carmen has bad news for me, she won't shy away from it. She'll stand with me as I figure out what to do next. Carmen grew up with a single mom, too, and lived as one for a year. She knows how to draft a Kraft Dinner budget Dash and I can live on.

"Here you go." I set down a steaming mug of tea on the dining table beside her and pull my chair up close, so we can both see her computer screen.

The way she's crunched the numbers looks promising. Sean bought a Porsche Cayenne less than a year ago. If I sell it, I can pay off my high-interest creditors and use the money my mom loaned me to get through the next six months, without having to list my house for sale. I have two extra bedrooms and a garage I can rent out for additional income. If the life insurance comes through, I'll have enough to pay off my debt and live for five years without supplemental income. That will give me time to go back to school, or at least to work my way into a better-paying job than what I'd have to take right now. In five years, Dash will be fourteen, old enough to get a part-time job if he wants things I'm not able to afford. It's hard to imagine five years from now, raising a teenager on my own, and I stop myself from trying to picture it. My grief counselor advised, "We don't know the future, no matter how much it feels like we do."

Presumably, Scott has filled Carmen in on the salacious details. "The first thing I'm paying off is boutique hotels and room service." I sound as bitter as I am. My request for itemized hotel receipts painted a nauseating picture: free-flowing prosecco and breakfasts for two; numerous single cups of coffee ordered for $17 apiece. *Leave the room, you assholes.* It was hard to reconcile the lavish overspending with my now having to pay for Sean's largesse with other women.

"Yeah," Carmen says, "poor Rebekah will have to foot her own bills now."

The blood goes out of my face and my jaw falls open. My chest feels tight, the airway pinched off like a bent straw. I'd thought the women were strangers he picked up or escorts he hired. Carmen registers my alarm. I push my chair back from the table so hard that one of the wooden legs cracks. I jump up to standing.

"Rebekah?!"

"Oh my God, Jess. I'm so sorry. I thought you knew."

"No, I found others, but not her. Jesus—she wasn't even in his phone." I'd checked. "I suspected something between them five years ago but— How do you know?"

"She's been phoning our house crying."

I gape. "To talk to *you*?" Carmen, Scott, Rebekah, and Sean had all worked for the same company at one point. They've known each other for years.

"Oh, hell no! To talk to Scott. I told him she better quit calling. I want nothing to do with it."

My head is reeling and suddenly I'm livid with Scott for keeping this from me. I cried on his shoulder and he chose to protect Rebekah instead of telling me the truth. By keeping her secret, he set me up for another fucking blindside.

"Do you know how long?"

Carmen's face shows two things: She shares my anger at the betrayal, and she's sorry for me, too. I stare down at the floor, trying not to be pitiful.

"I knew at the Christmas party last year. She was talking shit about you. . . ."

"About me?" *We've barely interacted.* "Like what? My weight?" I'd put on about twenty pounds since my thyroid stopped working and I'd been conscious of it at that party.

"No. She was saying what a bitch you were, and I was like, 'Why are you going off on Jess? Are you fucking Sean?' She went white as a sheet. She denied it, but I knew that night."

She was calling me a bitch? What did Sean say about me to her? My head is pounding.

"I told Scott they were having an affair and he was like, 'No way. Sean would've told me.'"

"No." I shake my head. "Sean would never have admitted it to anyone."

"So, when Sean died, Rebekah started calling and Scott was all 'Wow.'" Carmen's face mimics the expression of a naïve person mindblown by something obvious.

"For a smart guy, Scott's an idiot sometimes." I smile weakly at Carmen. "Sorry." She nods. "You know, when we were unpacking in Singapore, I found a note from Rebekah inside a journal she must have given Sean as a farewell gift." The yellow Post-it had said, "Thank you. I love you—Ryskah." I recognized the nickname as Rebekah's Skype handle and almost picked up stakes and moved Dash back home. "I told Scott about it because he was house-sitting for us then, and he was like, 'Oh, no, no, no! They're just friends! Rebekah says I love you to everyone all the time.'"

Carmen frowns. I don't think Rebekah says "I love you" to her very often.

"Scott's explanation sounded exactly like what Sean said when I confronted him." It's weird that their stories were so aligned when they weren't actually in cahoots. It shows what a skilled liar Sean was, skimming so close to the truth it was hard to perceive a difference. "I hate that I listened to those guys and not to my gut feeling."

Pacing around the dining room, I try to remember that Christmas party. It was a big formal dinner at the Hyatt. Sean had been seated between me and an attractive blond coworker named Maryanne. The two of them had an obvious bond and a lot of inside jokes. My spidey senses were way up about Maryanne: *Beware Rebekah 2.0.* As soon as the dinner dishes were cleared away, and everyone was getting up to mingle, Sean placed his hand on the small of my back and said, "Let's go do something fun."

We'd left the party and walked from the Hyatt to the movie theater in Eau Claire. Sean bought us tickets to *Birdman*, which I'd been dying to see. He held my hand during the movie. A surprise date night, overdressed in an almost-deserted movie theater! I'd felt seen, chosen, and in love with *my* Sean. We'd spent the drive home in lively conversation about the film. The evening had made my highlight reel for the year.

Now it looks like Sean wasn't choosing me, he was managing a wife/girlfriend/possible-other-girlfriend collision course. He'd seen enough sitcoms to know he'd better get me out of there before high jinks ensued.

I feel so duped; so manipulated. And I can't just *forgive* Sean for having an affair with Rebekah. He wasn't in a manic episode this whole fucking time. Five years ago, we sat on that marriage counselor's couch and put our cards on the table. I looked deeply into Sean's eyes and said, "Whatever passed between you and Rebekah, I forgive you."

Carmen has folded down her laptop and is straightening up the hard copies of the reports she made me.

"He never admitted it, you know." My voice wavers and my hands are shaking. "He let me hold his fat fucking face in my hands and forgive him. He just took it—" I slam my hand against the tabletop. Carmen jumps at the sound. "And as soon as we got back from Singapore, they just picked up right where they left off."

Blood is rushing all through my body. I can't stand being in this room. If I stay here, I will die.

"I'm so sorry, Carmen, and thank you for everything, but I have to go. Please tell my mom I'll be back before Dash gets home." I walk out, leaving Carmen alone at my dining table.

Backing out of the driveway, I have no idea where I'm going. *No more sucker punches. Please, no more.* Heading northward, I notice I'm steering myself toward Inglewood, where we used to live in a little townhome near the Bow River. When I get to Ninth Avenue, instead of cranking right toward our old place, I make a left-hand turn, and a minute later I'm at the storage locker.

―――――――

When Sean's mom and dad moved out of their family home into an independent-living condo, Sean moved some of their stuff into storage. Although Jack and Pat have both died, the family has never gone through the old shipping container to disperse the items. Sean kept the keys to the unit on the console of our van, and about once a month he'd say, "Gotta go check on Mom and Dad's locker."

I'd thought he was being dutiful, checking for frost and water damage, and keeping the dust down. Now I suspect that he was either lying about where he was going, or he was using the locker to store some things of his own.

The door of the unit is corrugated metal, with bright orange paint that's flaked off in places. *All right, Jonny, whadda we have behind Door Number One?* Meth lab? My Little Pony collection with man-size Twilight Sparkle costume? A human liver with fava beans and a nice Chianti?

I open the padlock and hike the steel door upward. The screech of rusty metal upon metal matches the frequency of my nervous system. At first glance it looks . . . *normal.* Furniture castoffs, boxes, lamps, and artwork I haven't seen for a long time. The detritus of a good life. I rummage around in the stuff I can reach: music boxes and Christmas ornaments, nothing untoward. The only sign of Sean's comings and goings are some ball-hockey nets and a few items that once took up space in our basement.

I feel relieved and also, oddly, disappointed—like I'd wanted to find a smoking gun or some kind of manifesto, revealing the inner workings of Sean's mind. I wanted a key to the heart of it all, but all I've found are some dusty leftovers from Sean's childhood home. The door screeches again on the way down. Sean's brother Riley was coexecutor of their parents' estate. I drop off the storage keys in his mailbox.

As I head home along Memorial Drive, my memory zeroes in on a time five years ago, the day our new mattress was delivered. Our bedroom renovation was finally done, and I'd spent the morning wiping down drywall dust, washing bed linens, and fluffing pillows, making the bed beautiful, like in a nice hotel. After preschool, I took Dash to IKEA to return an item and we stayed for a meatball lunch. The clearance table near the exit was loaded with pink and red glass candleholders. Perhaps I could delight Sean-of-the-grand-gesture by making our inaugural night in the bedroom memorable. Votives were fifty cents each; tealights, a quarter. I loaded up a big yellow bag and checked out with $20 worth of post–Valentine's Day discount romance supplies.

My friend Angie agreed to take Dash for an impromptu sleepover with her kids. I walked him to their house, and once he was settled, I came home, showered, shaved everything, and smeared my body with lotion. While my hair was air-drying, I peeled off sticky price tags and arranged the candleholders in clusters of three, along the ledge behind the bed, on each of our nightstands, and on top of the dresser. Even unlit, the little triads of pink and red glass looked pretty, like three-petaled flowers.

I styled my hair and did my makeup, following a YouTube tutorial for a smoky eye. The results were dramatic, but a little more goth than I was going for. Sean texted to say he was working late and I shouldn't expect him until about nine o'clock. I washed the eye shadow off and started again.

About quarter to nine, I changed into a red-and-black corseted teddy, wrestling with the hook-and-eye closures to get myself squeezed into the push-up bra. My boobs spilled over the top, practically hitting me in the chin. I belonged atop a piano in an old western saloon, someone playing Scott Joplin tunes in the background. I lit all the candles.

Arranging myself so deliberately into an object of desire was something I hadn't tried before, and I took cues from what I'd seen on television. The man was supposed to walk in at the perfect moment and sweep the lovely lady off her feet. TV hadn't shown me what to do if the man wasn't there yet, so I lay on my bed, playing *Angry Birds* on my iPad, clearing level after level, while the candles burned down and the room grew overwarm.

Eventually, Sean walked into his red-glowing bedroom and flipped on the light. I flinched. My eyes were strained from hours of staring at my screen in the candlelight.

Sean looked around and gestured toward all the candles. "Where'd you get all this shit?"

I jumped up to grab my robe, feeling overexposed and vulnerable in the bright light. In the bathroom mirror I saw what rubbing my eyes to stay awake had done to my makeup. Tiny black rivulets and sparkly flakes of pigment had migrated into my crow's feet. The overhead light shone hard on the gray roots at my hairline. I looked used up, an old tramp like Lola, the lounge singer from the Copacabana. I wrapped my fuzzy, frumpy bathrobe tightly around me, cinching it at the waist, and stepped back into the bedroom to answer Sean's question.

"I went to IKEA—"

"We don't need to be wasting money on all this crap."

"It cost less than twenty dollars." My voice was as soft as the chenille flowers on my robe. I walked around the bed to where Sean stood. His blue-checked dress shirt was crinkled after a long day of work. I could smooth it out. I reached my arm toward his shoulder. I could help him get past all this bluster. "I just wanted to make it nice in here for—"

"You do this all the time and I'm fucking sick of it!" He picked up a votive and whipped it across the room, where I'd been standing a moment before. The candle flickered out, but the holder smashed against the wall, sending shards of pink glass in all directions. Red wax splashed down the newly painted wall like spattered blood. The other candles flickered like gaslights.

I stepped back from Sean, anger rising in my belly. I dropped my robe and faced him in my lace teddy. "Look at me! *Look at me!*"

He looked.

"I spend my whole life waiting for you, trying to make things nice for you, and you *don't care.*" I lunged at him, both hands raised. "Why don't you care?" I slapped and punched at his shoulders. "What's wrong with you?"

Sean grabbed both my wrists and held my arms tight in front of him. He was a lot stronger than me and there was no getting out from the clamp of his hands. Neither of us had ever hit the other before. I wasn't trying to hurt him. I just wanted to get through to him. Sean held my wrists up in front of my face until the fight went out of them, then he lowered my arms, still holding them, gently. He looked into my eyes, his face empty of expression. "I don't deserve you."

That night, I'd been hurt and angry, but more than anything else I'd been bewildered. What had I done to provoke that fight? What I'd spent on candles, Sean spent at Starbucks every single day.

———

I could never make sense of that fight until now. What Carmen told me has helped me realize that while I was playing *Angry Birds*, Sean and Rebekah were in a romantic nest of their own making. If I'd gotten near enough to kiss Sean, I might have smelled her on him. Beyond that, Sean had come home to a lonely, candlelit wife who still loved him, who was doing her level best to delight him. He extinguished the candles before they burned him up in shame.

This missing piece helps me understand, but it also inflames me. The rage and betrayal I should have felt that night sear through my whole body. I'm driving past the Manchester Industrial area. *Don't deserve me? You don't deserve anything! I should dump your ashes in a ditch.*

The van fishtails on a patch of ice as I pull into my back alley. I straighten out and take my foot off the gas, coasting up the lane to my back garage. I slam the gearshift into park. The wooden urn containing Sean's cremated remains is stowed on Sean's workbench in the garage. A Phillips screwdriver makes short work of the four screws holding the lid in place. Inside is a clear plastic bag full of gray powder, sealed and labeled with an engraved metal ID tag. I slice the bag open with an X-Acto knife and scoop a handful of cremains into a green poo-bag from my coat pocket.

I march out to the backyard. Under the bristlecone pine, on a snowless patch of dirt, I spy a semifrozen pile of dog shit. My knees crack as I bend to scoop it up. A trickle of silty ash falls out from the shit bag into the soil below. I yelp and try to stop the dust from falling. *No, dammit, you don't get to be here!* But it's too late, the mineral powder has escaped into the ground and there's nothing I can do. I tie up the bag, stomp out the gate to the alley, and throw the mess into the black garbage can. "Piece of shit is as piece of shit does." I slam down the lid with a nervous giggle. I've spoken aloud without looking to see if any of my neighbors are out here.

I can imagine Sean watching me right now. He quoted Forrest Gump all the time. He'd shrug and give me a sad half smile, just enough to show his dimple. He'd say, "Touché."

It's not touché, though, and I know it. This isn't a proportional response. I've desecrated the remains of my partner in life. I put my hands over my face and press cold fingers against my forehead, rocking myself slowly back and forth. I'm, like, 99 percent sure what I've just done is a damnable offense. If God or his tally keepers are watching, that's a wrap for me. If anyone in the family finds out what I've just done, they'll probably disown me, too. I'll be entirely on my own. My hands are trembling now. Another nervous little laugh escapes, and behind it comes a wail, a tsunami of emotion.

I hurry back into the garage so no one will hear me keening. The yellow screwdriver and parts of the urn are strewn on the workbench. The slit in the bag of ashes looks like a gaping wound. *What have I done?*

"Sean." My face contorts with anguish and I swallow back tears. "Fuck. I'm so sorry."

My knees might buckle. I steady myself with both hands against the plywood counter. Sean built this. I can picture him in his cargo shorts, carrying in full-size sheets of plywood, single-handedly constructing all the shelves in here, then hoisting and Tetris-ing all these boxes into place. All our Christmas decorations. *Christmas.*

"Please, Sean." I'm talking to a wounded bag of gray powder. "I can't do this by myself. You were so strong."

The cremains feel dry against my fingertips, coarser than baking powder, grainier than salt. I take a pinch into my mouth. They mix with the teary water, a mineral mud on the back of my tongue. I swallow. The pasty residue coats my tongue. The chalky feeling lingers as I collapse onto the cold concrete floor. *Help me. Help me. Please God. Sean. Someone, help.*

Minutes or hours pass. When I hear my dogs padding around outside, I sit up. My muscles are cold and stiff. I dust myself off. A roll of duct tape is on a peg above the workbench. With it, I mend the bag of ashes and nestle everything back into the wooden urn, placing the engraved pewter tag at the cross of the tape. The ID number is face up: 67185. I screw the lid back on. Hugging the urn into my chest, I consider bringing it into the house with me. My stomach clenches. *Nope. Not yet.* I place the wooden box on the highest shelf of a rolltop cabinet, then close the cabinet and lock the door behind me.

Sean's spilled ashes aren't the only cremains in my backyard. On a summer morning in 2015, Sean and I rose at dawn to scatter both his parents' ashes beneath the hearth of our outdoor fireplace. A few weeks later, just before his ninth birthday, Dash came in from playing in the backyard and stood at the kitchen counter, pouring apple juice into a dark blue IKEA plastic cup. The top of his head was matted with sweat as he tilted the cup back to swig down the juice.

"Is it hot out there?" I screwed the cap back on the juice container.

"Not really. Can I have some more?"

"Water."

Dash went to the sink and looked out the window as he waited for the water to run cold. "I saw Grandma outside."

"Grandma who?" My mom was in Saskatchewan, and Sean's mom had died seven months earlier.

Dash held his cup under the stream of water. "Grandma Pat. Dad's mom." He took a long drink from the cup and filled it again before shutting off the tap.

I tried to stay cool with my next question. "So, did you talk to her?"

"No." Dash pointed with the hand holding the cup, sloshing a drip of water onto the windowpane, toward the lowered patio area by the fireplace. "The gate opened and Grandma came in, but then a big wind came and blew the gate shut and she was gone."

I popped outside and rattled the gate latch. It was firmly shut.

Sean was away working in Denver, but when we spoke on the phone, I mentioned what Dash had told me about seeing Sean's mom. I'd expected Sean to laugh it off, but he peppered me with questions. "Where was she? What did she want?" I took the phone back into Dash's room, then went to let the dogs out. I didn't overhear any part of their conversation.

Dash had mentioned it the same way I'd talk about bumping into someone at the post office. If he'd said, "Grandma said I should have ice cream whenever I want," I'd have known he was lying. If I'd seen it myself, I'd have known he was telling the truth. For me, it fell into the category of "kids say the darnedest things" and I might have forgotten it, if not for Sean's ardent curiosity.

Dash hasn't said anything about seeing Sean since he died, but I don't know whether he would have said anything about seeing Grandma Pat if I hadn't been standing next to him in the kitchen just then. Under a starry winter sky at the dog park on our way home from soccer practice, I take the chance to ask.

Dash is ahead of me, his parka unzipped, holding the chucker in its follow-through position, both dogs racing through the snow to find the orange ball. I sidle up to him.

"Hey, kiddo? Do you remember last summer when you saw Grandma in the backyard?"

"Yeah." Woodward returns and drops the orange ball at Dash's feet. Dash scoops it up and throws it down the field.

"Have you seen Dad?" The back of my mouth feels dry, like the question evaporated all the moisture in my mouth. I swallow hard.

Dash's eyes are shiny, catching light from the moon. He looks at me seriously, like he doesn't want to fail a test. I make my face as soft as possible. Any answer is okay.

He shakes his head. "No, but I don't think he's coming."

I nod. It sounds like Dash has already considered the matter. He doesn't sound dismayed by the absence of a visit. Not that *not* seeing a ghost should be disturbing. It's on the tip of my tongue to ask if he wants his dad to come.

"I think Grandma was coming to warn Dad." Dash scoops a ball of snow and throws it for Panda, then runs off, following its trajectory, boots crunching.

Holy shit. My heart pounds. I have no idea what my face has just conveyed to Dash, but his interpretation has left me stunned. I look up into the array of stars to find something I recognize. The Big Dipper is tilted with the handle down toward the earth.

Dash probably means Pat was coming to warn Sean he was going to die. Sean was still grieving his mom's death when he lost the job that took us to Singapore. I'd attributed some of his fragile emotional state and volatile behavior to the stress of those big losses. But what if Pat somehow felt her son's struggle and came to warn Sean about the way he was living? Had Sean felt her presence somehow? Is that why he was so interested in what Dash saw in the backyard that day?

THE COIN IN THE CREVICE

H ey, bud," I interrupt Dash at his desk while he's copying the scaly horns of a triceratops from his *How to Draw Dinosaurs* book. A basket of clean linens rests against my jutted hip. "Will you please help me change your bed?"

Dash moves Honda to the headboard and stacks his pillows on the desk chair. I pull off the blankets and sheets and slide the mattress diagonally across the white-painted bed platform. In the space between the mattress and the wall there's an icky accumulation of dust, hair, and pigmented flakes of dry-erase marker.

I grab an old facecloth from the basket and wipe the crevice clean. When I pull my arm back, a trapped coin rolls toward me, wobbling on its edge, then twirls to a stop with a soft clink. It's pewter gray; a little bigger than a quarter. I hold it out at arm's length—my focal range when I'm not wearing my glasses—to see if I can tell what country it's from. As my eyes focus on its etched markings, time stops.

When Dash was six years old, our family spent a day snorkeling off the coast of Thailand. We saw a clown fish, a real-life Nemo, in the wild. Dash spotted an octopus I was too slow to see. Afterward, we went to the island of Koh Lanta, to a little hillside cabin for the night. I popped

Dash into the shower and was lathering shampoo into his hair when I caught a scuttle of motion in my peripheral vision. I looked around, thought nothing was there, but then I saw it—three and a half floor tiles away—the height of a tennis ball. Four feathery brown legs bent in front of its bulbous oval body, the other legs retracted into the corner of the shower stall: a tarantula.

"Let's just rinse this shampoo right out," I said in a high, taut voice, as I cupped warm water at the base of Dash's hairline, flooding it back behind his ears to release the lather and the ocean salt. My other hand stroked the soft hair across his forehead, blocking his view, working by feel, keeping my eyes on the spider. I hated its being crouched in this tight space instead of out in the jungle where it belonged. *Is it poisonous? Is it scared and trying to hide—or is it readying itself to jump?* I held my breath as I turned off the water and hustled my dripping lad out of the bathroom.

This metal coin, now dislodged from its grotty dark corner, makes me hold my breath with the same wariness. The number 67185 is engraved across its diameter. It's the identification tag from Sean's urn.

Omigod. Dash has been snooping in the garage and I still haven't found Sean's weed stash. My heart is racing and I try to keep my voice level as I hold the tag up between my thumb and pointer finger for Dash to see. "How did you get this?"

"What is it?" His blond eyebrows are ever-so-slightly furrowed.

"I know it looks like a coin for your treasure box, but it's not, okay?"

Dash isn't looking at me, his eyes are still on the tag.

"And I don't want you going into the back garage by yourself."

"Can I see it?" Dash comes closer and extends his hand to take the metal token. He turns it over to examine both sides.

Since Sean died, Dash has been telling tall tales. A couple weeks ago, he said one of the bigger kids on the school bus had taken a plastic knife from the school cafeteria. On the bus ride home, as Dash told it, the kid pulled out the knife, threw a banana in the air, and sliced it into five pieces on the way down.

"Sounds like a real-life Fruit Ninja," I'd said, keeping it cool. But I'd mentioned the story to my grief counselor. She told me that Dash may have been transposing video games onto real life as a way of calibrating what is and isn't real in the wake of his dad's death. She said as long as he didn't stay in the story permanently and was always able to orient to a consensual reality, there was nothing to worry about.

The kind of lies Dash has been telling lack subtlety, as in, I could spot them from the International Space Station. The way he's interacting with this dog tag is different. He's tracing the edge of its circle with his left hand. His reaction seems completely genuine.

"Have you seen it before?"

He shakes his head. "Can I keep it, though?"

Keep a tarantula, caught in a mason jar, eight legs fighting to escape?

"I'm afraid not, sweetie. It's not that kind of coin." I extend my hand. Dash places the now-warm disc into the center of my palm. I close my fingers around it and hurry to the back door, where I grab the garage key and my slip-on shoes. If Dash opened the urn, I'll be able to tell, the same way I know from the peanut butter, knife, and crumbs on the counter when he's made himself a sandwich.

The garage door is locked. Inside, nothing has changed since I left it. The rolltop cabinet is still closed. The urn is undisturbed on the top shelf. I unscrew the wooden lid. A clear plastic bag of ashes, the stripe of gray duct tape. No ID tag on top. I lift out the bag: No ID tag in the box.

A possible explanation floods into my brain. . . .

"So, what, you're *haunting* us now?" I shriek at Sean's urn. Suddenly the placement of the tag, right under the spot where Dash wrote, *I miss you Dad*, feels like a deliberate stunt to get to our son behind my back.

A few evenings ago, I let Dash play on Sean's old phone. At seven thirty, a notification popped up: DASH TIME. Dash brought the phone out to the kitchen and held it up for me to see—his dad had made a daily reminder just for him. His face was flushed with pride and tight with the sadness he was holding back. He longed for Sean, and this tiny crumb of connection fed him in some small way. He mattered to his dad. He was important.

Dash's reaction gutted me. Not only because he was absolutely right: He was important and mattered to his dad more than he could ever know. But also, he was so innocent in accepting that tidbit of fatherly affection. I remembered days when seven thirty rolled around and the phone didn't ring. Knowing Sean had seen DASH TIME and swiped to ignore . . . it makes me livid again as I grapple to make sense of how the ID tag got into Dash's room.

Blood pounds against my eardrums. My gaze could burn two smoldering holes into the wood grain of Sean's urn. "You should have been there for Dash when you were *alive!*"

Everything inside me is tremoring, quaking like fault lines between my internal organs. I've been trying so hard to get level. I have so many secrets to keep. This is too much. If I tell anyone about this, they'll put me on full-time watch instead of the parade of drop-ins that have been happening since Mom left.

I'm not the only one who might be detached from reality in the wake of Sean's death. The other night, Dash and I were out at a family restaurant with Sean's oldest brother when he started talking some shit about levirate marriage, a historical convention by which a widow fell under the purview of the eldest brother's household.

Michael was just flexing some antiquated patriarchal muscle. But that freaky comment made Dash's eyes dart around the booth and prompted me to signal for the check even though our food had just arrived. No one's going to lean on some outmoded tradition and try to make me marry Michael, obviously, but his comments are a caricature of something I've picked up in other places: Not everyone is convinced that Dash and I can make it on our own. They have their own ideas about what's best for us.

What if people think I'm having a psychotic break? What if I actually am?

My fingernails dig into the skin of my palm. I open my hand and look at the dull metal dog tag, 67185 underscored by four deep red crescents.

So many times, Sean made me feel like I was crazy, just to throw me off his trail, but—*this?*

I slam my fist into the garage-door opener. The motor hums and the door rattles upward. I duck underneath and sprint down the alley. My slip-on shoes slap against the bottoms of my heels, and bits of wet gravel fly into the soles. Every stride gets grittier underfoot. The elastic waistband of my yoga pants slips. I clench the fabric with my free hand to keep my pants from falling down, galloping madly until I run out of wind. I stop to catch my breath, bent at the waist, just in front of a neighbor's black garbage bin. The lid opens with a whump. I throw the dog tag into a stranger's trash. *Get out and stay out.*

SPLINTERED CANDY CANES

I used mind power on my lunch today," Dash says.

I smile at him in the rearview mirror as I back out of our driveway. "Tell me more about *that*."

"Well, it was shepherd's pie. And it looked like a pile of yuck, but then I told myself, 'This is gonna be delicious.' And it was!"

I chuckle. "Great job, bud." I'm grateful his school cafeteria serves wholesome, hearty food that tastes good, even if the kids have to trick themselves into eating it. "You know, my counselor was talking about something like mind power to me. She said mindfulness helps grieving people stay in the present moment."

"What's that?"

"Like right now, you could be thinking about what you did at school, or about what you're going to do when we get to soccer. Or you could just be here in the van, noticing it's snowing, and we're talking, and it's dark out but we can see Christmas lights . . . ." I trail off and the radio fills in with David Bowie and Bing Crosby singing *pa rum pum pum pum*. Christmas is one month away. Two weeks till Dash goes on school break. My seat warmer is kicking out some good heat, and I lean into it as we slow down for a red light.

"Hmmm." Dash says. I presume he's taking in the billowing snow-man in the yard to our right. "That's where Dad failed in life."

Ulp. I turn off the radio and sit up straight, my hands on the steering wheel at a perfect ten and two. "What do you mean?"

"Well, Dad was always really fun, but then, sometimes . . . like when we were all at the dog park, Dad would start yelling and leave us there."

My guts drop. *I didn't do enough to shield him.* "Yes, Dad did that sometimes."

"It's like he couldn't see that it was a nice time, with our family, in the sunshine."

Omigod, this kid. The light has turned and I pull onto a long straight stretch of freeway. There's not too much traffic, and the drivers around me are taking it easy, with the snowy road. I think about my own dad, locked in the basement bathroom, me about the same age Dash is now. I wanted Dad to have fun with us, to play Frisbee outside. My mom tried to protect us, too, but I knew something was wrong, just like Dash knows now.

"You know how most of the time your stomach is healthy, but once in a while you feel bad and throw up?"

"Yeah."

"Your Dad's mood was like that. Sometimes he had a kind of mood sickness. It made him act in ways he didn't like." My stomach is turning over on itself. I glance at Dash in the mirror and his face looks faraway, like he's still in the park with the dogs on the sunny day, wondering why his dad ran off and left him behind. "Also, we didn't like it."

"Yeah, I didn't like it."

I tell Dash there are medicines for mood sickness, and there are peo-ple who can help us if we start to feel really bad. When we pull up at soc-cer, I take Dash into the building, but instead of going up to the viewing gallery, I get back in the van and drive through Tim Hortons. I sit in my vehicle with a decaf and wonder if I really believe that meds and a proper diagnosis would have made the difference for Sean.

I have respect and gratitude for the doctors, nurses, and caregivers who devote themselves to treating mental health patients. But I wonder if the whole model of characterizing some conditions as individual medical problems isn't flawed. In my late teens I played on an elite developmental basketball team, training for the Canada Games. By our third year, several of the girls on that team engaged in anorexic or bulimic behaviors. I purged after eating, but only on training-camp weekends and when I traveled with the team. That mental illness was, for me, context specific and seemingly contagious. To be clear, we players hid our disordered eating from one another. There was no direct social pressure to restrict calories, just the general perfectionist culture of a high-performing team.

Why are mental illnesses treated as individual problems when they're clearly also relational? The contributing social factors of abuse, trauma, and poverty are broadly known. Our collective thought-space is continually polluted—with everything from advertising and propaganda, to impossible-to-achieve expectations, to online challenges that result in people eating pods of laundry soap. How do we even gauge health with a baseline like that?

Sean once told me about a time in sixth grade when he took the bus after school to visit his mom in a Calgary mental hospital, where she was an inpatient. In the common room, they sat at a table, working on a worn-out jigsaw puzzle of Lake Louise. A man with a mustache was working on the puzzle, too. Toward the end of the visit, Pat told Sean he could have another Dixie cup of apple juice. When he came back, he set the waxy little cup onto the table. His mom had moved her chair next to the strange man. She told Sean the man's name and asked if Sean would visit if she moved into a new house, with the mustache man. Sean said, "No!"—and ran from the room; leaving the apple juice, leaving the puzzle, and leaving his mom behind.

Sean told me that story one time only, and we never talked about it again. But I've wondered if, as a ten-year-old, hotfooting it all the way back to the bus stop in 1977, Sean might have decided to never set foot in a mental hospital again. I've also thought about how categorically awful it must have been to feel as though the balance of his home life fell upon his shoulders.

I never want to put that kind of weight onto Dash. He's still a child. Yet he's so sensitive and perceptive. He knows things without being told. My desire is to give him as much of the truth as he can integrate, without being overburdened. Will it mess up his life if I tell him too much? If I don't tell him enough? There's no way of knowing if I've guessed correctly until he either grows up okay, or problems show up. The only thing I know for sure: his DNA is not his destiny.

When we get home from soccer, our house glows with twinkling lights. The extended Waite family surprised us by decorating last weekend. They seem to have followed Sean's meticulously laid-out plan for lighting all the eaves and ledges, with no messy cords dangling, and everything on a synchronized timer. Their act of kindness was a clear way to honor Sean, an enthusiastic partaker of holiday traditions. The house looks cheery and welcoming. I'm glad they did this, despite the marked contrast it creates with the inside of the house, which grows increasingly dungeon-like by the day.

I flip on the kitchen switch. One functioning bulb does its best to light the corridor. The other five bulbs have burned out over the last couple weeks. Dead pot lights are dull, unblinking eyes in the ceiling. Living with sixteen percent of the usual wattage, especially when it's dark sixteen hours a day, doesn't jibe with my commitment toward good mental hygiene for Dash and me. Before bed, I tour the house and tally up the number of dead bulbs I need to replace. Thirty-four.

In the morning, I buy a case of fifty long-life GU10 bulbs, and there ends the story of how I spent $600 on light bulbs in a single day. Afterward, I second-guess the purchase. If I end up moving, I'll never recoup that money. But if I stay here, I don't want to drag out the ladder every other weekend. Changing light bulbs was Sean's job.

Perhaps I wouldn't be thinking myself into a tizzy about the unexpected expense if I didn't also feel Christmas coming on, like a splintered candy cane being jammed down my throat. I now understand Mom's ambivalence toward Christmas after she became a single parent and my sister noticed Santa gave better presents to the kids with nicer houses. I'd always thought the financial strain was what bothered my mom. Now, the stark contrast between what is, what was, and what ought to be is enough to poison the figgy pudding.

THE CASE OF THE
MILLION MONEY SHOTS

A few days before my mom's scheduled departure, I flew to Denver to clean out Sean's apartment. My brother-in-law Bart (married to Sean's sister, Megan) pinch-hit to accompany me. A gentle giant, with a grounded, unflappable way of being in the world, Bart was the perfect companion. As we boxed up Sean's belongings, I opened up about what was really going on in my world. Bart was shocked and livid with Sean. *Good.* He was unsure how to tell Megan and wondered when and how to add such a complicating layer to her grief. *I know, right?*

Of Sean's five siblings, I've told only Ty. Of my fellow in-laws, I've told two: Erin (married to Riley) and now Bart. Each of them got roughly the same high flyover, and watching Bart grapple with my same questions felt reassuring. But now, I'm not sure who in the family knows what, or what drama might arise from secrets between husbands and wives.

In Denver, I found two surprises. On Sean's nightstand was a framed eight-by-ten print of our last family selfie. Seeing us huddled together smiling, right beside Sean's pillow, confused my suspicion that Sean was over being a family man. The sleeker, more sinister surprise lived in the entertainment console below Sean's wide-screen television: the slender silver hard drive that sits before me now, on our dining-room table in Calgary.

I've just dropped my mom at the airport, Dash is at school, and I have the house to myself for the first time in a month. The kettle is almost whistling for tea. Soon, I will discover what secrets are hidden in the Matrix of Porn.

———

Nothing staves off the Christmas blues like forensically analyzing a porn cache. I'm back at it for the fourth day this week. Now I know, for example, that the fake browser tab "News" leads to paid sites. Under that umbrella, "CNN" goes to Digital Playground, "BBC" goes to Brazzers, and so on. I'm no longer interested in the contents of any particular folder or file, but I'm curious about how this labyrinth was constructed. I'm looking for insights into Sean's state of mind and his interior life.

Today, I've found a toehold. When I arrange the folders by last-edited date, I can match together my memories of erratic or volatile behavior with Sean's online activity to see if they correlate. I look up my last birthday, when Sean came up from the basement and presented me with a gift bag at 7:00 a.m., while I was putting the kettle on, still in my housecoat.

"Happy birthday, hon." His eyes were bloodshot and his skin looked pale and waxy.

"Oh, wow. Yeah, thanks." I took the gift bag by its thin rope handles. A crush of lime-green tissue poked between them. "Do you want me to open this now?"

"Well, I'm already late for work, so . . ."

A dry tea bag was already in my other hand. I dropped it into my mug, then reached into the gift bag. Beneath the crumpled tissue, I felt the smooth plastic of a shrink-wrapped box.

My face must have given away some befuddlement because Sean said, "The rest of your present is coming later," as I held up a *Big Bang Theory* LEGO set.

Looking into his tired, red eyes, I discerned the etiquette: pretend we normally give gifts before breakfast; pretend Sean didn't buy this for himself; pretend it's not weird for him to give me a toy I don't like based on a sitcom I've never watched.

Gah, look how exhausted the poor guy is. So, he almost forgot my birthday—big deal.

"Thank you."

As soon as Sean left for work, I went downstairs and shoved the LEGO kit into the back corner of a cupboard, where I'd never have to think about it again.

Now I can see that in the predawn hours that morning, Sean had been cataloging porn. He'd started at 4:12 a.m. and stopped about fifteen minutes before he emerged into the kitchen—just long enough to realize the date, scrounge the basement for a present for me, and pop it into a gift bag. As I recreate a picture of that morning, I'm astonished he remembered my birthday at all.

Going back through the time stamps this way, a pattern reveals itself: During bad spells Sean would often be up working on "the matrix" between 2:00 and 5:00 a.m., and some nights he was at it for up to five hours. *Five hours.* While the depth and breadth of the human sexual imagination is vast, and more apparent to me now than it's ever been, by the five-hour mark things have to be getting a little same-y. This tells me the content wasn't driving Sean.

I try to imagine what it must have been like for him, late at night, sitting on a stool in the unfinished mechanical room in our basement, his laptop on the workbench in front of him, a second external monitor mounted against the pegboard wall in the corner. Surrounding him are carefully arranged tools: to his right, the brushes, paints, and sculpting tools of a model builder (a hobby he lamented not having time for anymore), and to his left, the full array of home-handyman equipment for his endless honey-do list.

So, let's say Sean's worked all day and been a dad for a couple hours and tucked me into bed with a microwaved hot pack for my feet. He's smoked some weed and fixed himself a plate of cheese and crackers, and after appreciating the internet images in the usual way, he's down to working on the porn cache. Files are downloading and he's dragging them into folders. His eyes feel dry. A little bottle of Visine is at the ready, next to the similar-size bottles he used to mix airbrush paints. He squirts a couple drops of lubricant into his ailing peepers. Tilting his head back, he feels a crick in his neck. He rolls his head around and shrugs his shoulders a couple times, then puts some cheese on top of a cracker and pops it into his mouth.

Outside of his awareness, as he's taken this microbreak to tend to his sore and tired body, Sean's laptop has been blinking a pop-up ad at him. It's a black square with white text, flashing, "Your wife doesn't love you." Sean turns back to the screen, clicks the nuisance out of the way, and keeps going. The downloads are almost done. Just a few more files to drag over. On the periphery, he hears the *vrmm* of a fan kicking in and smells the warm, dusty odor of the furnace igniting. The thermostat is programmed to come on at 5:30 a.m. Sean yawns. *Better finish just this last one before I shower.*

When I saw that ad pop up, I lost my breath. I felt cornered by a vast menace—a threat so palpable even the spiders in my basement might have scuttled away. That kind of powerful, nebulous enemy was lurking beneath my bedroom, working against me while I lay alone in bed, sometimes sleeping, sometimes waiting wide awake, hoping for Sean to return.

A stranger encoded lies about me and sent them to my husband in the wee hours of the night—the infomercial hours, when human defenses are down—trying to capitalize on his weariness, his loneliness, and whatever deep dissatisfaction kept him from sleep. I want to fight this foe, clash swords or use a scalpel to cut away the cancer of it, but it's too late. The battle is over. I lost years ago.

Sean probably registered those ads as a blip, an annoyance to click away. He may have set up blockers, but subliminal messages do their job anyway. They keep the slope slippery, the ground soft and squelching, so once Sean stuck his boots into the muck, he could never get out. *Your wife doesn't love you. It's okay. Stay here. Stay a little longer.*

And Sean stayed.

He stayed until the last possible minute, when there was barely enough time to shower and shave, then hit Starbucks for a quad-shot iced Americano on his way to the office. His razor-thin margins explain how I could wake up on a sunny April morning, open an adorable Easter video of our little niece Emma dancing with a chicken, and rush to share it with Sean, only to have him bark, "I don't have time for this shit."

He'd be out the door, and I'd be left ruminating. *Sean loves Emma. He loves cute, funny things. Why doesn't he have ninety seconds for me? Why is he being such a dick?*

Your wife doesn't love you. Your wife doesn't love you. Your wife doesn't love you.

The world Sean built on the surface—his career, our family, our beautiful home—all of that was matched in size and scope by his subterranean activity. The effort required to maintain both worlds is almost superhuman, and I don't know where he found the stamina. Sean didn't want to live as a servant to pornography—that much I know for sure—but for complex reasons I'm still trying to understand, he simply could not stop.

———

A few nights before school gets out for Christmas break, Dash and I go to see two of his cousins in their high school drama production of *The Little Mermaid*. Most of our extended family is packed into the overwarm theater. When Sebastian the lobster takes the stage, in his full suit of bright red foam, I stop bemoaning my itchy wool sweater. That kid must be boiling alive under the stage lights. The mermaid sisters have it easier, in their shimmering, sleeveless costumes. I'm looking at the tallest of the sisters, with her long neck and graceful arms, when her dress disappears. She keeps singing about being a daughter of Triton, unaware of her bare breasts and lithe, nubile body, fully exposed.

I blink and shake my head. The girl hasn't undressed, of course, and I wasn't *trying* to picture her naked. Her long slender neck evokes that of a young woman I saw on Sean's computer. My brain has conflated these two girls and supplied me with a composite image.

I feel dizzy and seasick. No one can see me in the dark theater, but if they could, I'd be as red as Sebastian. I'm looking at a *high school girl*. One of my niece's *friends*. My brain is toggling unbidden between fully clad people and their porn-star doppelgängers. This makes me ill, literally nauseous, but it made Sean . . . what? Turned on? Superpowered— privy to a fantasyland at less than the flip of a mental switch? No size or shape of body is unrepresented in the cache. Does that mean Sean saw everyone like this? Dash's schoolteachers? The women he considered for promotions at work? My mom?

My friend Kathryn has been coming to Calgary for follow-ups with her neurosurgeon, and I've sat in on every appointment. Visualization is one of the most important parts of her rehab. She uses a mirror to trick her brain into firing electrical impulses as though she's using her paralyzed arm. What she looks at directly affects how her nervous system functions and heals.

I clasp my fingers behind my head, lifting my hair. Releasing the trapped heat staves off my urge to vomit.

Sean used to say men and women were wired differently, and I don't dispute biological differences, but neurons in my brain are building shortcuts for me. I don't even have to double click. Sean's wiring was also cultivated by what he put in front of his eyes over thousands of hours of devoted attention.

I'm not willing to play pop-up-naked-person for the rest of my life, even if I have to leave the cache's remaining secrets unanswered. With the Little Naked Mermaid, my career as a porn detective has come to an end.

REBEKAH 2.0

When Sean was alive, we ate dinner as a family at the kitchen table, every night. Even when Sean was away on business, Dash and I would faithfully set the table for our evening meal. Now, we eat in front of the TV. I resisted the first couple times Dash asked, but the two of us are caught up on "How was your day?" before Dash has even finished his after-school snack. I have no appetite for food, and sitting at the dinner table, staring at each other while he eats mac and cheese and I sip a protein drink, feels intensely awful. Dishing up a plate for Dash and watching *Gilmore Girls* is much more pleasant. Their small New England town of Stars Hollow is such a far cry from Hogwarts or the Marvel Universe that it took me a while to recognize what Dash must like about the show: We're watching a family of two who eat takeout and leftovers in front of the television. Lorelai and Rory Gilmore laugh a lot. They pig out on junk food together—an aspiration I can get behind. The Gilmore girls seem to be doing okay, and so, in time, might we.

In some ways, finding out Sean's secrets has been weirdly edifying. It's given me a lens to what was really happening all those times when my spidey sense was going berserk. If I could have seen the truth sooner, I'd have been able to make better decisions, and I'd be in a solid place right now.

I've been withholding a big piece of the truth from Rebekah's husband, Brett. He and I were always friendly at company events, and we had dinner at their house a few years ago, though the gross manipulation that put the four of us around their family dining table still makes me seethe.

The night Carmen told me about Sean and Rebekah's long-term affair, I resisted the knee-jerk temptation to ricochet my pain onto Brett. Now though, I want to give him the gift I was denied: better information by which to understand his marriage. Things are swirling in his relationship with Rebekah, whether he knows it yet or not. I can offer him a tether. If he chooses not to take it, at least I tried.

A quick Google search and I've got a number for his employer. I hold my breath as the receptionist transfers the call. Brett probably won't be hostile, but if things turn sour, I can hang up. Butterflies slam dance to the hold music. I take a deep breath and rehearse my spiel: *Hey, Brett, it's Jessica Waite. I don't know if you remember me, but my husband, Sean, used to work with Rebekah. . . .*

A soft click, then Brett's on the line. "Jess, I'm so sorry about Sean." The compassion in his voice melts me. I slump back against the sofa.

"Thanks, Brett." His condolences have thrown me off my game. My resolve wavers, and I scramble for an excuse why I've called.

"I'm sorry I didn't go to the funeral."

I straighten my shoulders. "That's okay."

"Rebekah was out of town, and I said I'd go—to represent the family—but she told me not to bother."

Not to *bother*. Rage reignites in the pit of my stomach. When someone in Sean's world died, going to the funeral was nonnegotiable. You dress up, you show up. But some of us wouldn't want to *bother ourselves*, now would we. Brett wanted to come to the funeral to support *me*, but she stopped him.

"Brett, I'm sorry to have to tell you this, but Sean and Rebekah were having an affair."

He's quiet for so long, I worry we've dropped the call. From the little I know him, Brett's a real guy's guy. This blow must hurt, even at the most primal, mate-selection level. Brett's taller, fitter, with a full head of hair. I picture his giant cartoon fist pounding diminutive Sean into the ground like a hammer driving a stake. When Brett finally says, "Do you know how long?" I can tell he's doing the same relationship math I did. We talk for about fifteen minutes. I answer his questions as best I can, given the huge gaps in my knowledge. When I set the phone back on the charger, my hands are shaking. Hollowed out and still simmering, I grab my jacket and car keys.

At my counselor's office I barrel into it: "How dare she engage in a five-year relationship with him and then not even have the decency to go to his funeral!" I don't know their arrangement during our three years in Singapore, but my meter started running in 2010, when Rebekah first ran afoul of me.

"Are you saying you'd rather have had your husband's mistress at his funeral?" Her tone softens the pointed question.

"I wouldn't have looked at her stupid face." I quash the impulse to kick the corner of the squat oak coffee table between us. With so many people at that funeral, I was flanked on all sides. Rebekah couldn't have hurt me there. "But, yes. It's worse that she didn't go, and she wouldn't even let her husband come to support Dash and me."

My counselor says nothing, but pushes her black-framed glasses up on the bridge of her nose, and I notice one of her eyebrows is slightly raised. This woman has been around the block. Her skepticism makes me want to argue my point. "I have a control group!"

Maryanne, whom I'd red-flagged at last year's Christmas party as Rebekah 2.0, had come up to me after the service, looking dangerously distraught. I could tell she was wrestling with something, but—unlike with Slavo—I didn't encourage her to get whatever it was off her chest. Her shoulders were collapsed inward, and she wrung her scarf in her hands, almost hyperventilating when she told me if there was anything, *anything* she could ever do . . . And then, when Sean's stuff arrived the next day, I found an incriminating text thread between them that sealed my suspicions.

"There was at least one *other* 'other woman' there. So, I can say for sure, it's worse that Rebekah would be so disrespectful, just to cover her own ass." Remembering the exchange with Maryanne, I'm reminded how lucky I was not to have opened the box of Sean's personal effects the day it arrived. I'd never have been able to face everyone if I'd found his secrets before the funeral. I lean back in the chair and a small "Whew" sound escapes my mouth.

"Okay. So would you say that the quality of your anger is different today?"

I stop to consider. My rage usually feels like a white-hot coal in the pit of my stomach. Right now, it's volcanic.

"Well, I'm spewing."

"Yeah." She laughs. "Until today you haven't shown much anger in session, but you've told me you were mad at Sean. Today you're mad for him. There's a shift there."

Pfffff. "What a breakthrough. A different flavor of bile."

"Just keep tracking your anger," my counselor says as we wind up the session. "If it can move, it can move out."

I take out my debit card, wondering how much difference any of this makes. I feel better in the room, with someone listening to me, but as soon as I walk out, I'm back in the woods. Counseling is like setting a broken bone: it doesn't take the pain away, but it puts things in place so eventually they'll heal properly. It's hard to be patient with the process. I could be tracking my anger for a long time.

That night, the lava in my belly rumbles and I can't sleep. I think about Pompeii, how Vesuvius blew without warning, destroying everything in its path, burning villages and poisoning the sky. I can't live with a volcano inside me—it's eating me up, and it's not fair to Dash.

But what if I could turn this anger into a ballistic missile, fire it at a deserving target? Yes, that seems right. The anger inside me just needs a place to go.

And I know exactly where the bitch lives.

HO! HO! HO!

ext if you change your mind," Jenn says, and I give her a grateful nod. She's cute in a red and white candy-cane-striped top, and her recent pixie cut enhances her natural elfishness. "Really, any hour. Your bed is ready."

"Thanks, Jenn." Dash had zipped straight up to his eleven-year-old cousin Emma's room the moment we got here. NASA's Santa tracker was already running on Ty and Jenn's computer, and everyone's in the holiday zone. No point dragging Dash back downstairs for a maudlin farewell. "Have fun filling the stockings," I say. Jenn hugs me goodbye in the entryway.

I already know I won't be coming back to Ty and Jenn's tonight. My Christmas Eve plans include Rebekah. Just one more stop to go. The dogs are panting and restless in the back of the van. "Not long now, puppers!"

The parking lot at Sue Higgins off-leash park is almost empty, and I'm glad. Apart from picking up after my dogs, I don't have to pay close attention. My mind can drift, and the dogs can sniff and romp. I put earbuds in and cue up the FUSW playlist. We're midway along the looping trail when my phone pings, interrupting Nathaniel Rateliff & the

Night Sweats. It's a text from my friend Kathryn in Winnipeg: "Don't do it Jess."

Ahhh, Kath. Looking out for me. I don't reply. I'll answer her after it's done.

My counselor said the same thing when I told her about my revenge plan. It just goes to show . . . a person can hold advanced degrees in psychology and social work or be my bestie for twenty years and still be unequivocally, diametrically, 1 million percent wrong about what I ought to do tonight.

I'd already considered (and rejected) all their arguments before they even spoke them. I could not give less of a shit about the moral high ground, and whatever dignity I may once have had flew out the window a long time ago.

Here's the long view: When Sean said he was leaving us five years ago, he and Rebekah were already involved. Assuming they were both flirting with the idea of leaving their marriages and ending up together, they could have done it back then. That way, everything I'm dealing with now would have been *her* problem, not mine. He would have been cheating on *her*, he would have potentially bankrupted *her*, *she* would have been the one going for STD tests—and she probably still should. And I probably have some obligation to tell her that, but I don't have to tell her nicely.

I'd probably be remarried by now. My new, taller husband and I would have sat with the mourners at Sean's funeral and brought a lasagna for Rebekah, then taken Dash home to our stable and supportive household to grieve.

Besides, Rebekah never had to deal with Sean's bad moods, which became much more frequent and intense when they took up together— at least in part because she was skimming off the top, helping herself to the shiny and nourishing part of Sean and leaving Dash and me with the emotional dregs. I don't know if Sean and Rebekah broke it off for the three years our family lived in Singapore, or what their arrangement was at the time Sean died, but whatever fantasy Rebekah has about who Sean was, and how dreamy and wonderful their little romance was . . . all of that ends tonight.

We've hiked our way back to the parking lot. I raise the back hatch and towel off two furry bellies and eight snowy paws before letting Woodward and Panda jump in. No amount of toweling could stop the van from smelling like a wet-dog mobile, and I crack the window a smidge.

Were I to write back to Kathryn right now, I'd tell her there's one thing that matters to me, and one thing only: Rebekah is going to be smacked down by the truth and finally feel the consequences of her actions. However hollow tonight's victory might turn out to be, it'll be better than living as Rebekah's eternal patsy.

At home, I make hot chocolate, heating the milk on the stovetop instead of in the microwave because this is a special occasion. The wooden spoon swirls a slow creamy whirlpool. I watch it go around, using the back of the spoon to pop bubbles as they form. *Can I live with what I am about to do?* Pop. Pop. Pop. *Absolutely.* I spoon in the sugar, then the cocoa powder. The milk turns a smooth, sweet brown.

To be honest, I don't understand why anyone would try to call me off. My paragons of vengeance are fourteen-year-old Mattie Ross, who rode out with a U.S. Marshal to kill the coward Tom Chaney in *True Grit*; and Inigo Montoya, who spent his life pursuing the six-fingered man who killed his father. Those two showed impressive devotion to the cause. They'd scoff at my revenge plan. The only real malice in it is the timing: I'm trying to spoil Rebekah's Christmas Eve. In sympathy with that I say, *Boo-hoo.*

Woodward looks like a wooly little lamb curled up in his sheepskin dog bed. Panda follows me to the leather armchair in the family room, where he lies at my feet while I spread a blanket over my lap. I blow over the hot chocolate, then take a small sip. Yummy.

The shadows are long and the sun is about to set. Where is Rebekah right now? I try to imagine her, cozily settled into an armchair beside a roaring fire, surrounded by everyone she loves. Her husband, Brett, quietly contemplating divorce, sits in the chair farthest from her. Her son and daughter are eating fresh-baked cinnamon cookies, from the same batch as those they'll put out on a plate for Santa later. A twinkling, fresh-cut pine tree stands in the corner. Michael Bublé croons "White Christmas" in the background.

Into this picture-perfect imagined scene, I send the opening salvo from my phone.

"Ping."

In my imagination, Rebekah's text-alert sounds but she ignores it. Anyone she wants to talk to is already in this room.

I've prewritten my message so I can copy and paste it in sections and send them in a rapid barrage. I enter the text as fast as I can, stabbing the SEND button over and over with my pointer finger.

"Ping." *That's annoying,* thinks Rebekah.

"Ping." *Maybe I'll just see what's up.*

"Ping ping pingpingpingpingpingping . . ."

Ho! Ho! Ho!
Just so you know, your "lover" was mentally ill and his affair with you was a manifestation of his bipolar disorder.
If you thought you were special, think again.
He had other girlfriends and was even paying prostitutes.
As a courtesy to your husband, advise him to get tested for STDs.
If you thought he loved you, ask yourself, "How could anyone love something they were so deeply ashamed of?"
Sean hated himself and was overwrought with guilt and shame over you and all his other whores.

At this stage, as I picture it, Rebekah is panicking and has locked herself in the bathroom, trying to delete the messages as fast as they

pour in. Her stomach is heavy with dread and she's fighting off tears as
she reads . . .

You made him sick . . .
and sicker . . .
and sicker . . .
until finally his heart gave out.
Now his son has no father.
That little boy's hero, his Santa Claus, is gone forever.
What a waste.
I honestly don't know how you live with yourself, knowing how you
    cheated his family and your own.
My Christmas wish? That your children find out what a worthless,
    selfish, life-destroying coward their mother really is.
Merry Christmas, Ryskah.

Ryskah was the pet name I'd seen her use on the Post-it to Sean, an
obvious allusion to her first name. I used the term of endearment as the
double tap to make sure the zombie is really dead.

Years later, when I look back on my text attack, I'll read it as, perhaps,
a little heavy-handed. But then I'll remember, at this point I'm still a
month away from receiving the autopsy report and finding out what
caused my strong, vibrant husband to suffer his heart attack. On this
night, just six weeks after Sean's death, it's still unfathomable to me that
he is actually gone.

At any rate, I've struck an angry blow against a deserving target. My
heart is pounding with adrenaline and I feel like a boss . . . for about five
seconds.

Rebekah hasn't replied. Of course she hasn't. She wouldn't. My stomach sinks as I realize I have no way to be certain she even got my message.
She could have blocked my number and not received anything past the
first line. I'm a full-on idiot for thinking so carefully about what I wanted

to say, and not paying any attention to how easily I could be dismissed. Again. Ignored. Again.

I jump up. Panda springs to his feet with me, tail wagging. I find Sean's computer, log on to his Skype account, and resend the whole message in the chatbox to "Ryskah," this time adding the line "Let me know you have received this message."

I look out the window. The sky is a deep purple blue and the street is decked out with glowing trees and houses. Smoke billows from my neighbors' chimneys. Across the street, a man carries a laundry basket full of presents up the walkway, while two little ones in matching parkas run ahead, racing to be first to ring the doorbell. Every few minutes, I check Skype for a reply, but there's nothing. After half an hour, I call Rebekah's cell: straight to voicemail. I leave a message: "It's urgent you answer me." I call the family's landline and leave another terse but polite message. I don't want to escalate, but I'm not going to stop until she acknowledges me. I communicate this to her clearly.

Sean was once Rebekah's boss. Did she use him as a reference for her new job? This is extreme, and not what I first intended, but I do not feel sorry for what I am about to do. It doesn't take long to sleuth out Rebekah's work email.

> Subject: *Immediate acknowledgement required. Possible HR concern.*
> *Rebekah,*
>   *This is serious and you need to acknowledge that you have received and understood this message.*
>   *Messages like this don't belong in work email accounts.*
>   *There's just no privacy, and this shouldn't be your employer's business, should it? Unless you were sleeping with your previous manager and he gave you a reference for your job there. But you wouldn't do something unethical like that, would you? I'm sure you would have wanted to land your job on your own merit and not have slept your way into it. . . . "*

I hit SEND.

Well, lo and behold. What in the bleak midwinter do we have here? An incoming email!

Jessica,

Please accept this response as acknowledgement of your texts, voice-mails and emails.

Any subsequent attempt on your part to reach out to my husband, children, family, friends, employer and professional associates will re-sult in legal action.

Rebekah's scared. I can tell by the way she's trying to threaten me. *Good. I hope she's fucking quaking.* She has no legal leverage over me. I could prove my allegations against her if I had to, and while I'm sure she feels harassed right now, so would anyone with all those wings beating around their face—that squawking, flapping, pecking mess of chickens coming home to roost. Besides, Rebekah would never dare to bring an action against me because it would expose what she's done. What she's got at stake, I've already lost.

I should stop now. I know I should, but I don't want to let her think her empty legal threat has intimidated me.

I write back, "Eek."

It's over, now. I've won. My hands tremble from the adrenaline. There's no one to high-five. No one wants to celebrate my ugly victory with me. My calculated ballistic-missile attack morphed into something more deranged, and I didn't like how it felt to be so obsessed. But I stood up for myself and off-loaded some responsibility onto Rebekah. I clap my hands together, then clasp them behind my head and stretch out my neck, pulling the elastic off my ponytail. A sour, sweaty smell wafts out from my hair.

I strip off my shirt, then the rest of my clothes. In the shower, hot water softens the tight muscles in my neck and shoulders. The bristles of my body brush feel scratchy but good, scrubbing my back, my legs, all over. This wasn't my proudest hour, but I don't regret it.

Until tonight, Sean boosting Rebekah's career hadn't crossed my mind. If he promoted her over someone equally deserving, or his glowing recommendation tipped the scales in her favor, that's one more reason to be disappointed in him.

If my message gets flagged by an HR professional at Rebekah's new workplace, so be it. I didn't intend to attack her professional life, but I also didn't create the ethical problem my email points out. If Sean's name is in Rebekah's personnel file, she put it there. Rebekah and Sean were both in senior management at big corporations. They knew better, and if they thought they were too clever to get caught, then let this be a reality check.

I watch the trail of shampoo bubbles run down the drain. The lavender scent lingers in the steam, even after all the lather has gone. Bending forward, I squeeze the excess moisture from my hair, then work in a creamy dollop of leave-in conditioner I almost never use. I towel off and flop into bed. My wet hair soaks into the pillow. I'm asleep before it dries.

A MATED PAIR

I wake up rested and relieved. Ty and Jenn will give Dash an excellent Christmas morning. They'll make Sean's traditional breakfast of pigs in a blanket. They'll feign surprise over Santa's gift to Dash. I don't have to do any of that. I don't even have to pick up my twenty-ton anvil of anger because I dropped that thing on some bitch's head last night. It feels good to stand up and stretch my arms overhead, open the blinds, and see a clear blue sky, the trees sparkling with hoarfrost.

I check the temperature: -25C. *Yikes.* I check the bathroom mirror and see my bedhead. *Double yikes.*

Once the dogs are fed and I've called Dash and my mom, I bundle in warm layers—covering my Medusa-like hair with a toque—and load the dogs in the van. Sean's sister, Megan, and Bart have invited me to meet them at Sandy Beach, a park at the end of the street where all the Waite kids grew up.

I turn onto Riverdale Avenue and feel my heart thumping under the wrap of my chenille scarf. The canopy of trees glitters in the sun, forming an archway of delicate frost as I pass Sean's childhood home. Every Christmas morning, Sean would add our tote box of presents to the avalanche of gifts spilling out so far from his parents' tree, they blocked the front door. It didn't matter if you were a born Waite or a passing acquaintance, you'd find something under that tree with your name on it.

Jack would have breakfast ready, and soon the house would be bustling. The grandkids (plus Sean and Jenn wearing jingling elf hats) would pass out the gifts, and the noise would dull to a murmur as everyone opened their presents. Someone would throw a ball of crumpled wrapping paper toward the garbage and "miss," pinging one of his brothers in the head. Then we'd all bundle up and walk along the river to Sandy Beach, a nice bit of shoreline on the banks of the Elbow River. Sean and I walked here every Christmas Day.

I dab my eyes with a Kleenex and wrap my scarf mummy-style around my face. After smearing a frostbite-preventing wax onto their paws and snouts, I let the dogs bound onto the snowy trail. Megan and Bart are already here. Our cold Gore-Tex jackets rustle against one another as we hug. It's about ten o'clock, and no one else is here. We walk through the frosty trees beside the Elbow River, snow crunching under our feet. Ice creaks on the river, and the dogs' collars jingle when they loop back through the forest to find us.

As we approach a curve in the pathway, Bart extends a long arm upward, pointing to something on a branch, midway up a cottonwood tree. A bald eagle. I stare at the crown of white feathers, meeting the espresso-colored body like a ruffed collar. Its wings are drawn up, shrugged shoulders under a dark brown cloak. From this angle, it almost looks like Bart could reach up and pluck one of the white tail feathers tapering below the branch. Not that anyone would dare: those talons.

Sean took a picture of every eagle he ever saw. Going through boxes of old photos to make the montage for his funeral, I came across countless pictures of the sky, the sky, a blurry wing, sky with treetop, brownish blob in the clouds, more sky. This amazing creature is sitting perfectly still and it's *right there.* Even my crummy old iPhone 5 should be able to get this photo, if the battery can stay alive in the cold.

I'm wearing mittens over my gloves, and I strip off one item at a time, stuffing my pockets, working slowly enough not to startle the eagle, and quickly enough not to freeze. I open my phone. *C'mon, battery.*

As I raise the camera, the eagle fluffs out its feathers, and I think it's readying to fly. Instead, it turns to give me its full, majestic profile. I look into its pale-yellow eye. Click.

My fingertips pulse with burning cold, but the rest of me feels warm and excited by the encounter. We keep walking along the riverbank.

"Cross over? Or turn back?" Bart asks at the suspension bridge.

I turn to see what Megan thinks, but her blue eyes are huge, peeking out from under the knitted ribbing of her multicolored toque, tracking something in the other direction. I follow her gaze. The eagle soars silently across the bend in the river. It lands on a pine bough. Above it, in the same tree, is another, larger eagle.

When I taught English in Japan, I once showed my high school students a picture of Sean and me at Tokyo Disneyland. The sassiest girl blurted, "Nomi no fufu!" Her classmates looked shocked and shushed her. It means "couple of the flea," a slang term for the female being larger than the male. Beside me in that photo, Sean was shorter, even if you included his Mickey ears. We fit the bill, but there had to be a noninsect species that could represent us. Spotted hyenas were candidates, as were blue whales. When I ran it by Sean, he said, "Bald eagles, hands down."

Woodward barks, a series of sharp, staccato woofs. I follow the sound, backtracking. Woodward runs back and forth along the river's edge, sounding the alarm. Panda is in the river. The white underside of his chin pokes like a periscope out of the churning dark water as he thrashes to get back up onto the ice. I sprint to the snow-covered shoreline, drop my purse, and brace myself for the hypothermic plunge. *Megan and Bart will call 911 if they need to. Our puppy will not die on Christmas Day.* As I step onto the ice, Panda gains purchase and claws his way out. He runs, tail between his legs, back to the trail and bolts for the van. I run behind, cold air burning my lungs.

By the time we get to the parking lot, tufts of Panda's fur have frozen into icy pyramids over his whole body. He looks like a giant frozen hedgehog with hoarfrost whiskers and eyebrows. I wrap my pupsicle in a blanket and give him a hug. "It's okay, boy. You're okay." Woodward jumps into the back of the van beside him, a furry big brother to warm Panda up.

Back home, I text Megan and Bart. With our abrupt departure, I didn't properly say goodbye or thank them for venturing into the frigid morning to meet me. They've got teens at home and Christmas traditions of their own. It was gracious to make room for me. I add, "Either of you guys ever seen an eagle there in winter?"

"No. Not even in summer. Too close to downtown. We were just talking about how cool that was."

Wow. I ask Google what bald eagles are usually doing on December 25. Mainly, they gather off the coast of British Columbia and Alaska. In early spring, they travel, alone or in pairs, to find a nesting site. They shouldn't be here for months yet. The two eagles we've just seen might be literal early birds, scoping out riverfront real estate, looking for a place to make their family.

A mated pair of bald eagles. On Christmas Day. At Sandy Beach.

LUNCH WITH TY

Just before noon, I luck into a parking spot near Vintage Chophouse. It feels good to be downtown, wearing nice jeans and a long wool coat, feeding the meter as if I'm a regular person, not a brokenhearted wreck, plagued by sleeplessness. Every night it's some version of the same dream: Sean comes home, weary and smiling. He sets down his bag and stands in the doorway. My whole body recognizes him joyfully, the way I've seen a German shepherd meet a soldier home from deployment. I smile and rush toward Sean. "Where were y—" Then I remember what he's done.

Lying awake after that dream is when the marching orders come. Do-gooder tasks that swirl in my brain and won't leave me alone until I act. Though they all feel urgent, some are futile and none of my business: *Teach Jenn to drive in case something happens to Ty. Urge every friend to get their paperwork in order.* If people are mocking me behind my back— "Jess tried to make you do your will yet?"—I deserve it, but I can't stand the idea of my dearest people ever having to live through the bureaucratic hellfire I've endured the past few weeks.

There's been one silver lining to my meddlesome ways: I confided in a good friend about my insurance woes and she was inspired into a conversation with her parents. She helped them get their financial house in order, and just a few days later, her dad died of a heart attack. November 24. Not even three weeks after Sean, and not even a week after getting their insurance business settled. My friend's family is still reeling with the awful news, and money will never ease the pain of their loss, but her mom will have more options down the road.

That may or may not be the case for me. I'm still waiting to hear about my life insurance claim. They won't begin the adjudication until after the autopsy report is sent from the medical examiner, whose office is backlogged and short-staffed. In the meantime, I'm keeping an ear to the ground about job opportunities, and acting on my marching orders. Today's agenda: apologize to Ty.

I should never have asked Ty to change his tribute to Sean. Every night when I can't sleep, I rewatch the DVD of Sean's funeral. Propagandizing myself with paeans to Sean hasn't resolved my anger, but I have noticed this: every aspect of Sean's personality came out at that service.

Standing at the podium, Ty told a story meant to illustrate Sean's love of travel. "Sean's first adventure was to England. While working a summer job at The Bay, Sean had injured his thumb and was eventually offered an insurance settlement for his pain. Sean cashed the check and—without telling anyone—went to the airport, bought a ticket to London, and left. No luggage. No worries. He spent about twenty hours there . . . walked around . . . ate a couple meals . . . napped . . . a couple museums . . . back to the airport . . . back to university."

Ty looked out at the congregation, making sure everyone was suitably astonished by the audacity of the trip. He held eye contact for a long moment, then held up both hands, ten fingers splayed wide. "Ten years!" The look on his face was incredulous. "It took ten years before Sean told me that story." Everyone laughed. Our Sean. Our adorable rascal.

Sean had told me about the London trip much earlier, during the Golden Week we spent together in Japan. We were sitting cross-legged on the floor, our legs under the blanket of a heated kotatsu table in Sean's apartment. A tall silver can of Asahi Super Dry between us, poured into short glasses. Cold beer and warm feet. Cozy.

Sean said, "I did a covert trip to London once." His eyes sparkled.

Covert. Like it was a spy mission or something. "What do you mean?"

"I was at UVic, and I got a check for ten grand. *Ten grand!*" He grinned wide and threw his shoulders back into a shrug, palms up, like, what do you expect?

He told me about the British Museum and how he saw . . . he drew in a breath and said in a hushed voice, *"The Rosetta Stone."* His eyes were rapt and glossy. I was captivated by every glorious detail, and the conversation spun into a deeper one about the effects of colonization. It moved me that a person could do something so seemingly frivolous and end up enriching me through the vicarious experience.

When Sean and I were still in that same getting-to-know-you period, he told me proudly of his mom's First Nations advocacy work. Then his story digressed to a time when he was in grade two and his dad came home to a hungry household.

"Where's dinner? Where's *your mother?*" I pictured Jack as a tall, imposing man in a dark suit, slamming a frying pan onto the stove and trying to open a can of Spam without getting jelly on his tie. The phone rang. Sean hopped up from the table to answer. It was a collect call from Arizona. Sean accepted the charges.

"Daaarling!" Sean's singsong impression of his mom's greeting was spot-on. He spoke quickly and breathlessly, repeating her words as fast as they'd come at him back then, "I'm so glad it's you. Listen, sweetheart, there's a very important protest down here, you see, they're trying to build a dam—" Sean felt an upward tug on the receiver as Jack yanked the phone away from his ear. Sean was left to guess the rest.

A medically qualified person might point out that impulsive decision-making, like taking unplanned trips to London or Arizona, could be symptomatic of bipolar mania. I can't know what impulses, feelings, or chemical drivers motivated Sean and Pat to take trips without telling anyone, but I can recognize patterns. Watching the funeral video, I understand Sean as the same person all the way through his life. He didn't suddenly become a villain. None of what he did was because of me. He wasn't even living a *secret life*, not in the truest sense of that term. The shadowy aspects Sean hid from people were, in many ways, just shameful expressions of the same traits that gave him the vitality and charisma so many people adored. This matters to me.

There's a slight hitch in Ty's eulogy, right in the place where he changed the speech. It's clear the edit cost him something, and it cheated the mourners out of the most powerful expression of healing Ty could have delivered. I want to make amends.

The hostess leads me to a table where Ty's already seated in a black leather booth, typing into his BlackBerry. His cheeks are still ruddy from having walked here. As I pull up my chair, my sense of purpose collapses. This mission feels too earnest and overwrought. "Happy New Year! I have good, evil news," I say with a grin. "I'll tell you after we eat."

Ty's quick with the menu, and I can tell by how friendly he is with the server that he comes here a lot. I order the same thing he's getting, a steak sandwich, which will be easy to pack up and make into a dinner for Dash. We catch up over the meal. After the server has taken our plates, and we've each ordered a coffee, I lean closer to Ty. "So, guess who caught her husband in the hot tub with another woman?"

Ty raises his eyebrows and nods for me to proceed.

"My old pal Rebekah." I lean back in my chair with a wicked grin. *Yay, Brett!*

"What?" The surprise on Ty's face is delectable. "How do you know?"

"The gossip gods smiled on me." Carmen gifted me this bit of intel when I took her out for dinner as a thank-you for putting together my financial plan.

"Wow." Ty taps his fingers on the table, considering the tangled web of it. "You know, I creeped that Rebekah out on Facebook. She's pretty hot."

My fingers wrap around the handle of my fork, clenching into a white-knuckled fist. I'm about to stab Ty in the eye with it when he adds, "And her husband is *way* better looking than Sean."

"Yes." I let go of the fork. "And taller. I've met the man. Been to his house."

"So did you ever think about—y'know?" Ty's deadpan, trying to get my goat.

I look at him squarely. "I've fucked people for stupider reasons than that."

Ty bursts out laughing. I laugh, too.

"Anyway, no. Hot-tub woman took care of the nasty bit for me. Besides, I had my own revenge thingy on Christmas Eve."

"You went through with that?" I'd alluded vaguely to the plan as my reason not to sleep over at their house. I only mentioned it to Ty. I don't think Jenn knows about any of this yet. Someday one of us will tell her, but it's still too soon for me to talk to Jenn about it. She's a candid, unfiltered person who says exactly what she thinks. Most times that's endearing, but I'm still raw and not ready to face other people's opinions of my situation, or to risk having my worst pain become an anecdote among the wine moms on a Friday night. I think Ty knows that and has kept my drama in confidence, for the time being. "How'd it go?"

"She threatened to sue me."

He reaches for his BlackBerry as though he's about to summon a lawyer. I shrug it off. "It's over. I call it a win."

I stir my coffee. Half a cup left. Ty will have to go back to work soon. "Listen, Ty, I'm sorry for bringing you into all this. It's ugly and painful." A fountain of emotion rises in my chest. I pull a packet of Kleenex out of my purse. "You'd just lost your brother and you didn't need to know." I steal a blurry look at him and his eyes are shining, too. I slide the Kleenex packet to the middle of the table.

Ty doesn't reach for the tissue. "Jess, you and I are going to be friends for the rest of our lives, and if I didn't know that, then I wouldn't know you, would I?"

His words drop into my body like a magnet, pulling in the untethered, scattered bits of myself, like iron filings. No matter what happens the rest of my life, those will be the most important words anyone ever says to me.

Ty called his younger brother "the single best person I have ever known." I'm sitting at this table with someone who's willing to carry the burden of Sean's disgrace, to suffer the pain of it, just to *know* me. That means I'm worth knowing. It means I'm worth *something*. And Ty said it so easily, without a moment's hesitation.

Back in 1997, when not all telephones had call display, Sean prank-called me from the sidewalk outside our house while I ran back inside to grab something. I picked up our landline. "Hey, Jess," I heard "Ty" say. Sean didn't have to disguise his voice to impersonate his brother. We had a two-minute conversation—*How's Jenn? Did you call to gloat over destroying Sean in the hockey pool?*

Sean must have laughed at my facepalm as he revealed the prank and watched me hang up on him through our picture window. That night, I told Sean, "If anything ever happened to you, I'd have to call Ty sometimes, just to hear your voice."

With Sean gone, that impulse is so much deeper and more intense than I ever imagined. Being with Ty feels like the antivenom after a snakebite, lifesaving relief from the agony of missing Sean. It's not just the resonance of their shared voice. Their sense of humor is identical. When my STD test results came back negative, I texted Ty, "STD-free! Should I make that my Facebook banner?"

He wrote back instantly, "Damn. I lost the pool."

I laughed about that for a week, and remembering it makes me want to laugh now. No one else would dare make that joke. No one else would know it was the *only* response that would help me see the absurdity of the whole damn thing. No one else, except Sean.

I look across the table at Ty. He's fought back his tears, and a fond smile crinkles the lines around his eyes. He's so familiar to me, and such a comfort. But he's not Sean. And he's not a proxy for Sean. He is only himself, and I'm glad to know him.

Ty asks what's next for me. I take a sip of coffee and swallow it down hard. *A hideaway cabin,* I want to say. *Wind. Trees. Wandering the woods with Dash and the dogs. No people. No time pressure.*

"I've decided to do a masters of counseling psychology." My undergrad was in psychology and English, so it makes sense to put my grief to work, though academia is antithetical to the wilderness my heart is calling for. "But, I'm so daft right now, I have to check if my shoes match before I leave the house." I tell Ty I can't even concentrate long enough to read a novel, which I'll have to confess to my book group next week.

"They'll still love ya."

I hope Ty's right.

DEATH BY REMORSE

Dash races into the pyramid-shaped building ahead of me. Fish Creek Library has just reopened after New Year's Day. Of the many people here, I'm probably the only one who chanted, "Reintegrate with the outside world," as a way of getting out of the house.

Dash hands me his parka and heads off to see what's new from Rick Riordan. I spot two chairs together and hang our coats on the backs, then wander for a browse. I'm standing in the literary-fiction section when the tops of my cheeks go numb, like dental freezing gone amok. My head feels tingly and faint. The first time I ever felt like this, buying sheets for my dorm room at age eighteen, I blacked out and fell onto the person behind me in line at Sears. I crouch down and put my head between my knees. If I lose consciousness, at least I won't tumble into the stacks.

I breathe through my nose. In and out. In and ooooout. The industrial carpet smells like rubber and papery dust. When there seems to be enough gravity to tip me toward staying in the library, I open my eyes and stare at a nub of gray carpet. Still crouching, I lift my head. My vision is blurred. *Did I eat today?* No. *Do I have my period?* Yes. *It's probably just that.* It will pass, but I should eat something soon.

I look around. The books on the shelves are fuzzy and indistinct. My eyes zoom in on the one thing I can see clearly, a small green heart on the spine of a book. Focusing closer, two little buttonholes peek out from its glossy green face. The text above it is glossy, too, in watermelon red, all lowercase: *the list of my desires.*

Huh. I recognize this book. I held a copy in my hands a few months ago, when Sean was alive and I was still excited by things like voting on book-club selections. My friend Melody suggested this novel by Grégoire Delacourt. We're meeting to talk about it on Sunday morning, four days from now. I stand up. Whoosh goes a head rush, but it passes. I pull the slim volume off the shelf and read the first line.

"We're always telling ourselves lies." *True dat, Grégoire.*

I flip to the end. This book is only two hundred pages long. My plan had been to show up on Sunday without even trying to track down the book, assuming everyone would understand. There's a big advantage to reading it, though: I'll have something to talk about, other than how I'm *doing.* Besides, I voted for this book, the opener is intriguing, and it's pretty much just offered itself to me. How can I argue with something so easy?

I take it back to the children's section and find Dash still browsing. I give him a fifteen-minute warning. He groans, "We just got here." He's right and I'm sorry, but I need to get some food into my system soon.

I find our chairs and open the book. Jocelyne, the novel's protagonist, is a middle-aged woman living in a small town in France, taking stock of her life. On page six, by way of introducing her husband, Jo, she says, "He dreams of a flat-screen TV instead of our old Radiola set. A Porsche Cayenne. And a nice fireplace in the living room. A complete set of James Bond films on DVD. . . ." My heart rate quickens with these details. Everything Jocelyne's husband covets, my husband already had. Jo thinks those things will bring him happiness. I already know they will not. His appetite will grow in proportion, so getting a Porsche Cayenne will create a void slightly bigger than a Porsche Cayenne.

For most of our time together, Sean and I didn't own a car, which wasn't always easy in a sprawling city with long, cold winters. Our first vehicle was a VW Jetta, which we traded in for a minivan two days after Dash was born. Sean generally left the van for me and continued to cycle or ride transit to work most days, even after he was promoted to senior management. When he wanted to buy a nice vehicle, I supported the decision. He'd worked hard and his salary would afford the purchase.

In hindsight, cycling was part of what kept Sean level and grounded, and when he started driving everywhere in an ego-feeding-machine, I'm sure some things became better for him—ease of picking up other women comes to mind—but in other ways it added to the strain. I resented the Porsche by association and drove it only once—back to the dealer, to sell it for a $39,000 loss after less than a year.

No luxury item is going to save Jo from the truth of who he is, but like most people, he seems willing to stake his future on the hope it will. I'm hooked into the story and hustle Dash through the checkout so we can get home and spend the afternoon reading.

At home, I throw a protein shake in the blender. A friend sold me a bulk pack of this nutritional formula and I've been living on the shakes for a while. It's easier than forcing myself to eat, and the only downside is feeling cold all the time. I premake a sandwich for Dash, then pop a straw into my "lunch" and settle into my favorite chair with a hot pack and a blanket. I jump back into the novel, and when I feel a nudge under my elbow, it's almost dark. Woodward's brown eyes are expectant. I give him a scratch behind the ears. Both dogs follow me to their empty bowls.

Man, this book. It's uncanny, the parallels it has with my own life. Jocelyne and Jo have lived through some tough times. Things aren't perfect between them, but Jocelyne has resolved to choose the modest, imperfect life she has, over a big change that would improve their material circumstances.

Over the last few years of his life, Sean's career took a meteoric rise. At each juncture, when a new opportunity came up, we'd talk through it, find ways to rebalance the load between us. Countless times I told Sean, "You don't have to work so hard. I'm happy to get another job and you can take time off or take a position that requires less of you."

But some part of him wanted to know how high he could rise. Part of him was born to build. People ribbed Sean for "playing with LEGO," but he built models as a way to satisfy his drive to create structure. Doing that organizationally, as CEO of the midsize company he was about to lead, wasn't something he could have walked away from.

In the novel, Jo finds a check his wife has hidden and realizes it's his ticket to the big-player life he's always dreamed of. He goes for the money, abandoning the marriage, leaving Jocelyne betrayed and humiliated.

I scoop kibble into Woodward's stainless dish, then into Panda's labyrinthine plastic slow-feeder. Both dogs are on their haunches, eyes fixed on the bowls in my hands. Poor Panda is so excited he's faking the sit, his butt hovering a couple inches off the floor, black tail sweeping across the tiles. I smile, looking into each of their eyes, but neither dog can see me right now. They heard food falling into the bowls, they can smell its fishy odor. The object of their desire is so near it commands their full attention.

"Okay!" I set the dishes down.

In one sense, the husband in the story, Jo, is not so different from my two beautiful mutts, now happily munching away. He could only see the thing he wanted, and he went after it. His belief that money could quench all his desires blinded him to the life he had. Now, the mother of his two grown children is in a psychiatric hospital, fantasizing about how beautiful the blossoms of red would look, swirling into the bathwater, if she slit her wrists.

I can picture what she's imagining. The beauty in it, I mean. One of my earliest memories is standing on a kitchen stool, filling a jug with cold water from the tap. I'd use both hands to lift the heavy pitcher onto the counter, then tear open the Kool-Aid packet. That first instant: when a sprinkle of dull powder became a burst of blue, a swirl of deep pink, a streak of red . . . pure alchemical magic.

I'd be lying if I said I haven't imagined how good it would feel, fading into nothing. Part of the reason I'm defensive when people who bring casseroles poke at the rotten vegetables in my fridge is that I suspect at some level they know this, but no one asks. We creep around in the subtext, wary of one another, watching. I will not do what Jocelyne is imagining, but I relate to her fantasy, where candles flicker and a glass of red wine rests beside her on the ledge of the tub. Feeling the warm caress of the bathwater, the brief pressure of the deep cut, seeing that first bloom as the water changes color, then closing her eyes forever.

But I can also see the scene from another angle: the red blossoms long gone; the whole tub a brown-edged crimson; Jocelyne's face a distorted white moon. I can smell the ferrous, visceral tang that fills the nose of the person who finds her. One of her nurses. One of her children. The police.

When my dad died, the police warned my sister and me not to visit his apartment. "Hire a professional restoration service," they advised, and my uncle did that for us. He found someone else to clean up, as a mercy.

There will always be a witness, Jocelyne. Someone will put on a hazmat suit and a long pair of rubber gloves. Someone will reach into that bathwater and pull the plug. You can never do it entirely alone. I direct these thoughts to the protagonist in my novel, as though she's still teetering on the brink, as though her decision has not already been made.

I open the door and let the dogs out into the yard. A hint of woodsmoke from a neighbor's fireplace wafts in with the cool evening air.

———

Given my ambivalence toward life right now, it's probably a good thing I'm double-dipping on the counseling front. I see one counselor for grief at Hospice Calgary and another in private practice for everything else. *Everything else* usually means anger, but today it means "So, this weird thing happened at the library."

I tell my counselor about *the list of my desires*, how the book and its surrounding circumstances are still swirling in my mind. I don't go into the whole backstory about it being my book-club pick, but explain how my field of vision went blurry except for a little green heart on one book's spine, and the story turned out to be about a husband who betrayed the living fuck out of his wife and then died of remorse.

"I mean, it doesn't say those exact words, but the dude *dies* of *remorse!*" I've tilted my head and opened my hands in a gesture meaning *Are you getting this?*

If she's surprised by the coincidences or my sudden changes in perception, she doesn't show it. Her face has had the same open, neutral affect this whole time.

"Do you think Sean died of remorse?"

I snap my head straight up and narrow my eyes, like she's trying to trick me. "You mean will his autopsy report say, 'Cause of death: remorse'? Of course not. I know that."

"Is it important to you how Sean died?"

I tuck my chilly hands under my hamstrings. My fingers warm up a smidge, trapped between the back of my legs and the rough tweed upholstery.

"Yes, if he had illegal drugs in his system and it would invalidate his life insurance." I pull my hands out and clasp them together. One of my knuckles makes a loud crack. My heels lift and drop as though I'm walking on the spot. "And, yes, if it was a side effect of Viagra, because that would be devastatingly stupid."

She nods. I appreciate the affirmation.

"But otherwise, not really. I mean, they're going to say a heart attack caused by X, and the medical examiner can only know as much about X as Sean's frozen body can tell them."

She hears the frustration in my voice. Her mouth was already forming the small O of a question before I finished my sentence. "What is it you think the medical examiner might be missing?"

I lean back on the love seat and look at the ceiling. "I don't know. . . . To me, it seems like Sean's head did him in, at least as much as his heart." My own heart hurts, remembering our drive to Denver and Sean's breakdown in the parking lot three months before he died. "And I know it's not the most scientific explanation, but there's more to it than just things we measure, like high cholesterol, you know? And no one seems to track that, or even to care. I wish a doctor would have asked me about Sean's life. The hospital wouldn't even give me the doctor's *name*."

"That must have been hard for you." My counselor's elderly father is hospitalized now. We've had to juggle appointment times as she cares for him. Her black-framed glasses don't fully conceal the dark circles under her eyes. She understands the exhaustion of waiting for information, feeling at the mercy of a system.

"Yeah, it sucked. And the first thing anyone ever asks"—I shake my head, remembering all the times this has happened—"is 'How did he die?'" I say the question in a mocking voice, like everyone who's ever asked me is an idiot. They're not. It just pains me to give an answer I'm not confident is true.

"So, you're more interested in reconciling how he lived with how he died?"

Reconciling. There's an interesting word. She's onto something and I nod, slowly, but can't think of anything useful to say. I feel more riled up and frustrated than I did when the session started. The bills for the ambulance and hospital have started finding their way to me. There's a $960 invoice for performing four minutes of CPR before pronouncing Sean dead. I don't even know if he was alive when they attempted the resuscitation. For-profit medicine is unconscionable.

I finally tracked down the doctor, by his name on the invoice, and have left three messages, but no one will call me back. There's no point in talking about any of this in a counseling session. I'm not paying $180 an hour to bitch about bureaucracy. I glance at the wall clock, ticking its way around. The session is almost over, anyway. I reach into my purse and pull out my wallet and leather gloves.

We schedule an appointment for next week. I'm zipping up my coat when she says, "By the way, what happened to the wife?"

I don't follow and give her a puzzled look.

"In the book you mentioned. The one whose husband died of remorse."

The wife. Jocelyne Guerbette, proprietor of a haberdashery in Arras, France. My fictional sister-in-abandonment, whose little green heart-shaped button was a beacon for me. I pull my shoulders back and straighten the scarf around my collar.

"She makes it."

SOUL MATES ARE BULLSHIT

There are drugs in my house, *somewhere,* and per my marching orders in the night, I'm hunting them down. I've unloaded the freezer, checked inside every container, even opened a nostalgic TV dinner. Stalactites of frost hung from the thin plastic film, over rectangles of mashed potatoes, pale sliced turkey, a frozen gravy blob. No weed.

I text a couple of Sean's buddies. One claims to have no idea. The other says check his hockey bag.

Fluorescent lights flicker above me in the cold garage. When I unzip Sean's black duffel, a sulfurous stink gets me in the face. *How does hockey gear maintain this foul odor even when it's frozen?* I lift out shoulder pads, cup, rolls of tape, an old towel. No weed. No closure.

The bag gets stuck as I try to wedge it back under the counter. Shifting things around, I spy a briefcase behind a file box. The leather is stiff and cold in my hands, and beige with dust, except where my fingerprints leave black smudges. Marijuana is illegal, but it's not fear of the law making my pulse race, it's this queasy feeling of dread mixed with the potential for vindication. A perverse feeling I've become familiar with: not wanting to find the evidence because that makes it all true, and being thrilled to find it because I fucking *knew* it.

Finding the drugs means Dash will never stumble upon them. But there's something else I'm searching for: some verdict on whether I was an idiot for devoting twenty years of my life to Sean. My hackles went up when Rebekah came onto the scene; I wondered how many kinds of pussies Sean thought there were. My intuition got me close to the truth, so many times, but where is the thing that will tell me for certain?

The briefcase zipper opens smoothly. In the main pocket is an old black pen and two empty file folders. I slip my hand into a side pouch and feel something smooth and plastic. It crinkles when I slip it out. It's a Blue Mountain Arts greeting card, still covered in protective cellophane. I wipe my dusty hands on my pants and remove the plastic. The card stock is rough and heavy, like handmade paper, painted with a moonlit scene in purples and blues.

To My Soul Mate

I am so glad that you are a part of
my life. It is a privilege—to know
you, to share myself with you, and to
walk together on the paths that take
us in so many beautiful directions . . .

I had heard of "soul mates" before, but
I never knew such a person could exist—
until I met you. Somehow, out of all the
twists and turns our lives could have taken,
and out of all the chances we might have
missed, it almost seems like we were given
a meant-to-be moment—to meet, to get to
know one another, and to set the stage for
a special togetherness.

When I am with you, I know that I am
in the presence of someone who makes my
life more complete than I ever dreamed it
could be.

I turn to you for trust, and you give it
openly. I look to you for inspiration, for
answers, and for encouragement, and—not
only do you never let me down—you lift
my spirits up and take my thoughts to
places where my troubles seem much further
away and my joys feel like they're going to
stay in my life forever.

I hope you'll stay forever too. I feel like
you're my soul mate. And I want you to
know that my world is reassured by you,
my tomorrows need to have you near, so
many of my smiles depend on you, and my
heart is so thankful that you're here.

My thin yoga pants don't protect from the creeping chill of the concrete
as I sit down cross-legged on the garage floor. The price tag on the cellophane shows this card was purchased in Singapore, which means Sean
bought it between 2011 and 2014.

Back in Canada, the summer of 2013, Sean and I celebrated our fif-
teenth wedding anniversary. Our little family took a weekend trip to a log
cabin overlooking a meadow full of wildflowers and tall alpine grasses.
The Kootenay mountains rose up in the background. On the Saturday
night, Sean made dinner while I took Dash and the dogs to swim in the
pond. It was early July, not long after the summer solstice, and when we
got back, the sun was still high, casting a golden light on everything.

"Can we keep playing outside?" Dash asked.

"Yes!" I hung our towels over the timber deck rail. "Keep running around until you're all dry."

Sean didn't hear me come back into the cabin, and I stood watching him in the kitchen as he cracked an egg into a bowl and whisked it into Caesar salad dressing. I could smell the fresh garlic and the char of barbecued steak wafting through the screen.

Sean hummed as he worked, relaxed and happy in his baggy blue T-shirt with the RAF roundel on the front. He noticed me and smiled, then poured two glasses of prosecco into tall flutes he must have remembered to pack from home. "For you, my love," he gave me a glass and led me outside, his hand on the small of my back.

We ate at a picnic table he'd set, with a bud vase of wild daisies in the center, and when he went in to get dessert, he came out with a small robin's-egg blue box tied with a silver ribbon. He got down on one knee and took my left hand in his. "Jess, when we started out, we had nothing. I couldn't afford to buy you an engagement ring, but you didn't mind."

I shook my head and smiled.

"I could never have imagined how amazing our life together would be. You could have had anyone, Jess, but you chose me." His eyes were shiny, just like mine. He turned my hand over and set the box inside my palm, resting his hand on top. "And you keep choosing me. I love you. Thank you for marrying me."

I undid the ribbon and opened the lid. Inside was a Tiffany diamond solitaire ring with a platinum band. Sean slid the band onto my finger. A perfect fit. "I forgot to bring the card, so I'll give you this instead."

He took both my wrists in his hands and lifted me to standing, then rocked onto his tiptoes and gave me a kiss that left me weak-kneed and breathless. When he unwrapped me from his embrace, I giggled, "Yeah, that was better than a card."

From the concrete garage floor, so far from that golden summer day, it occurs to me this could be the card. What it says about taking his troubles away and lifting his spirits is something Sean said to me almost weekly.

The message alludes to an unlikely meeting and a beautiful journey together. Sean bought it at a time when we were living a charmed and exotic life, one degree north of the equator, where frangipani blossoms fell into the water and floated around us at night when we'd sneak down to the hot tub together and share thoughts about the day. A bookie would give long odds that it *isn't* that card.

But it's not signed.

I read through it again, imagining Sean bought it for Rebekah, or Maryanne, or anyone else but me. It's just a sappy message. Anyone could think it was for them. That's the whole point.

"I hope you'll stay forever" doesn't sound apt for someone you're already married to. Unless Sean already had some sense that the center would not hold. The doubt in my stomach is bitter and sickening. I push myself up from the cold floor. *Soul mates are bullshit. You just marry whomever you're with when your biological clock starts crowing, and woe to you for the rest of it.*

I move to throw the card away, but hesitate, holding the cold metal handle of the garbage-can lid. I've already thrown away all the cards and letters Sean ever gave me. I did it on a sunny afternoon, the summer we moved back from Singapore, a full year before that awful Denver road trip. We'd been living in the chaos of construction and moving boxes. I got bewitched by the magic of tidying up. Two decades' worth of cards and love letters Sean wrote, just for me. Heaps of card stock. Pretty Japanese paper, fluttering into the recycle bin. Loving sentiments, charmingly sprinkled with spelling mistakes. I've cursed Marie Kondo ever since, but it was my fault for doing the hardest thing first. Someday, I might want to look at this card again. I put it inside the cabinet, on top of Sean's urn, and pull the rolltop down.

Dash and I have finished watching *Gilmore Girls*. Now, we eat dinner in front of *The Big Bang Theory*, a sitcom about young scientists who also eat a lot of takeout. Our dinner routine has evolved to suit the new show. Dabbing—the celebratory dance move where you turn your head like you're about to sneeze into the crook of your elbow—is big these days. As Barenaked Ladies sing, "Our whole universe was in a hot, dense state," I carry the meal out from the kitchen. Dash dabs in time with the final "Bang!" and then we begin eating. It's a lively and adorable form of grace. We've just started watching when my mom calls.

"You'll never believe it, my dear," she says. "I shot a hole in one today."

"No way!"

"Right from the get-go I just felt it. I haven't been golfing well since I got down here, but when I hit that shot, I thought, 'Things are turning around.'"

"The TSN turning point!" I laugh.

She laughs, then we're both quiet on the line. "But not just for me, honey. Things have been going from bad to worse for a while now. We needed a win. Things will turn around for you, too. They will."

I let out a long, deep breath. I want to believe her, but I don't see it.

A few minutes later a text comes in from Ty.

"You guys come with us to Disney. Family Day weekend." Ty, Jenn, and Emma had to cancel their November trip to Los Angeles to attend Sean's funeral. They must be rescheduling it now, making their travel plans for mid-February.

Dash is loading up the last strands of spaghetti from his plate, eyes on the TV screen. *The Big Bang Theory* is set in California. Penny's wearing a cute tank top. I've been in heavy sweaters for months. Being at Disneyland over Valentine's Day would be less of a drag than staying here. Maybe my mom was right. Things could turn around.

THE SEAN SHOW

Welcome aboard, Mr. Waite, Mrs. Waite, Mrs. Waite," the flight attendant greets Ty, Jenn, and me as we board our flight to Los Angeles. Dash and Emma have a five-day school break, and our two families took this same trip last year, when there were two Mr. Waites and we looked less like a polygamous family.

Jenn wants to finish the novel she's reading and volunteers to take the seat next to a stranger. "You can be First Wife on the way there," she jokes, as I buckle in next to her husband.

Ty and I haven't talked since our lunch together, when I apologized for telling him Sean's secrets. I wrote to the whole family two weeks ago to share the coroner's conclusion: cardiac sarcoidosis killed Sean. It's an autoimmune condition in which white blood cells form small clusters called granulomas and embed themselves into the tissue of the heart. Sarcoidosis can affect any organ, but inside the heart it's almost undetectable. That explains why nothing showed up on Sean's ECG. An hour on the internet told me everything I could absorb about the disease, and I parsed the salient points into the email I sent the family.

It was a relief to know there was nothing sketchy or humiliating about the circumstances of his death, and a surprise to find out that, like me, Sean had been living with an autoimmune disorder.

After takeoff, when we've folded down our tray tables and taken our paper cups from the flight attendant—tea for me, coffee for Ty—he asks how things are going. I admit how scared and lost I've been feeling.

"I spent twenty years living in *The Sean Show*, y'know?" He nods and takes a sip of coffee. "Our life was exciting. We had adventures."

"You sure did." Ty was a big part of them. He knows.

"We were a team, and I was good at my role, but it wasn't exactly a résumé builder."

My unfortunate career planning feels like a gargantuan mistake. On paper, I'm a middle-aged housewife with stale references who's been out of the paid workforce for almost ten years. My mom raised my sister and me to be independent, but I'd wanted Dash to have a parent at home, and Sean was doing so well. . . . Now, I've squandered my mom's good example and put myself in jeopardy. "I'm just not sure how to get my feet back under me."

"Well, it's *The Jess Show* now. You're in charge of you."

I set my tea down harder than intended, and it slops onto the tray table. "*The Jess Show* sucks. No laughs, no sex, no intrigue. Just desperate, mopey bullshit. I'd cancel it if I could."

"But you're going to Disneyland," Ty says with a charming smile. He's not patronizing, just trying to muster a bit of joy around the escape to his happy place. This getaway is meant to be a bright spot for Ty after three long, dark months. For me, it's different. When our families went on this trip together last year, I noticed that six was the perfect number on the rides: Dash and Emma strapped in together, Ty and Jenn, Sean and me. In the photos, we all looked silly and delighted.

I put on a smooth, deep voice-over: "In this episode of *The Jess Show*, Jess cries into the empty seat next to her on the Matterhorn, the Teacups, It's a Small World . . ."

Ty points an imaginary remote control at me and presses a button.

"Not changing the channel. Just muting until *The Jess Show* hires a new writer."

I smile. He gives my hand a single, comforting pat. "Don't worry. We'll rotate the empty seat."

At 6:45 a.m., even the bounciest kids in line for Disneyland are a little subdued. I glance down at Dash's blond head, still a bit tousled from bed. He leans in close to Emma and whispers, "Churros," in a dreamy voice. Emma giggles and says it back.

At the park entrance we discover a change: Disneyland has implemented airport-style security screening. Uniformed guards and pat-downs feel off-brand for the "happiest place on earth," but this is the world we live in.

I hand our tickets to the gate attendant and pass through the metal detector. The two kids zoom past me, racing to catch their first glimpse of Cinderella's castle. Jenn speeds after them and I look back to find Ty.

He's been held up at the gate. A guard has his bag open on top of a folding table. Tiny beads of sweat glint from the back of Ty's shaved head, though the morning air is still cool.

Sean's head used to bead up like that. It happened almost instantly when he ate spicy food, and sometimes when he was triggered by stress. Ty stands perfectly still, hands at his sides, watching the security guard check his bag. Finally, the guy lets him go. Ty crosses purposefully to where I'm waiting. His face relaxes a little when he gets to me.

"Why'd you look nervous? You packing heat?" He's not a gun owner, but it's never too early for a little ribbing.

"Sean's in my pocket," he says, as though referring to a packet of pretzels stashed from the plane.

I search his blue eyes for a hint of the joke.

He pats the side pocket of his gray cargo shorts. When I divided the ashes and gave some to Ty, we never talked about intentions. His expression is neutral. My mouth is still hanging open. "Why?"

"I'm scattering him off Space Mountain."

I freeze. Ty once told me he wanted his own ashes scattered off that particular roller coaster, but I'd laughed it off, assuming he was kidding.

"For real?"

He nods.

"Right now?" My mind reels. Disneyland is Ty's happy place, not Sean's. We had a wonderful joint family vacation here last year, but Sean's attitude toward theme parks was ambivalent at best. He didn't like the crowds, and he complained about the artifice. It's hard to imagine Sean being okay with this plan.

Yet, here's Ty. He's crossed an international border and passed through a battery of security with a Ziploc bag of powder in his pocket. Here's Ty, the big brother Sean adored beyond measure. Five years is a big age gap, and when Sean was little, he followed Ty everywhere. Lots of times, Sean got told to scram, but no matter how pesky he'd been all day, if Sean ever felt scared in the night, Ty always let him crawl in next to him. When they got older, if Sean needed backup, Ty was there.

Scattering ashes from a theme-park roller coaster seems fraught with spiritual and logistical complications—maybe even legal ones—but I'm in no position to tell anyone what to do with Sean's cremains. Ty has come here with a big agenda. I need to get onside.

"All right." I start toward Jenn, who's up ahead, beckoning. "But you're sitting at the back."

———

Space Mountain has changed since last year. It's now an immersive *Star Wars*–themed attraction called Hyperspace Mountain, replete with characters, movie props, and sci-fi sound effects coming at us from every direction.

Waiting in line, I remember watching every *Star Wars* movie with

Sean. When he heard John Williams's score, Sean's eyes would twinkle with wonder and anticipation. He'd bounce around in his seat. It never got old for him, though he watched the entire series at least once a year, expanding the ritual to include every new movie in the franchise. I used to tease him about having a completist contract with George Lucas. Sean would just grin and call me a "stuck-up, half-witted, scruffy-looking nerf-herder"—the ultimate signifier of sexual attraction.

When our group gets to the front of the line, Dash and Emma board the railcar up front. I sit in the middle with Jenn. Ty's in the back. The safety bar comes down over the tops of my shoulders, pressing me down snugly. How Ty has conceived of moving his arms freely enough to release the ashes, I don't ask. The car inches up the steep incline, pressing my shoulder blades back against the seat.

We launch forward, first into total darkness, and then we're in outer space. Points of light are all around us, even beneath our feet. The *Star Wars* theme begins and we accelerate into hyperdrive, propelled into a world where good and evil are clearly defined—a world where Sean was only ever a Jedi, good-hearted and true.

Pictures of Sean flash into my mind, from a time before I knew him. He's ten years old, running around the grass in his backyard with the neighbor's German shepherd, waving a green lightsaber, driving Zack the dog into a playful frenzy. Then Sean's in the den, around the same age, practicing his violin and wearing a blue T-shirt with the white iron-on lettering MAY THE FORCE BE WITH YOU. These images arise from photos I've seen, and childhood stories Sean told, but they're as clear as any scenes I've witnessed with my own eyes.

The five of us twist and turn, laugh and scream our way through our final ride with Sean. A cold trail runs into the hair on my temples and splashes into my ears: the effect of g-forces on tears.

The ride ends. The safety bar lifts and we're herded toward the exit. I catch Ty's eye. He nods.

I would never have thought to make this pilgrimage for Sean. Half an hour ago, if consulted, I'd have discouraged the whole endeavor. But this brotherly mission was the right thing for Ty, and therefore the right thing to do. Sean was never mine alone. It takes all of us to let him go.

Later that day, we drift through the dark bayou into the skeleton-filled caves of the Pirates of the Caribbean. The kids are up front, Ty and Jenn in the middle, and I'm in the back with the empty seat. We can hear drunken pirates carousing in the port ahead, but before we reach them, we must pass through a dark cavern, candlelight flickering against a pile of human skulls. I reach forward and tap Ty on the shoulder. He turns around.

"When I die"—I knock on my own skull, then point to the heap just a short toss away—"you'd better up your game."

———

Homebound at LAX, I hear my name paged over the airport loudspeaker, calling me to the Air Canada desk. I talk to the gate agent, then find Ty, Jenn, Emma, and Dash, sprawled across four airport chairs, each on separate devices, our carry-on bags piled in front of them. "They offered me an upgrade. But there's only one seat, not all of us."

"Take it," Jenn says. "We've got Dash."

Part of me feels I should protest, but Dash is happy with them. Jenn sat as odd man out on the way down so I was going to be on my own anyway.

On board and seated in the back row of business class, I tuck my iPad into the seat pocket. When I look up, a sliver of perfectly sculpted male torso is just to my right, between a black T-shirt and the waistband of some washed-out jeans. The man is tall and I can't see his face as he stretches to put his bag in the overhead compartment. I look away before he can catch me noticing, but I'm blushing with how completely I've noticed.

I reach down to get something out of my purse and come up with a pen and notebook. He's sat down beside me.

"Hello," he says. *Crikey, that accent.*

"Hi." I smile and turn to face him. *Holy shit.* He's Hemsworth hand-some. I avert my eyes before his perfect symmetry blows out my retinas. "Kiwi?" I ask, about his accent, with a side glance.

"Ay yeah. Everyone always guesses Aussie."

"Yep. I'm Canadian. I get it." He might have been Aussie, for all I knew, but if I'd guessed wrong, I wanted it to be in favor of the oft-overshadowed country.

"You been to New Zealand then?"

"I was in Auckland in 2011 when the All Blacks won the World Cup. I'm in love with the haka."

He lifts his fist and smacks his forearm with the other hand and makes a deep *hyah* sound, flaring his nostrils and sticking his tongue out all the way. His eyes are huge and bulging. It's a fierce gesture—from Maori lineage—meant to generate a fighting spirit. But even with that grimace his face is still ridiculously attractive. It's too much. I start giggling and cover my face with my hands, then cross my legs because I'm laughing so hard.

He's on his way to Vancouver to shoot a pilot for a television series. He tucks the script into the seat pocket. I can't make out the title without my reading glasses. I had twenty-twenty vision until just a few years ago, when I turned forty. *Sigh.* I look around the cabin. The flight attendants seem about to secure the door when someone I recognize gets on board and sits in the front row.

I nudge Hemsworth guy. "Goldie Hawn's up there. You should intro-duce yourself."

Now he's blushing. "Nah." He smiles and tilts his head. "She's superfa-mous and I'm kinda shy." He pulls out his script and appears to study it.

Once the plane is in the air, I set up my iPad on the tray table and play the iOS version of a board game. Hemsworth notices. "You playing Dominion? I'm designing a board game m'self."

"Really?"

He pulls a notebook from his bag and shows me what he's working on. I give him feedback on what I like and don't like about the mechanics of the games he's drawing on as influences. I know most of them. This feels like a victory for nerd girls everywhere.

"Do you live in Vancouver?" Hemsworth asks.

"No, just connecting on to Calgary."

"Ah, too bad." He shakes his head. "I was gonna ask if you wanted to come by and play-test my design."

Play-test his design. I'm sure he means it literally, but I'm awash in entendres. I turn my mouth down to suggest, "Darn it all."

When we land in Vancouver, I tell Hemsworth, "I hope your series gets picked up." And I mean it. That show, the name of which I do not know, is now the reason I pay for cable.

————

We're barely off the plane when we discover our connection is delayed eight hours. Getting out earlier is impossible. We huddle for a second, looking at one another. Ty says, "Commodore?"

Ty and Jenn met at Commodore Lanes and Billiards in 1993, just after Jenn graduated from high school and used her Burger King savings to fly as far away from Saint John, New Brunswick, as she could get without a passport. Ty used to manage the place. We stash our luggage in lockers and take the SkyTrain down to Granville Street.

The new owners have decorated with kitschy memorabilia and terraria, giving the place a quirky, overdone charm. They've also installed an electronic scoring system, so you pay by the hour instead of by the game.

Sean used to bowl here, in a Wednesday-night league, after beer and wings with his yuppie buddies at O'Doul's. It's strange to be in the place that held Sean's life on the cusp of our meeting. He left this life to move to Japan, beginning the era of our life together. My red-striped rental shoes are cream-colored where once they might have been white. Sean and I had the same-size feet and I wonder, as I tie the laces, if Sean ever stood here in these shoes.

Dash is a novice bowler. Each time he lofts the ball or sends it trickling into the gutter, a different one of us tries to help him correct his technique. The rest of us are rusty, but nobody cares. This is much better than being stuck in the airport. Ty's winning until the ninth frame, when I somehow hit a hot streak and finish with three strikes in a row.

"You ended on a turkey!" Ty says, and I don't know if he's congratulating or insulting me, but he sounds excited.

The next game, I bowl strikes the first four frames. Each time, I choose a different ball, hold it in close to my chest, take a deep breath, and look at the five pins. I know, as soon as I let it go, the ball will keep a straight line, then curl to connect with the headpin, knocking the rest down. This must be how my mom felt when the sweet spot of her nine iron connected with her dimpled yellow Titleist. She just knew from the get-go.

It feels amazing to be *in the zone*; not just the bowling, but being upgraded to business class, bumping elbows with Hollywood types, and finally getting to see this old haunt. Not only does the Commodore hold the origin story for Ty and Jenn's relationship, but it gives me a feeling about the life Sean had before I knew him. It's like finding a new/old piece of him that fits perfectly into a puzzle I hadn't even known I was solving.

Dash throws a gutter ball and bursts into tears. He's been trying so hard, and after three days of Disney excitement, he's worn out. He runs toward the bathroom, trying to hide his crying. I go after him, meaning to console him and coax him back, but he isn't ready. He doesn't want my help, or my reassurance, or even my presence.

I leave him on a bench to compose himself. Back at our lane, the scoring monitor has gone blank. Our session timed out and the game is over. My stomach drops. I'd bowled seven strikes in a row. Ten is a perfect game. How long might my momentum have carried?

As we ride the SkyTrain back to the airport, Dash is in a better mood. He and Emma schooled Ty in a game of foosball, and our Commodore trip ended on a good note. Still, it's hard to shake my own feeling of letdown. I'm ashamed over how much I wanted to keep bowling. Not because I was feeling competitive . . . it was being adept, surprising myself, feeling *lucky*.

To feel in a groove and then be yanked out of it, to be elated then frustrated, a success then a failure, is discombobulating and painful, like being *Freaky Friday*-ed into Sean's old life, only to have the spell wear off too soon. I might be able to tolerate my own grief if I could have moments of freedom interspersed, but being entwined with a child on his own emotional roller coaster, I don't know when I'll get to feel untempered, untethered joy again.

———

Sean's frequent-flier guest vouchers get us into the Air Canada lounge. It's about 10:00 p.m. when we flop into the wide love seats and leather chairs. I try to doze off but a phone pings behind me. My ears perk up to the conversation of a businessman whose seat backs onto mine.

"Wifey says there's a snowfall warning for Calgary tonight. Up to twelve inches." The man pronounces Calgary as two syllables, *CAL-gree*, which makes me think he's local to the city.

That's a grim forecast. I hope we make it out before the weather causes further delays. The guy composes his text reply out loud: "Hope . . . you . . . packed my . . . swimsuit. . . . Sydney's . . . gonna be . . . hot."

His buddy bursts out laughing. "Did you really write that?"

"Nope. Went with my standby: 'Hang in there, babe.'"

My face gets hot. I've received hundreds of "hang in there" texts from Sean over the years. The second-last message he ever sent said, "I know this is a hard day, hon. Hang in there." I took those messages to heart. They gave me encouragement and made me feel less taken for granted. Sean told me all the time how much he valued my contribution to our partnership.

"Smart." Buddy chuckles.

"Wifey can't stand shoveling snow." The businessdouche laughs.

"Y'know, I feel so guilty, I think I need another drink. Want one?" Both men walk to the bar counter to help themselves to free alcohol while I glare daggers into their backs.

When I didn't go back to work after Dash was born, people couldn't stop telling me how lucky I was. And I *felt* lucky, not having to wake him up early and bundle him off to a day home. Getting to see every milestone, kiss every boo-boo myself. But I also sacrificed for that luck. I gave up my own income, career advancement, status—and not just social status—even the dynamic within our marriage changed when I became financially beholden to Sean. His peers didn't constantly remind him how lucky he was, to be able to grow his career, and network, and travel all over the world while a trusted and competent person took care of his home. I hadn't realized the steadfast partner made such an easy target for casual mockery.

I get up from the leather lounge chair and walk to the window. The sky is dark, but the lights on the tarmac are colorful, airplanes and support vehicles moving to and fro. Going home means going back to being the only one to pick up milk when we run out, the only one to soothe Dash's tears, the only one to shovel snow. But I know how to do it because my mom showed me. I know how, also, because I've been doing these things on my own for years while Sean traveled and worked his sixty-hour weeks. *Fuck those entitled assholes. I* will *hang in there.*

I set my phone alarm for half an hour earlier, so I can shovel our sidewalk before getting Dash off to school. A text comes in from my friend Lianne, a neighbor who's been checking on our house while we were away. "Welcome home! Can I pop by tomorrow? Someone left a package on your porch."

REVERSAL OF FORTUNE

I 've shoveled, fetched my dogs from the kennel, and am unpacking gro-
ceries when the doorbell rings. "Lianne!" She steps into the entryway
and we hug while the dogs sniff at her legs. Her blond hair is cut into a
fresh bob. "You look great! Love the new do."

"Oh, thanks." Lianne smooths down the back of her hair with her
free hand. She's holding a FedEx envelope in the other. "How was your
trip?"

"Kids had a blast. Want to come in?"

"Wish I could, but we're on the run." She gestures toward the driveway where her husband is waiting in their Volvo. "I just wanted to make
sure you got this." Lianne hands me the envelope.

I nod and look at the return address. *Great-West Life.* My stomach
feels untrustworthy. "It's from the life insurance company."

Lianne's expression is both somber and gentle. "Yeah. That's why I
wanted to get it to you right away."

I run the soft pad of my thumb along the ridge of folded card stock,
slowly, as though it's hypnotic.

"Do you want me to stay with you while you open it?"

Her offer startles me. Not that I'm surprised Lianne would be sensitive and kind, but if I'm giving off a vibe that suggests I need support to do something as simple as open an envelope . . .

"Thanks, Lianne. That's okay. You've got things to do."

I've never had a big sister, but Lianne's tender look as she heads out the door makes me feel like I have one now. She says, "I'm five minutes away."

I steady myself on the mat in the entryway, holding the envelope. The insurance agent, Nick, had said he'd call with any news of a decision. I took my cell to California but never checked our landline. The dogs follow me back to the kitchen where I pick up the phone. Seven new messages: one from the library, two telemarketing scams, four from Nick.

I put the unopened FedEx envelope on top of a growing pile of papers on the window ledge. Nick's most recent message was from this morning, while I was out picking up the dogs. He asked for an urgent callback. Stomach heavy, I press his digits into the keypad. "Sorry, Nick. I was out of town."

"Whoa, I'm so glad you caught me, Jessica. I was just about to issue a stop payment on the check."

It's the check. I knew it might be, but it could also have been a registered letter denying the claim. "I just got it."

"Well, I'm glad it's in the right hands now. So, how do you feel?"

I feel queasy and numb. My hands are freezing and not connected to my body. Those aren't the right answers. "Relieved, I guess."

"It can take some time to adjust." He must hear in my voice I'm not uplifted the way I imagined I would be if this settlement came through. "Lots of people feel some pretty big emotions when their claim pays out."

I sigh. "Listen, Nick, thank you for everything you've done." Gratitude wells up as I imagine the claim-review process he must have sat through. This policy earned one month's premium. Every detail of Nick's decision-making would have been scrutinized. "I know this is every broker's worst nightmare. You must have really gone to bat for me."

"I just did my job. It was your husband who looked out for you."

After Nick hangs up, I sit, holding the phone, swiveling back and forth in my chair. The envelope on the counter comes in and out of view as I swing my knees slowly from side to side.

I pace around the kitchen, put a loose spoon in the dishwasher, take a jar of spaghetti sauce downstairs to the pantry, change loads in the laundry, go back up to find the dishwasher wide open, realize I forgot to start the dryer, notice the spaghetti sauce on top of the washing machine. It's no good, skittering around the house like a free radical.

The library's message said my hold was in. I put on my boots and coat and wrap a long knit scarf around my neck. As I walk toward the library, the sunlight feels good on my face, even with the bracing wind. My tricky stomach settles in the fresh air.

Back in November, Carmen wrote up two financial plans. One was based on this outcome: the best-case scenario, where I could pay off all my debts and—so long as I wasn't foolhardy—live for five years without supplemental income. Many more life options have just become available to me. . . .

But if I open the envelope, Sean is never coming back. Some part of me still feels like he's away on a business trip. Any minute now he'll walk in the door, like he does in my recurring dreams. Taking that money means agreeing to something I don't agree with. Not at all. I want to renege, give it all back, call it a mulligan. *Sorry, just kidding. Can I have my husband back, please?*

The library's hold section is just to the right of the main doors. Normally I'd browse a bit, but I've only got about half an hour before Dash gets home on the bus. I go straight to the shelf alphabetized for "W" names and find the book: Alix Ohlin's *Inside*. The snow globe on the cover feels like a good metaphor for my life since Sean died, bleak and snowy in a hard-shelled bubble.

Walking to the self-checkout, I pass between racks with the book covers displayed outward. New releases and librarian-recommended picks. In front of a turquoise-and-yellow book, I halt.

The background blurs, leaving only the blue-and-yellow book in clear focus. I blink but my field of vision doesn't correct. The pretty blue stripes are variegated, forming the wavy surface of a rough sea, with a yellow ship rolling in choppy waters. It looks *bigger* than the book next to it, as if I'm seeing it through a magnifying lens. I pick it up and read a blurb from Patrick deWitt on the back: "A generous and wise tale, told with Evison's trademark verve and charisma, *This Is Your Life, Harriet Chance* is a deeply felt and deeply comforting novel."

Deeply comforting. Sold. I check out both books and tuck them under my jacket in case it starts snowing again on the walk home.

———

Jocelyne Guerbette, the fictional French haberdasher in *the list of my desires*, hid her life-altering check in a shoe in her bedroom closet. Mine hides in plain sight, still in the FedEx envelope on the kitchen-window ledge, for three days. On the fourth day, I get a call from Nick. "Okay, I'll deposit it right now."

Sitting in the kitchen, I swivel my chair toward and away from the cardboard envelope. *Just pick it up.* The smooth packet is so light it could be empty, but my chest is heavy with the weight of what's inside.

A few weeks ago, when my mom sat in this very chair and told me why she had left my dad, it came out that his drinking had been bankrupting our family. I was either too young, or the situation wasn't yet far enough gone, for me to notice any status difference with my friends on Vancouver Island, but in Weyburn, I knew we were broke.

We'd left with nothing and started over with hand-me-downs from our cousins, instructed to count our blessings for every scrap. My mom carried two and sometimes three low-paying jobs. Financially, she'd have been better off on welfare, but she had a strong work ethic and didn't want to model a life on the dole. We never suffered the desperate poverty I've since seen in other places, and looking back, it's almost comical to remember feeling so ashamed of our lowly status in a town where the grandest building was the old mental hospital, but it was the eighties and we were living in a material world.

Back then, I was certain more money would solve all my problems. *Goodbye, patched jeans. Hello, Fancy Ass.* A check like the one I'm holding would have made life more comfortable for my mom and helped gawky-adolescent me fit into Weyburn Junior High.

But I know better, now, what money can and cannot do. My problems have shape-shifted to fit whatever socioeconomic altitude I've found myself cruising. And it's not just me. The years I spent as an insurance appraiser took me into the private spaces of hundreds of extremely wealthy people. I saw oral-chemotherapy meds on bathroom counters, secret recycle bins in bedroom closets full of empty wine bottles, shelf after shelf of self-help books promising solutions for all the ways human beings suffer. Rich people still have problems, they just have more money to throw at them, and more elaborate facades to hide behind.

This money, which amounts to three years' salary for Sean, lifts me out of widowhood's economic hardship. Yet, I'm no more deserving than anyone else, and no more deserving than I would have been if the claim had been denied. I already knew how to live the hardscrabble life I've avoided. Work hard, live frugally. Growing up, our fridge, pantry, and Mom's bank account were empty four days before payday. My mom borrowed and repaid the same $200 to her parents monthly for years. "This is silly," they said. "Let us give you the money." My mom refused. She wanted to make a go of her own life. No handouts.

With this insurance payout, I'm afraid the people who've rallied around me will leave, assuming all my problems are solved, just as I would once have assumed the same thing. Some might even resent me for cashing in, never understanding what this money has actually cost.

The cardboard pull tab zips open and I slide the paper out of the envelope. It feels ordinary, a piece of paper and some ink. Handling it does not require a shower, or the donning of special attire, or a waiting coachman and horse-drawn carriage. The bank is five minutes away. I slip on my shoes and drive there in my grubby duds.

Ahead of me at the bank, people fidget and check their phones. I catch my reflection in the silver ball on top of a stanchion. Unwashed hair and yesterday's wrinkled jeans. I look, as my mom would say, like a ragamuffin. I glance down at my scuffed and dirty dog-walking shoes. *They could treat me as suspicious, the check as a possible forgery.* Maybe being here did require special clothes, after all.

When my turn comes, I set my driver's license, bank card, and the check onto the counter. The teller is a woman around my age. I notice a budding hangnail as I slide the paper across to her waiting manicure. "My husband died." My voice is neutral and not too quiet for her to hear. "This is the life insurance check."

"Oh, sweetheart. I'm so sorry." She looks at me, hesitating. "I'll just call the manager over to receive the deposit."

We stand looking at each other and I can see pain in her eyes. *I am Typhoid Mary, spreading misery wherever I go.*

"I'm widowed, too." Her lipstick, a sad smile.

Oh. It's not pity in her eyes, but recognition. Suddenly I can really see her—a human being, not a bank teller. She's not just receiving this check, she's receiving me and my entire unkempt, conflicted reversal of fortune. "I'm so sorry," I say. "What was your husband's name?"

"Paul. It was seven years ago. He was thirty-seven."

"Sean. Three months ago. Forty-seven."

How are you now? I want to ask her. *Do you have kids? Do they remember Paul? Can they sleep at night?* I try to transmit all my questions through our extended moment of eye contact. As she takes me in, I wonder if I'm a reflection of how far she's come. To me, with her decent job and professional manner, she's a beacon of hope. Life goes on.

"SIGNS"

S o, another weird thing happened at the library." I assume my Everything Else Counselor will remember the episode a couple months
ago, when I almost fainted in the stacks. I hold the blue-and-yellow book
up, so she gets a clear view of the cover. "It was so weird. I got some great
books for Christmas—ones I was dying to read—but this one jumped
the queue."

"So, you felt compelled to read it right away?"

"Yeah, but why would I?" I show her the back cover, which is all praise
for the author, nothing about the story.

"What was important about it?"

"Well, the plot for one thing. It's about this new widow, Harriet,
who finds out her husband won an Alaskan cruise in a silent auction just
before he died. She decides to go anyway, with a friend. Turns out the
husband bought the cruise for himself and Harriet's *friend*."

"So, they were having an affair."

"Correct." My counselor never takes notes during the session. Right
now, I wish she did, so she could drop her pen in surprise. Instead, she
shows no reaction at all. She rests her chin on the bridge of her pressed-
together fingers.

"Harriet's all alone on the ship, beside herself with this horrible news, while everyone else on board is having a fabulous vacation, and then the *ghost of her husband* shows up to apologize to her. . . . " I'm amping up, advocating for the relevance of these made-up characters. "He's already been in trouble with the higher-ups for breaking the rules of the dead. He'd put a can of WD-40 on the breakfast table and moved his slippers to a place where she'd trip on them, trying to get Harriet's attention."

"Okay."

"So, appearing to her on the cruise was, like, his third strike." I take a breath, gathering the biggest detail of all. "Her husband was willing to forgo his place in the afterlife, just to apologize to her."

A solemnity drops over me as I say these words. When Harriet got her apology, I'd stopped reading and punched the air in celebration. *Vindication!* Here, in the presence of an objective third party, the weight of the husband's sacrifice hits me in a way it didn't when I was caught up in the drama of the story.

"And then, after the husband has disappeared, and the ship is about to pull away from the port in Ketchikan, Harriet sees"—I swallow hard— "a pair of bald eagles."

"And you saw a pair of eagles on Christmas Day."

I nod, glad she remembers the salient point. I can still feel that frozen morning and see the eagle fluffing its feathers against the cold.

"So"—she opens her hands as if to receive something from me— "what do you make of it all?"

A whoosh of breath lifts the loose fringe of hair around my face. "Well, of course, it's not a big deal to see eagles in Alaska, but this is the second book that's felt directly related to my life. It almost feels like divine providence or, y'know"—I tilt my chin down and look up at her— "a sign?" I curl my top lip slightly, like the word *sign* is a wood louse, crawling around the drain on my laundry room floor.

She nods. "What would it mean if it wasn't a sign?"

I bristle, then feel surprised by my irritation. I'm not saying signs are real, and it's not like I want her to say that either. If she jumped to those conclusions, I'd never have come back after the first appointment. But still, I checked with a librarian to see how many books are in circulation at Fish Creek, and the chance of me stumbling onto *the list of my desires* was 1 in 136,000. To have something similar happen, *again*—the odds are infinitesimal.

I look toward the ceiling, considering her question. "I guess it would mean this kind of thing happens, and everyone looks for answers, so I'm not alone."

"How does it feel to think in those terms?"

I shrug. "Mixed, I guess. . . . On one hand it's good, less isolating. At least two other people understand what I've been through and cared enough to write books about it. On the other hand, I hate to think about my situation being so run-of-the-mill."

She says some more things, and I say some more, but while our surface conversation plays out, a busy little secretary in my mind is labeling a file "Talking about Signs" and sealing it shut. The secretary thrives on gold stars. Every session, her efficiency makes me better at gaming counseling. I know exactly what to say to feel dandy for the hour I'm in session, with the empathetic presence who listens and nods as I put forth my big ideas about healing. If a counselor tells me, "You're doing really well," I bask in the sense of achievement, but the afterglow is gone before I've even started my car. The other 167 hours per week, I feel tired and lonely and have minimal resolve and no clear idea how to enact my grand plans for "not becoming a bitter old hag." Soon, I'll notice this tendency and decide I've exhausted the option of talk therapy.

For now, I set my bag on the passenger seat and stand Jonathan Evison's novel upright. The turquoise-and-yellow spine pokes out of the top of my gray tote purse like a small companion, riding shotgun. My copilot.

HALF YOUR AGE + 7

What I want is to peer through the fish-finder from the safety of the boat, no line in the water, every single toe kept dry. But this is the age of surveillance capitalism, and no site will let you browse without surrendering your personal details. When the questions pop up, I hear Hannibal Lecter's voice: "Quid pro quo. Yes or no, Clarice."

Honest Answers to Online Dating Questionnaire
Status: Separated*
Profession: Unemployed**
Yearly Income: $20,000–$25,000
Hobbies: Crying, napping, flooding periods***
Fave Book: They jump out at me in the library.
Fave Food: I only eat protein shakes. Hope you have a good blender.

Come and get me, boys.

---

*Separated by DEATH, and fuck you for trying to call me a widow.

**Also, bitter that the lame but socially accepted term *stay-at-home mom* only applies if one's husband is alive.

***Menstruation is not a hobby. *However*, interminable hemorrhaging keeps you busier than you'd think.

Lying in bed at night, the same topics—loneliness, parenting, sex— recirculate in my mind. It's not like I even want to date. I don't. It pains me to imagine kissing anyone else, let alone showing my naked body to someone new for the first time since my early twenties. Ever since I sat next to that handsome young actor on the airplane, though, I've started to wonder what the possibility of dating means for me. If I didn't have Dash, I might enact my Wid-Ho phase, taking comfort with any number of warm bodies, making up for lost time. Ultimately, though, that path would leave me just as lonely with a mound of extra sheets to wash.

When I thought Sean's work was sapping his libido, I was willing to settle for whatever flirty, playful exchanges passed for our sex life—even though they didn't always translate into the satisfying intimacy I wanted. Knowing he gave himself away to everyone else but me? The rejection seemed bottomless, but at its core is this roar that drives me to consider dating before I'm ready, just to see if I can.

The other big question is whether there's anyone out there worth shaping up for. If so, what would make him want someone so broken-hearted and confused? I'm afraid of porn now, and pot, and even cell phones, for how easy they make it to hide what you're doing from someone sitting beside you in the same room.

When you date online, you have to supply the age range you're looking for. I heard there's a formula some men use: half their age, plus seven. By that math, guys my age will be looking at twenty-nine-year-olds, and I'll be on the radar for seventy-four-year-old men.

This whole space grosses me out. It's online shopping *for people*. The dudes in these photos hold up dripping fish and rest their elbows against big, shiny pickup trucks, brandishing a version of masculinity I don't register. They remind me of those inflatable noodle-men at the entrances to car dealerships, waving their arms in the wind. *Right this way, ladies.*

My own profile, were I to make a real one, would have to be even salesier than these. A realtor covering up a former grow-op. Bleach everything, spray it with Febreze, hope no one notices the spores of heartache and distrust hiding in the insulation. After about half an hour, I delete my shell profile and shut down my computer. There's only one person I want, and he was never who I imagined him to be.

TINFOIL HAT CLUB

It's spaghetti tonight, with garlic bread and a green salad made mostly of iceberg lettuce. Volunteers smile from behind long plastic tables, holding tongs and ladles, serving us cafeteria-style. The garlic bread is the first food that's smelled good since my abandoned bowl of chicken soup five months ago. I ask for two pieces. For the past few Thursdays, Dash and I have been coming to the Kids Club program at Hospice Calgary. We eat dinner with other families who've experienced the death of a parent. It's the one night a week I don't have to think about what's for dinner: a small, enormous reprieve.

When we're done eating, a counselor hands a frame drum to Nora, a seven-year-old with short curls and huge dark eyes. She hits the drum tentatively, with a leather-wrapped stick. The beat gets louder as Nora warms to it; the deep *thum-thum-thum* spurs the other six kids to line up behind her. Dash files in, second from the back. Nora drums the young ones out of the room and down the hallway to their session room.

When I signed Dash up for this program, I mistakenly thought the parents met for coffee while the kids were counseled. I'd been avoiding any kind of group therapy, assuming other widows don't have a daily practice of listening to Fuck You playlists dedicated to their dead spouses. But it turns out there's a program for us, too. The eight-week syllabus covers parental versions of the children's curriculum.

This is our fourth week. Five widowed moms sit in a circle around our counselor, Carly. I'm wearing a sparkly purple barrette in my hair and a David Bowie T-shirt. Prince died today, and I don't have a Prince T-shirt. I wish I did. Or a raspberry beret. When we go around the circle to check in, I say, "I'm sad Prince died, sorry." I mumble the apology, imagining it makes me a jerk, to privilege a celebrity death in a room with five dead husbands.

Carly says the passing of public figures can create the rare occasions when our death-denying culture comes together to mourn. "When people seem overly distraught about the death of a famous person, they may actually be mourning a loss in their personal life, too."

It's an interesting take, and it makes sense, especially when I put it together with something else I've noticed in recent weeks. On Friday nights, I've been taking Dash to a community drumming circle. When my massage therapist recommended it, I shook my head. *No way. Too hippie.* But then she said, "They do a round of drumming called stress release where they turn off all the lights and you just whale on the drum and scream your head off."

Screaming into the dark was something I could get behind.

We went to the first drumming session of the New Year. Dash took to it right away. I could almost see it working through him. He pounded along until his hair was damp with sweat. I wept almost the entire time, but I didn't feel self-conscious because everyone was doing their own thing and there was no expectation of social conversation. All I had to do was choose my drum, a djembe, hit its taut skin with my hand, and feel its percussion meet that of dozens of other drums playing together. In that space, my tears came as a gentle catharsis, not like the gut-wrenching sobbing I did at home on my own. I can see how mourning a loss becomes more manageable when it's blended into an expression of sorrow from a whole community, even if the focus is ostensibly on a famous person. It's a more generous view of celebrity deaths than I held before.

"Tonight," Carly says, "we'll be talking about continued bonds. After a parent dies, kids often wonder about identity questions, like, 'Am I still my dad's son?'"

She's still talking, giving other examples, but my thoughts stick with this first question. Dash hasn't asked anything like that yet, but Father's Day looms. I don't know if grade four teachers still get the kids to make something for their dads in class, or if Dash will want to, or how to handle that.

Last summer, as Sean was preparing to start commuting between Calgary and Denver, he found an old glass jar shaped like a teddy bear and filled it with little reminders of the ways he loved Dash and the fun times they had together. Dash put the memory jar in his closet, and I didn't realize he'd been dipping into it until he found me in the kitchen and held out a crumpled slip of paper, wordless with tears. I read Sean's note: "Future plan: Teaching you to play baseball."

I wrapped Dash in my arms and held him until his crying was done. *Fuck me. Why didn't I go through those notes?* Failure to shield: the great and unavoidable crime of mothering.

I'm lost in this memory when a question from Carly breaks through. "Has anyone noticed their light bulbs burning out more frequently?"

I raise my hand. Other hands go up as well, and there's a round of nervous laughter as we recognize the same questions in one another's eyes.

"I didn't used to ask about this," Carly says. "It's not strictly part of the syllabus, but story after story kept coming out in groups, so I introduce the topic now."

"Thirty-four," I say. "I figured my house was falling apart." I look overhead at the fluorescent lights in the conference room, daring them to burn out, for the cheek of it.

We go around the room. Everyone has a story about clusters of lights burning out.

"Okay," I say, "but could they not magically mow the lawn instead? Changing pot lights is a pain in the ass." It's the least guarded and friendliest conversation we've had as a group. After the session, I feel a sense of camaraderie. These experiences are so common, Carly made sure to normalize them. If grief counselors hear this stuff all the time, why does no one talk about it in polite society?

When I brought signs up with my individual counselor, she redirected without hesitation. It hurt a little, to have my seedling question yanked from the soil before it could take root. This has to be part of why people don't share; it's too delicate and subtle an experience to risk putting forth. It's not like I'm desperate to believe. I'd be happy to find a rational answer, but I also don't want the evidence tampered with or destroyed, which happens by default if we can't be forthright.

The truth is, it's not just burned-out light bulbs. Sometimes I hear music or a voice in another room, and when I search out the sound, the radio has come on by itself. I updated the stereo's software. When that didn't stop it, I powered down the sound system altogether. The TV in the kitchen came on by itself, so I donated it to a thrift shop. But I can't easily get rid of the motorized projection television in the basement. A few times now, Dash and I have been in the same room upstairs when I felt a small vibration in the floor and heard the motor hum as the retractable screen lowered from the ceiling. When I went downstairs, the screen was down and the remote control was in its cradle. Both dogs followed me to the basement, which meant that neither of them could possibly have bumped the remote or done whatever far-out series of events could cause a dog to turn on a television.

I've been handling each of these events as a one-off, unwilling to look at the mounting pile of data, unwilling to connect it all back to my conversation with Sean on the night we saw the owl. If, somehow, Sean is causing the disruption to my home electronics, I'm no longer interested in the overture. If he were alive, I wouldn't be taking his calls, especially if he drunk-dialed, which is what this feels like. And if it's not Sean, I don't want to come off as part of the tinfoil hat club. I need credibility if I'm going to reestablish myself in the work world or ever get a date or even hold on to my friends.

Frankly, I want the weirdness to stop before it upsets Dash, and before his friends notice and we get a reputation for living in a creepy house. Could I call an electrician? "Uh, yeah, hi. So, can you please fix my stereo? But sometimes it's the TV . . . and, oh, I forgot to mention, my cordless phones act up sometimes, too. Do you hear that static at your end?"

Maybe we should move, but I can't bear the ordeal, and Dash loves living here. A change of scenery might help. When good friends offer the use of their mountainside condo for the Father's Day weekend, I gratefully accept the ticket out of town.

SIX MONTHS OF KINDNESS

I'd hoped Ty and Jenn could come with us to Canmore for Father's Day, but Ty has to work and Jenn's away in Italy, the fruition of her fortieth-birthday gift from Ty—a holiday to wherever she wanted, all by herself.

Happily, Emma can come anyway, and we pick her up early Friday afternoon. It's a glorious summer day, and we arrive in the mountains in time to swim, while sunshine still bathes the courtyard pool. The chlorine smell is sweetened by the surrounding pine forest, and the kids dart under the water until their eyes are red and fingers pruny. When we get back upstairs to the condo, I notice a text from Ty saying he's been able to get away after all. He'll be here shortly with pizza. My heart leaps with joy and relief. It was easy to envision Father's Day including the things Sean loved in life—spending time in the mountains, playing games, floating down the river—but the logistics of planning, packing, and driving here have sapped my energy. Turns out I can't celebrate fathers and stand in for them at the same time.

Ty brings the dinner, and the fun. After pizza, we play a few rounds of the card game Cheating Moth, and the kids hoot with laughter, trying to hide cards up their sleeves or under the table without getting caught. When the game ends, we all retreat to our rooms. The condo setup is perfect for us, with two large bedrooms flanking the common living area in between. Once Dash is tucked in, I slip into the living room and turn on the floor lamp next to the fireplace. Ty sticks his head out from Emma's and his bedroom door. "I'm gonna hit the hay, too."

"Actually, Ty, can I talk to you for a minute?"

He closes the bedroom door and takes a seat in the armchair across from me. My pleading look is something he must recognize by now. I've been stumbling over a problem Ty might be able to solve. Why did Sean lie when he didn't have to? So much of what he hid from me, I would have been open to, and Sean knew it. I talked to Scott about it, and what he said made sense, but Sean and Ty thought so much alike, Jenn and I used to joke that they shared a brain. Without coordinating, they'd buy the same shirt and wear it to the same occasion. Only Ty's insight can verify Sean's thought process.

"There's something I want to ask you. I mean I don't *want* to, but . . ."

He nods. Permission granted, but get to the point.

"Okay, so I'm truly sorry." I've been twisting the tassels on a decorative pillow in my lap. My fingertip looks pale as a deep-sea creature, already bluish below the nail. I unwind the string from my knuckle. "You're the only person who really knows how Sean thought, and I have to know—"

I can see the struggle in his face to endure my awkwardness. He's had a long week of work and single parenting with Jenn away. He probably just wants to play a game on his iPad and go to sleep.

"There were times when things were distant between Sean and me. Like, physically . . ." My whole guts are cringing. I fix my eyes on a space between the brass rivets on his armchair. "And I asked if he wanted to consider opening up our relationship." I peek back in Ty's direction.

His eyes have widened a little but he doesn't open his mouth. My face is getting warm. I take the pillow off my lap.

"Sean was adamant: *no*. He wouldn't even pursue the thought." I take a deep breath. I have to know why Sean would cheat on me when I was willing to negotiate an honest nonmonogamous relationship.

"I know Sean might not have wanted to risk me falling in love with someone else, but at the same time he was never jealous or possessive of me. In almost every other way, he tried to support me in being happy. Like how you are with Jenn. You just gave her a dream holiday for her birthday, y'know?"

Ty nods. "I can see that."

"So, I offer Sean an open relationship and it's a hard pass, but in the meantime he's full-on extracurricular. My question is, Why steal something that's offered to you as a gift?"

Ty sighs, slouches forward, and looks at the coffee table. "I don't know, Jess."

I lean back in my chair, watching him. He's on the hook for something that's not his problem and not his business. It's not fair, but I can't let him off. We sit, both squirming inside, until I realize Ty might not have a ready answer to such a complex question, but he'll have an opinion.

"Scott said the person Sean was with me was the man he wanted to be. Opening up the relationship would mean acknowledging this other part of him existed."

"It's that." Ty sits up straight, shoulders back as if an army sergeant has called him to attention. "One hundred percent."

I study Ty's face, trying to discern whether he means it, or whether he's giving the best answer to appease me and let him get to bed. His face is plain, not smiling, not searching to see if he's sold me. His eyes are relaxed and his body language is open. He looks more solid and less guarded than when I first asked.

I'm sitting straighter, too. "Okay. Dismissed." I give him a mock salute.

Ty smiles. "Goodnight, Jess."

In bed I mull it over, looking for holes in Scott's theory and scanning for deception on Ty's part. I can't find anything. Maybe Ty couldn't answer at first because he couldn't place himself in the shadowy, troubled part of Sean's mind. No one who loves Sean—including me—wanted to acknowledge it. Sean had a genius for compartmentalization, but past a certain point, compartments do not hold. Reckless, rampant desires bust through, operate unchecked, and take over a person's life.

———

Father's Day, we eat a fancy brunch at the Banff Springs Hotel, then head back to the condo to change into outdoor duds for a rafting trip down the Bow River. We did a boat tour of Lake Minnewanka yesterday and saw a mated pair of bald eagles riding thermals at the end of the lake, but this float trip is the weekend's main event. Before we left Calgary, I filled a little heart-shaped leather pouch with Sean's ashes so Dash could release it to the waters of the Bow, the same river we visit with the dogs almost every day.

As I tie up my hiking boots, my stomach gets jittery. If Ty hadn't come for moral support, I'd never have been able to pull off this excursion. Even with him, I'm shaky.

But because Ty's here, everywhere we go this weekend, we look like a mom, dad, and two kids. We are that. And also, of course, we are not. The guide on the rafting trip will have no inkling about the people we're missing, Jenn far away in Tuscany, and Sean dead. It's hard to gear up and go into a world that's bound to assume the wrong things about us.

At the put-in spot, I double-check the clips on Dash's life jacket, then hand him the heart-shaped leather pouch. He tucks it into his pants pocket.

The raft can hold ten people and there are only five of us, so it's easy to find a comfortable seat on the inflated yellow rubber benches. The guide gets us moving and starts into a local-history spiel. I wish he'd be quiet so I could think my thoughts, but Ty engages, and since he's paying attention, I don't have to.

This river is sourced by snowmelt, running off the steep and jagged mountains that surround us. I drop one hand into the clear water. It's hard to associate the fluttering whitish tendrils beneath the river's surface with the aching chill in my fingers. I watch my trailing hand until the pain becomes unbearable, then dry it on my jeans. Dash is perched on the edge of the raft, in perfect position for his ceremonial task. "Do you want to release Dad's ashes now?"

"I already did it."

"Oh." I try to keep my face neutral, but I'm disappointed. I'd imagined a collective moment, my gaze following the floating heart along the water until it traveled out of sight.

But it was Dash's task and he's done it without needing my instruction, my sense of portent, my sentimentality. He's said goodbye to his dad, again, in his own time. This won't be the last time he lets Sean go. In Kids Club we learned that children keep reconciling the death of their parent at every developmental stage, until finally, as adults, they can process the loss in an adult way. I don't look forward to "grief on repeat" like a record skipping through Dash's every life stage, but I can already see how he's changing.

Dash's teacher emailed me after the high school biology teacher dropped by their classroom with a sheep's heart. The school encourages enrichment across grade levels, and the biology teacher took the opportunity to share the heart with Dash's class, pointing out the atria and ventricles, showing the fourth-graders how veins fed different parts of the sheep's body. "Dash, naturally, had questions about what might cause a heart attack and how blockages happen," the teacher's email said, and she assured me she'd watched Dash for emotional cues, but didn't see anything worrisome. He seemed interested and engaged.

That night, I'd asked right away, "Anything unusual happen today?"

"Nope."

I skirted around a bit, trying to draw out anything he was curious about, without poking a sore. He didn't volunteer a word. When I said, "I heard there was a sheep's heart in class," he said, "Yep." That was it.

He used to talk openly about every little thing he saw and did, how he felt about it all. But he's turning inward. I was the same at his age. Puberty or grief? It's impossible to tell. People say how resilient kids are, but I'm not convinced. I think we grow around our obstacles, like tree roots inching along the edge of a boulder. Dash will be okay, but he won't grow into the same person he would have been if Sean had lived. Just like I'd have been different if my childhood hadn't been disfigured by alcoholism. Dash's thoughtful, introspective nature will help shape him, too. I'm trying to learn how to trust that.

The guide takes a group picture with my phone. Against the blue-gray backdrop of mountains and sky, we're a burst of primary colors: red life jackets, blue jeans, yellow raft. Four smiling faces: a makeshift family who banded together and got Father's Day done, just like we did at Christmas and Valentine's Day. I make the picture my Facebook banner so Jenn will know: our little team has kicked another holiday's ass.

The morning clouds were still pink when we pulled onto the highway, but now they're white and billowy over the vast horizon. Dash is asleep in the back of the van, and I have six hundred miles of prairie highway left to cross before we get to my mom's tonight. Normally, I dread this long drive on my own, but today I'm grateful for the open road, and the time to think through what the hell just happened.

Yesterday, the whole family gathered for an inurnment ceremony at Union Cemetery. Sean's brother Riley and I worked together to get adjacent niches for Jack, Pat, and Sean. Laying Sean to rest with his parents gave me a lot of peace. Whatever his faults, he was a loving and devoted son, and because we'd helped his parents in their declining years, I was afforded a special relationship with my in-laws.

After the service, everyone went to Kam Han for dinner. When Jenn stepped out for a smoke, I went with her, wanting to hear more about her trip to Italy. Leaning up against the brick wall outside the restaurant, I asked if she'd seen the picture of Ty, Emma, Dash, and me on Father's Day.

She took a long drag on her cigarette. "Yeah. I almost left a com-ment"—she made air quotes—"'You moved right in there.'"

The words warped and wobbled through me like I was sheet metal, struck with a mallet. Jenn was kidding. I faked a laugh. Thinking about it now, I can understand how Jenn might have seen the rafting photo in a homesick moment. It was naïve to assume she'd understand that, in my eyes, Jenn was a part of that picture.

But for fuck's sake, I'd just locked what was left of Sean into a tiny metal box. Forever. One might say I was feeling a little raw. And Jenn's joke wasn't just ill-timed. It felt like a warning shot.

Even ten hours in the car isn't enough to sort it all out, and at my mom's kitchen table that night, after Dash has gone to sleep, I sip a cold beer with Clamato juice and tell my mom what Jenn said.

Mom raises one eyebrow and presses her lips together in a tight line. "I warned you about that."

I gape. She's never said a word about Ty and Jenn. I thought she'd be baffled, not stern like a schoolmarm.

"I told you, remember? Not long after Sean died. You've got six months."

Oh my God. She did tell me that. She said my friends would be nice to me for six months, then start seeing me as a threat. That's what happened to her after Carl died. I was sorry Mom had felt people turn against her, but I assumed it was a peril of Golden Girl culture. I never believed my friends would turn on me. I never thought *Jenn*.

Jenn and I have known each other for twenty years. We joined the Waite clan the same Christmas, befuddling everyone as newcomers with similar-sounding names. We've ridden elephants together in Indonesia. We got tattoos together. I guess the whole sister-wife thing went sour before I gave credence to the expiry date.

"So, you're saying I got a bonus month from Jenn?" I can feel the pinch in my eyebrows.

"Pretty much." Mom gets up to freshen her drink.

This is so much worse than I thought. I know how it feels to lose out to a rival. I never want to make Jenn, or anyone else, feel that way. Likewise, I never want to be on the receiving end of another joke like the one I heard yesterday.

Just outside the window, two hummingbirds dart around a hanging feeder. Mom keeps a sixty-six-ounce jug of what she calls "hummer juice" in the fridge. These two birds have an unlimited supply of nectar. They could both feed at the same time, but the larger one keeps chasing the smaller one away.

I'm not after anyone's husband, but that won't quell my friends' territorial instincts. It's not personal, just human nature. Ty can't be a go-to for me anymore. And not just Ty. Almost all my friends are married. Mom is right. Seven months into widowhood, I'm not just a third wheel, I'm an oil slick.

LET IT BE

Horseback riding on the Fourth of July, my mom's suggestion. Eighteen years ago, she was mother of the bride at my wedding to Sean. Today she's Grandma, making memories for Dash and his cousins Hannah and Isaac, who are visiting for a few days. The five of us wend our way through sun-dappled birch trees on horseback. My spotted brown mare has an appetite for the tall grasses we're riding through. We were told not to let the horses graze, but after wrestling mine back five or six times, I give up the fight. She takes a mouthful of wild grass and trots along, chewing contentedly, the rest of the way.

Back at Mom's, with a few happy horse pics to cheer up my Facebook feed, I turn on my laptop. I open the email at the same time Mom presses the button on her answering machine. We hear each other say, "Ohhhh, Mary."

Beautiful Mary. My dad's sister. It's hard to imagine the world without Mary shining in it. She had oral cancer. We knew this was coming. And yet.

Driving, driving, driving home. Ten hours back across the prairies so I can drop off my dogs and catch a flight to Victoria for Mary's service. Mom's kept Dash and will bring him home in a few days. Emerging from the van, late at night, back muscles locked and aching, my left foot drags a little with each step. I hurt. I *hurt*.

The next morning I'm on a massage table, face down. The therapist holds the soles of my feet with a firm, warm grip. She comes around and places her hands on the crown of my head. She sniffles. I open my eyes and see her bare feet and tie-dyed genie pants.

Dammit. This woman has a cold and now I'm gonna be sick for Mary's funeral. Great.

I've been coming to this clinic for years and I thought I'd seen every therapist who works here, but I've never been with this one before. When she met me in the lobby, she said her name was Jolene. Her wide colorful hairband held a fountain of dark hair away from her face, and she wore dangling crystal earrings.

"Sorry about the sniffles." She stops touching me. I hear a Kleenex being pulled from the box, then a spritz, and I can smell essential oils in some kind of hand sanitizer. "I work with energy as well as massage. You have so much sadness and trauma trapped inside you, it's making me tear up."

What? She's crying? I feel caught out, and at the same time there's such mercy in her recognition. My state of being has brought this young woman to tears.

"I'm sorry." I lift my head out of the face hole and crane my neck to see if she's okay. "I lost my husband seven months ago. Things have been really hard. I'm so sorry you have to feel all that."

"Oh no. No, I don't feel it. I just release it. With your permission I can help you."

"Okay," I say, not sure what I'm agreeing to. I close my eyes, but tears trickle through the space between my lashes. Before long, my mouth, nostrils, and each of my eyelids is closing and opening intermittently while a stream of fluid pours from my face.

I feel soft pressure over the crown and base of my skull, a hand hovering just about my head, a humming sound, something vibrating. My thoughts give way to a sense of ancient time. Time of cosmos and universes. No future . . . just everything, patiently, all at once in black and swirling pink cloudbursts and expansive white rays of an infinite past, like my mind has inhabited the Hubble telescope and merged with everything it can see.

The hands over my body change position: flicking, whooshing, then held over the space between my shoulder blades. My chest fills with warmth. Golden warmth radiates out to every part of my body. It's love, and it's everywhere for just enough moments to kindle a pilot light in the part of me that's flagging and unsure how much further I can go on my own.

Hands moving again, working over the small of my back . . .

I open my eyes. A puddle of snot and tears shines from the floor like a yolk-less egg. *Omigod, Jolene could slip in that. She's in bare feet. I should warn her. No, too embarrassing.* "Could I please have some tissue?"

I wipe my soggy face and drop the tissues strategically, traffic cones to steer her away from the mess. I don't want her to think I'm just a drooling slob. "My aunt died yesterday."

"Yes. I'm sorry." There's a metallic tink and I feel a vibration just above my tailbone. *What the hell? Is she playing one of those brass-bowl thingies on my back? This is weird. Weirdy weirdness . . .*

Tap, tap, tap. The mallet strikes the edge of the singing bowl and rings hard into my sacrum. There's a sudden release. A crack in the dam, and a trickle of *I'm okay* runs up my spine and down the backs of my hamstrings and out my toes. Just a trickle, not a flood. But a little okay goes a long way.

Time's up. The massage, or whatever the hell that was, is over. The room is dim, with only the light of a Himalayan salt lamp in the corner. I feel disoriented and heady, but much more relaxed than when I got here. When I bend forward to mop up the puddle, my back doesn't hurt, and getting dressed again is fluid and pain-free. I'm redoing my ponytail when Jolene knocks.

"About your aunt?" Jolene holds the door open just wide enough for her head to peek through.

"Yes?"

"Well, she was here, and she's doing *great* now."

My eyes twinge against the brightness of the lobby light.

"She feels connected to you through past lives. If you're open, she's available to you as a spirit guide." Jolene smiles. One of her crystal earrings sprays colors against the wall.

"Oh. Okay, thanks." I give her a weak smile. I don't believe in past lives, but Auntie Mary *did*. She had an aromatherapy side hustle. She lived with a new (additional) rescue cat every time I visited. She reminded me of the actress Teri Garr: beautiful, quirky, and funny. The New Age accoutrements added to Mary's charm, but I didn't buy it. Likewise, with my first impression of Jolene.

But something *happened* just now, on the massage table. I'm not walking with a limp anymore. And it's not because Jolene reefed on my muscles or manually forced things back into place. She barely touched me.

Jolene steps back into the room and gives me a hug. "You're a beautiful soul. It's okay. I'll meet you out front when you're ready."

I've had back troubles since I was a teenager and seen dozens of massage therapists over the years. None has ever come back into the room to relay a message. *If Jolene was trying to reassure me in my grief, wouldn't she have said the message was from Sean?* I told her about his death at the outset of the appointment and didn't mention Mary until close to the end. I slip my silver bracelet back onto my left wrist, just below my recent tattoo. Jenn and I had researched artists and gone to the tattoo shop together. We were both going to get elephants, but the night before the appointment, I changed my mind. Three words are inked onto my left forearm.

LET IT BE.

CHICKEN STICK

Mary's number one piece of dating advice? Smile at one hundred men per week. Of all her wisdom, I shall not partake of this particular strand, but it's occurred to me that my finding a boyfriend could neutralize the threat I pose in social circles. Even if I'm self-enforcing it, I don't want to be iced out forever.

Last time I dated, in my early twenties, I was openhearted and ready to be fascinated by people I met out in the world. Online, now aware of dating as a job interview for sex, just weeding through the résumés feels like a chore. And that's nothing compared to the task of getting ready to go out. Now, it takes hours just to get to "beauty base zero" and that includes steps like dyeing my eyebrows, tweezing places that never used to grow hair, and applying primer (Polyfilla for the face) before even starting with makeup. The process requires more time with a magnifying mirror than I would ever care to spend.

I'm using a decoy profile with the scantest possible information. I don't admit to being widowed because I'm afraid of being targeted by scammers and creeps. I've met a few men for coffee or lunch. Most were nice but didn't make the next round of interviews. One, an ultramarathon runner who seemed pretty pissed at his ex, texted after lunch to let me know it was between me and one other candidate. I conceded the position to her.

First meetings are grueling because I have to confess the lie—I'm not separated, but widowed—which means the man inevitably asks how Sean died, and how long it's been. Then, even if they don't ask outright—which most do—the question "Isn't it too soon to be dating?" hangs over the table between us.

And they're right, eight months is "too soon" because I'm an emotional wreck who doesn't trust the world or the men in it. But changing that will take time, and meanwhile my appearance is deteriorating quickly, evidenced by the heroic effort it took to get ready for the stupid coffee in the first place. Who knows what I'm going to look like after years of daily crying, the stress of raising a teenager, and the hormonal ravages of menopause?

If I'm willing to put in the work, shouldn't I be allowed to try to meet someone trustworthy and kind, even if it's just to prove that such a person exists? Staying faithful left me starved for intimacy in my marriage. Shouldn't I be able to offer myself as a sexual partner to someone I'm attracted to, even if I'm not in shape to make a great life partner right now?

I don't ask, off the bat, "How long since your marriage crapped out?" And even if I did and phrased it in such a coarse and brutal way, it still wouldn't contain as much judgment as what they're asking me. The standard of "too soon" applies less strictly to breakups than death, and less to men than women. So, when they ask, I answer in the gentlest possible way, "I fulfilled my marriage vows. Not everyone can say that."

Tonight, I've polyfilled because I've invited Mack to my backyard for a fire and a light dinner. I'm deliberately keeping him outside because this is his final round of interviews. He arrives with wine and a small bag that probably contains his shaving kit, telling me he thinks he's already got the job.

He's not a viable long-term partner for me, nor I for him. He's fit and handsome and smart, but I sense something secretive in his manner, a wobbly afterimage in his facial expressions, which makes me doubt his sincerity at times. In that way, he reminds me of a Ray Liotta character, charming, but vaguely sinister in a nondescript way. I don't fully trust him, but we've been out a couple times and our banter has been engaging and I can tell he loves his kids.

We've kissed once already, after a movie date, where we took separate vehicles to the theater. Driving home afterward, I still felt the quickening of the kiss—teenage butterflies—and in that heightened state, I was physically aware of his car following behind my van as I drove home on Macleod Trail. Glancing into his headlights in my rearview mirror, I wondered what he was feeling, and whether he would text when he got home. I drove carefully, signaling the right distance ahead of each lane change, aware that my taillights were speaking directly to him. Mack's car made the same lane changes I made and took the same turns, and when I turned onto my street, I watched carefully to see if he followed, planning to drive past my house and lose him if he did, but he kept going, and I laughed at my overwariness.

I'd suspected we lived near each other when he suggested the "north patio" of the coffee shop at Willow Park Village for our first meeting. He confirmed it, by text, the night of our first kiss. We're neighbors. If he'd wanted, he could have walked here to join me for the fire on this sunny evening.

I guide Mack into the backyard and point out the woodpile, asking if he minds chopping a few pieces of kindling for the fire. Watching him perform a manly task will help me decide about tonight. "While you do that, I'll open the wine and bring out a charcuterie plate."

"Do you have a chicken stick?" he asks, confusing me—*Is he asking for satay instead of salami?*—and killing any budding lumberjack fantasy. He wants something he can use to hold the logs in place without risking a finger. I find a suitable length of one-by-four in the garage and rest it against the chopping block, next to the ax.

As the sky darkens, the fire glows pretty orange and warm yellow, and when Mack opens a second bottle of wine, it becomes tipsily apparent the evening will end in the bedroom—which it does—and I'm overjoyed with my body for remembering what to do, and not breaking down into shuddering sobs. This feels like such a victory (truly, no woman has ever been more proud of herself for getting wasted and having sex with a near stranger) that I agree to meet him again at his house, this time sober, and the result is a mutually humiliating sexual experience, after which he leaves for a scheduled trip to Kilimanjaro. On his return, he ghosts me—or tries to—but we shop at the same Safeway and our sons' sports competitions will put us in the same bleachers for years to come. It's by the chicken stick, which I now use to chop my own kindling, that I remember the man to whom I gave my widowed-virginity.

———

Sean and I were curled together, spooning under the feather duvet he'd brought from Canada to Japan. He was naked and I was wearing his T-shirt, which he'd offered after tracing the goose bumps along the side of my arm. A rooster crowed outside his apartment window and Sean said, *"Ko-ke-ko-ko,"* which made me giggle.

"You're speaking rooster in Japanese."

"I'm better at animal languages. You should hear me speak gorilla."

"Let's save that till morning." I yawned. We hadn't slept yet, even as the predawn light illuminated goldfish shapes on the wall. A Matisse poster took up almost the entire vertical height of Sean's loft. We were lying face-to-face, both on our sides, mirroring each other. He propped his head up and asked, "How did you lose your virginity?"

I told him about my high school sweetheart; the late-summer night when he hollered goodbye to his parents, who were watching Super Channel in the basement, and the two of us walked out the front door of his house holding hands, heading out on a date, as far as they knew. He led me into his backyard, and we sneaked back into the house through his bedroom window.

Sean laughed at this, and I said a little more, getting lost in the memory of that boy—our earnest fumblings, my good fortune to have loved a scrawny little dork who loved me back. We were sweethearts for two years, two months, and five days. He'd told me that, the number of days we were together, when I broke up with him. There was still fondness in my voice as I recounted it to Sean. I noticed my tone and stopped reminiscing, worried I was striking the wrong chord with my new boyfriend. Sure, I'd only agreed to go out with Sean for four months, but I could still show regard for his feelings.

I looked into Sean's face and was surprised to see him gazing at me. *Gazing.* Giving rapt attention to my story. I felt adored, and it was too much, the intensity of his affection. I deflected with every English-conversation teacher's standby, "How 'bout you?"

"Well, when I was fourteen, I took the bus to Chinook—"

Oh my God. His story was starting with a kid on his way to the mall. I propped my head up, matching his posture.

"I went to Wizard's Castle, which was a big arcade at the time, and there was this Moonie chick there. She was about twenty-two—"

"Wait, Moonie? Like the cult?" I remembered the news stories: mass weddings and blind devotion to the Reverend Sun Myung Moon. Flirting with unattached young people was a hallmark of the cult's deceptive recruitment strategy.

"Yeah. But she didn't really get into that until after. She had long hair and flowy hippie clothes and beads like everyone used to wear in Banff in the seventies." He smiled at the memory. I pictured some Stevie Nicks wannabe lurking around the Tron machine. "Anyway, we started talking and I ended up taking her home."

"On the bus?" I scrunched up my nose and let out a nervous laugh.

"It was the afternoon on a weekday in the summer. No one else was home." The rooster crowed again in the background, spurring Sean on.

He folded the duvet around his chest. "She showed me how to do *every-thing*. A *bunch* of different positions. I was fourteen so my recovery time was really fast." He said this like *dreams really do come true*.

I wanted to jump in a time machine and call 911.

"When we were done, she started telling me about this great place she lived and how I should come check it out, but by then I'd lost interest. Ty came home and asked who she was. That scared her away."

"Did you tell Ty she was trying to recruit you into a cult?"

"Nah. When it happened, I wasn't really paying attention to that part." The sheepish way he said it made me laugh. It must have been a wondrous experience, through his teenage eyes.

"I didn't even tell my friends." Sean shook his head. "She was long gone and I knew they wouldn't believe me." He sighed, his lips closed into an almost smile, just enough to make his left cheek dimple, a little oval in the half-light, a blur in the smoothness of his face.

Putting the pieces together now, I speculate about what cross-pollinated for Sean in that encounter: wild fortune, danger, illicit thrill. I don't think Sean should necessarily have felt victimized, but processing such an intense experience all on his own, at fourteen, and keeping it all a secret . . . how could that not have influenced his budding sexual identity and future appetites? The arc of repercussions for formative events is long. "No harm no foul" doesn't take that into consideration.

I wonder if Sean's adoring look as I shared my virginity story was partly an attraction to the purity of young love, imagining what it might have been like to share your first time with someone who cared for you, instead of being the target of a statutory rape.

There was a longing for innocence in so much of what Sean did: the way he embraced childlike wonder; the way he showed up ready to be awed by the world. In many respects, Sean lived a deeply earnest life. His deceit has been so unbearable because, most of the time, he was almost embarrassingly wholesome. Scott still does an impression of Sean as a rebellious teenager: "So then I called in to the PBS telethon and challenged all the other high schools. . . ."

Sean trusted me enough to confide deep, formative moments of his life. He told me things he'd never shared with anyone else. When I asked Ty about the Moonie chick, he remembered seeing her, but had no idea he'd thwarted a possible kidnapping. Without Ty's intervention, Sean might have ended up leading the Moonies to multiplatform success in the digital age.

CAMP WIDOW

Fans in Blue Jays gear cram onto the Union Pearson Express, packing the train as we approach downtown Toronto. Gleaning from their buzz and banter, I realize tonight's game could decide the American League Championship. *Man, I'm out of the loop.* I hadn't even realized the MLB playoffs were underway.

I've been up since 4:30 a.m., but the fan energy invigorates me with the juice I need for the last leg of this journey: finding Camp Widow in the Marriott at Eaton Centre.

When a friend told me about Camp Widow, I'd pictured a circle of black-veiled women sobbing kumbaya around a campfire and rejected the notion out of hand. But as we moved toward the end of the summer, it dawned on me that "getting through the first year" has been a false target. Sean's not going to jump out of a cake to congratulate me on surviving a calendar year without him. When November 4 rolls around, nothing will change in my day-to-day except that people will assume I've moved on and stop helping me. That's happened to a large extent already. Rightly, everyone needs to get back to their own lives.

On Labor Day weekend, I hosted a barbecue to thank everyone who's brought us meals, babysat, fixed broken things, and helped in a million big and small ways. I hired photographer-friends to do family photos for the guests, mainly as a thank-you gift, but also because, now that my six-month grace period is over, I won't be participating in our friendships the same way I used to. I'll treasure their photos as much as they will.

Lots of people offered to help with the party, but I wanted to do it myself, to repay my debt, and to prove I could. It took two weeks to get everything ready, and the day after it was over, I boxed up serving plat-ters, chafing dishes, and enough glassware to serve cocktails to Lower Manhattan, and donated it all, officially retiring myself as a host.

After the party, an article about Camp Widow popped up, but this time I double-clicked. It's a conference with a menu of events for par-ticipants to tailor their own experience. Some sessions appealed to me: Writing through Grief; Love after Loss; Signs and Synchronicities. Even a stand-up set called "My Husband Is Not a Rainbow" performed by comic Kelley Lynn. Widow comedy. *Yes.* I asked Megan and Bart to take Dash for the weekend and they agreed, so I've sent myself off to Camp.

In the hotel's beige marble lobby, a Camp Widow sign points to where I'll need to go in the morning. My shoulders drop. I've made it. I pass my driver's license across the counter to a dark-haired woman. "Calgary, huh? You've come a long way."

She slides the key card across the counter, then steps out from behind the desk, arms extended, head tilted in the question of a hug. I give a slight nod and let go of my carry-on. She wraps her arms around me, bringing me in so close I can smell the spray starch in her uniform collar. In the warmth of her soft body, I feel every mile I've traveled, not just today, but since the day in Guy's Café when I ordered a bowl of chicken soup, not knowing I'd never eat it. Her hug is a warm, nourishing meal, eleven months after the fact.

At Camp Widow we wear lanyards telling others how long it's been since our partner died. It seems a weird badge to broadcast, but I quickly realize what a tedium-saving device it will be. It also allows us to scan for others whose loss is as fresh or weathered as our own. When I see ladies with 10+ YEARS on their tags, I shudder a little, realizing just how *forever* grief must be.

The Signs and Synchronicities workshop is set up for about thirty people, with sturdy metal-legged chairs arranged in a circle. A woman around thirty sits closest to the door. I sit down next to her and introduce myself. Her name is Leigh, and her name tag confirms what I'd have guessed from her youth. She's LESS THAN ONE YEAR into her loss, just like me.

"When did you get your tattoo?" she asks, and pushes her sleeve back to reveal her own similar tattoo, freshly inked to the same place inside her left forearm. Turns out we got them the same week, which leads us to discover our husbands died the same day, November 4, 2015. Brian was a firefighter, paramedic, and EMT instructor. Their son, Henry, is only a few months old. My heart breaks, doing that math. I miss the facilitator's opening remarks, pondering a final trimester heavy with grief, a delivery room with no daddy.

"I keep finding dimes on the passenger seat of my truck," says a short-haired woman with glasses. "They can't be outta my pocket 'cause I never sit there." Finding coins is common, Abigail Carter, the workshop's leader, tells us, so common it's the origin of the phrase *pennies from heaven*. I scrunch up my eyes, trying to reconcile her etymology against what I'd always understood the term to mean: a windfall, not a sign from beyond.

I originally mistook the dog tag I found under Dash's whiteboard for a coin, and it's on the tip of my tongue to mention this example to the group, but I don't want to have to explain why I kept Sean's ashes in the garage, so I keep the story to myself.

Abigail invites questions for the last few minutes. A woman with tightly curled silver hair, who'd been silent all session, says, "My neighbor, *Colleen*, keeps coming over with messages from Marv." Her hurt and confusion are louder than her actual voice. In the subtext, I hear, "Should I tell Colleen where to shove it?" and beneath that "Why her, not me?"

"It's hard," Abigail says, "when we don't have a direct experience of our loved one and someone else says they do."

The woman makes one slow nod.

"You don't have to believe her. And you can ask Colleen to stop telling you when she thinks she gets a message."

The woman's expression doesn't change. She holds eye contact with Abigail.

"No one knows how these things work, exactly. Some accounts suggest strong emotion can block our receptivity, so fresh grief makes us like a cell-phone tower that's jammed. The signal meant for us bounces to the nearest open tower."

The woman's face softens. Just a cell-phone tower, not a personal preference. It's something to consider. But with a switchboard so prone to overload, how does anyone know who a message is from or who it's for?

One night, back in October 2009 when I was sleeping in a separate bedroom from Sean, I was jolted awake after my dream in progress "changed channels." It felt as though someone had cranked the dial on an old radio tuner. First a haze of static, then a clear signal. I couldn't see anything, but someone was there. "Are you Perry?" I asked. Perry confirmed it was him.

Perry was an old boyfriend who'd recently moved to Calgary and "poked" me on Facebook, but I hadn't replied. Things were too strained in my marriage to consider rekindling an old acquaintance. The next day, I learned Perry had died overnight, by suicide.

The flash of contact was brief, but the feeling was like a burst of leftover love. I held on to it, assuaging my guilt over not having been a friend. Now, I wonder if I might simply have been the nearest cell-phone tower. Perhaps I've done something worse than Colleen in withholding a message of love from Perry's family.

A whole order-of-operations problem becomes clear in my mind: First, do I acknowledge what I'm perceiving as real? If so, how do I discern who's trying to communicate and what they're saying? Who is the intended recipient, and are they open to the communiqué? Will it comfort them, piss them off, or freak them out?

Gah. I thought relationships with the living were complicated.

I skip the Sunday-morning events to have brunch with Jeff, Sean's childhood best friend, and his wife, Monique. They were in Cambodia when
Sean died, so couldn't attend his funeral. They walk in through the big
glass doors off Bay Street, and I cross the lobby to greet them. Monique
still looks just like Princess Diana, and the only thing different about Jeff
is his hairstyle.

We hug. I pat the back of Jeff's smooth dome. "Hairdo by Gillette,
huh?"

He laughs. "I shaved it in Southeast Asia, for the heat. Then I liked it.
Sean was always ahead of the trend."

We sit in a booth at the hotel restaurant and order brunch. I catch
Jeff up with the Waite family goings-on, which leads to him reminiscing
about their high school days.

"I remember sleeping over at Waite's one night. There were a few of
us. Sean took the floor and I crashed in his single bed. When I woke up,
I saw he had this picture of Tyrone taped to the underside of the shelf
above his bed."

"You mean, where most guys would have a picture of Farrah Fawcett?"

"Yeah. He had a picture of his *brother*, and no matter how much I
razzed him, he never took it down."

I laugh, but my heart melts. Ty would have been away at UBC then.
Sean must have really missed him. To keep that picture up through a fire-
storm of teenage gibes . . . It makes me remember the depth and loyalty
with which Sean loved his people. Some part of me recognizes he loved
me like that, too, despite the many occasions I've had to doubt it.

Our coffees have been topped off for the third time. Jeff takes the
check when it comes. "Let me charge it to my room," I say, but Jeff
insists. He and Monique are moving to Hong Kong soon. It's not clear
whether our paths will cross again, though I hope they will. I'm thinking
about the right way to say goodbye.

"I wasn't going to tell you this, Jess," Jeff says, voice low, "but I've been to this hotel once before."

I tilt my head, not sure why that would be a secret.

"Sean stayed here, back in the GreenPoint days, when he was slinging tax software with Cam. We ate right here." Jeff gestures to a section of the restaurant a few feet away. "It used to be more of a sports bar. We watched a Leafs game. It's the only other time I've ever been here."

Monique's jaw hangs open, and she stares at Jeff. I guess he didn't disclose this on the drive over, which makes me wonder about his instinct to keep it to himself. Did the memory feel private, or the coincidence?

Over the years, when I've visited historic places, I've imagined the people alive and breathing in the place I stood—William Shakespeare at the Globe Theatre, Mahatma Gandhi at Gandhi Smriti, even my favorite author, Margaret Laurence, at her childhood home in Neepawa, Manitoba. Knowing Sean's been in this hotel restaurant drops me into the same feeling.

I can picture him, from that era, in his faded Levi's, a black computer bag over his shoulder, stepping out of the elevator, crossing the lobby. Unlike famous people, who I know only from photographs, I can see Sean from every angle. I can hear him laughing, ribbing Jeff as a turncoat for becoming a Leafs fan. I can smell the pint of Heineken he'd have ordered in those days. My chest remembers the rectangular press of the PalmPilot in the breast pocket of his leather jacket.

Camp Widow is designed to help remember the dead. To knit the dismembered pieces of our relationships back together. As part of the registration, you're supposed to submit a photo of your partner. Their face meets you on the memorial wall at the entrance to the main conference area. I didn't partake in any of the opportunities to presence Sean into this space. I came here for myself, to learn from people who've survived and have come back to shine a light for the rest of us. And yet, here he is anyway.

Sean was here.

FIRST ANNIVERSARY

At Camp Widow, Abigail Carter, who lost her husband in the World Trade Center attacks on 9/11, also led a session called Love after Loss, which, knowingly, began with recommendations for discreet online shops selling good vibrators at fair prices. My big takeaway from her session was a confidence-inspiring rundown on how to write a good dating profile. Step One: Admit you're a widow. Step Two: Know what you want.

I repurpose an old journal to write about what I'd hope for in a new partner. After lots of scribbling it comes down to the two things I pleaded for in almost every quarrel with Sean: kindness and respect. Not the sexiest qualities in the world, and hard to discern from pictures of freshly caught fish, but at least I have some idea what I'm looking for. I update my profile to something genuine, just to see what happens. I don't actually want to date, but also, I don't want to be alone forever. I don't want Dash to be deprived of having a father figure, and at the same time I won't let any new man near him.

I remember a Sunday morning, in the old rental house my mom, sister, and I lived in the summer I was thirteen. The first one awake, I'd helped myself to the last of the milk, dripping the dregs over my Honey Nut Cheerios. I stuffed the empty milk carton into the garbage, packing it down so I wouldn't be the one who filled it (and therefore had to take it out). Air whooshed up from the bag, with the sour, bitter odor of decaying spaghetti and smoke butts. Gagging, I turned away. There, beside the garbage can, was a pair of knockoff Adidas shoes. Men's shoes, the tongues splayed out through loose gray laces.

My mom's bedroom door, just off the kitchen, was still closed. I froze, understanding I was in a direct line between those shoes and their owner. I tiptoed past the sneakers and slipped out the side door, closing the screen gently so its too-tight hinge wouldn't slam the door shut and wake them.

On our front landing, the Saskatchewan sun blasted me as I ate my breakfast. When the screen door slammed, I shrank back against the stucco, bits of stone and brown bottle glass poking into my bare shoulders. I was conscious, then, of the sleep set I was still wearing, a cotton spaghetti-strap top and short-shorts, and I crossed my arms in front of my chest, listening to the gravel crunch under the man's feet. An unfamiliar brown car was parked in front of our house, and I hoped the man would get straight into it and drive away, but he noticed me and walked up the steps.

He looked at my empty cereal bowl, like he expected me to move it to make room for him. I kept my arms crossed. He sat down on the step below me and stretched out his legs. His stupid shoes had four blue stripes instead of three. His hair was fine and wispy, with scaly patches of scalp showing between the strands.

"So," the man said, "what do you think of it?"

The night before, Mom had put on lipstick, gussying up for a cabaret at the curling rink. *What I think is, you are a drunken mistake. And you must still be drunk if you think I'm talking to you.* My scowl was reflected in the man's mirrored sunglasses, and seeing it made me narrow my gaze even more. "Think of what?"

He tilted his head and made his face slack. "Hing ko wha?" he said, as though his tongue were too thick and slow to enunciate my words back at me. His mimicry made me feel I'd teleported into the world's worst after-school special. I sat sullen and silent until the man walked away.

That was the only incident of waking up to a rando in our house, but the number of times that will happen to Dash is zero. I'm not angry with my mom. I have empathy, now, for Bonnie the human woman: a thirty-something divorcée, with two adolescents, two jobs, and a microscopic dating pool. As my old diaries tell it, all my mom's boyfriends were duds until Carl, who became my stepdad when I was an adult. I imagine Dash will feel similarly ambivalent about anyone who alters the covalent structure of our little dyad. For now, I'll make an honest-to-goodness profile, and if it gets a nibble, we'll keep it between me, him, and the keyboard.

———

Yesterday was the first anniversary of Sean's death. Dash and I visited the cemetery, then had the family over for dinner. We collaborated on a jigsaw puzzle and read through the masses of condolence cards that came in for us over the last 365 days.

Today is Sean's death anniversary plus one day, which makes it—according to me—Get Out of Judgment Jail Day. It's a warm fall afternoon. A cyclist pulls up and I recognize it's William, the man I've come to meet.

I arrived a little early for our date at Pies Plus Cafe and am watching from my van. He's wearing linen shorts and a blue fleece pullover. When he takes off his helmet, a tuft of salt-and-pepper hair lifts off his forehead. He doesn't smooth it down or check himself out in the side mirror of a parked car. I'm attracted to his unselfconscious way of being, like he knows the make or break of this meeting doesn't depend on the reliability of his pomade. While he locks his bike, I walk over to meet him, so he doesn't have to cross the threshold alone, wondering if I'm going to show.

"Favorite Things" per William's profile:
Eating souvlaki in restaurants on Corfu
Sipping on miso with seaweed and tofu
Cold beer on hot days, my toes in the sand
These are a few things that make me feel grand.

I don't like tofu, but I do like clever rhymes, and his made me laugh. I also thought referencing *The Sound of Music* showed a degree of masculine confidence. It's shocking to articulate the basis upon which one makes decisions when dating online.

Seated at our two-person table, William's quiet. *Wow.* He sure is. But I'm quiet, too, so I understand boisterousness doesn't equal personality. Besides, I've spent much of the past year wishing the noisy, frenetic world would shut the fuck up. The server sets down our coffees. William passes my mug to me, even though it's within easy reach. He looks at me with big hazel-brown eyes, like Ponyboy Curtis from *The Outsiders*. Eyes I was dreamy over, as a tween.

"So, you've read *Restless* by William Boyd," I say. Much as I cursed the profile process when writing mine, I bless it now for the small-talk fodder. I've read Boyd's novel, too, and remember the plot, about a woman who worked as a spy during World War II, creating disinformation to help the war effort.

"Yes. It sure has interesting parallels with the current media circus." He's talking about American politics—Clinton vs. Trump. The election is three days away. As we chat, I can tell our views are aligned enough that, come what may, we could have reasonable conversations about current events. I've missed having Sean—a hawk-eyed political observer—around to debrief the astonishing series of world events. It feels anchoring to have a grounded conversation with William about how weaponized disinformation and propaganda are nothing new.

William asks me to a movie. We go midweek. That Saturday, he invites me for a walk around Glenmore Reservoir, where we see a cute brown furry creature climb out of the water and scurry along the rocks. It's slimmer than a beaver and shorter than an otter, and we guess that it must be a mink, though neither of us has seen one in Calgary before. I love seeing something novel in a place I've been many times. When we say goodbye, William touches the tattoo on my left forearm. I feel a jolt of electricity.

His profile didn't list a bunch of deal-breakers, but tattoos were one. "Problem?"

He shakes his head.

"Aha!" I smile. "Anything else not true on your profile?"

"No, it's all true. I'm making an exception for the Beatles."

Before bed, I log back on to the dating site for a snoop at William's profile, now that he's verified the truth of everything.

He's logged on recently, too, and changed the whole page: "I've met a wonderful lady here and I hope it lasts. . . ." He goes on to give encouragement and pointers to whatever lonely hearts see his profile before the account lapses. He does not intend to renew.

Uh-oh. The poor guy likes me.

New problem. I like him, too. But I'm just trying to get my legs under me. I'm not prepared to be anyone's "wonderful lady." Go on the odd date when I can get a sitter? I'm your girl. More than that . . . we should probably break up. Rookie move, is it not, to stick with the first person one meets on the way out of jail?

HE'S RIGHT HERE

A couple weeks after Sean died, a friend gave me a sympathy card with a green-gray twist of dried sweetgrass. I understood her intention. As Robin Wall Kimmerer describes it in *Braiding Sweetgrass*, a ceremonial smudge "washes over the recipient in kindness and compassion to heal the body and the spirit."

My mother-in-law left us a beautiful smudge fan: the wing of a hawk, with a handle of beaded deer hide, but she never taught us the ritual, probably because we never asked. Smudging has endured, despite the tyranny of colonization, through the resilience of indigenous peoples, but without ancestral knowledge, the healing power of sweetgrass seemed unavailable to me. I tucked the small bundle into a drawer with our spare candles.

Every so often, though, over these sixteen months, I've been opening the candle drawer and lifting the sweetgrass into my hand, wondering about its potential to release trapped energy. I think about it when the sound system comes on by itself, or the lights flicker and sizzle with a buzz of electricity. I ask around, trying to find a teacher, and one of my widowed friends refers me to her neighbor, Lisa, who is smudging a home near me this Sunday. Lisa says I'm welcome to come and learn.

The house is a seventies-era suburban bungalow, the same vintage as my own home. Lisa, a tall, dark-haired woman, opens the door and invites me to join her and two other women around my age. She gives a cursory explanation of what we'll be doing and asks us to follow four principles: Lead with gratitude. Approach with humility. Honor the land and the spirits of the land. Intend this work for the highest good of all beings. She arranges twiggy-looking stems and dried silvery sage leaves into an abalone shell. "I gathered this sage from a nearby grassland and asked its permission to be burned in today's ceremony."

Lisa lights the sage and a strong-smelling herbal smoke rises up from the shell. Her face drops into peaceful solemnity, eyes gazing downward. She seems to be addressing someone or something, but no language escapes her lips. Lisa uses a feather to waft smoke into the high and low corners of the living room, where the oak floor gleams and not an item is out of place. The kitchen is equally spotless. Either this house is being staged for sale, or the owner is of Sean's ilk in keeping a spare and tidy living environment.

When we reach the home office, Lisa invites each of us to feel the space an inch in front of the bare wall, and then an inch in front of the computer screen. I go first, and it's subtle, but I do feel a slightly fuzzier sensation in the space between my fingers when my hand is in front of the screen. I take Lisa's point: objects emit energy. We see things because photons bounce off them and reach photoreceptor cells in our eyes. Electronic devices emit both light and other energetic frequencies. That's science.

We move to the main bedroom, and as I stand at the foot of the bed, noticing its perfectly pressed pillow shams, Lisa wheels around and looks right into my eyes. "Did your husband die?"

I feel like a fawn, lifting its head to discover it's wandered out of the forest into a clearing. Eyes from the periphery make the hairs on my arms stand up. I nod and pull the sleeves of my sweater over my wrists.

"He's here right now," she says.

I'm standing off-kilter, all my weight on my left foot. I have no idea what my face is doing. A cool breath draws in through my back, just below my shoulder blades, like chilled air that's bypassed my mouth and nose, gently penetrating my lungs.

"Did you feel that?" Lisa smiles wide. "He's hugging you."

What I felt was not a hug. It was a slight chill and a sense of disorientation, nothing like a hug. Not at all. And I wouldn't even want a hug from Sean, especially in the middle of a group lesson. Everyone is looking at me. They probably expect me to rejoice. I fake a smile and say, "Mmm, not sure." I regret coming here.

Lisa doesn't seem to register my apprehension. She's still smiling. "It's so cool when they show up like that."

The room feels too small and I wish for fresh air instead of sage smoke. I pretend to read the takeaway sheet Lisa gave us at the start— "Instructions for Smudging at Home."

"Lisa, this house is so clean and tidy. . . ." I'm trying to change the subject, but as I start to speak, the image of my mechanical room flashes—porn-laden computers, bins and bins of stuff. "How do you smudge a cluttered space?"

"Right. So, you need to remember, objects hold energy. The more you clear things out, the better. But if you don't have that option, just do the best you can."

We leave the bedroom. Lisa wafts smoke along the hallway behind us, completing the smudging of the main floor. The four of us gather in the front entry. "We'll repeat this same process with the basement," Lisa says, "But if you want to leave now, the lesson is complete."

I take the opportunity to bail.

Driving home, I try to decipher what just happened. There are multiple ways Lisa could have known about Sean. The friend who referred me could have mentioned it; Lisa could have looked at my Facebook page or googled my name and seen his obituary. She could have staged the whole thing to up her credibility as an intuitive. I don't think Lisa set me up as a sucker, but as P. T. Barnum said, there's one born every minute, and two to take 'em.

I did feel a little jolt of sensation, but if Sean was really there, wouldn't he have known I wanted an apology, not a public display of affection? And wouldn't he have made himself visible to me, instead of another woman? I don't like the feeling—not quite jealousy, not quite resentment, but a close cousin to both.

I get home, thinking I'll smudge right away, while Dash is at a friend's house and the process is fresh in my mind. Lisa sent us away with some sage. My grandma's crystal ashtray would work in place of the abalone shell. I go downstairs to find it, but when I open the laundry room door, the stark contrast of this room with the pristine home I've just left makes me recoil.

Sean has been gone for sixteen months, and I've fallen into "emergency cleaning" when people pop over. All the stashed piles of stuff are down here, not to mention the heap of laundry on the floor. It's Sunday. Dash needs clean clothes for school tomorrow. I drop the smudge bundle onto the counter and start a load in the washer. The timer expects me back here in forty-five minutes. I trudge upstairs for a quick nap.

What Lisa said, about Sean appearing in the smudging session, shook me up. My friend Kathryn used to see psychics and fortune tellers from time to time. "C'mon," she once tried to coax me to tag along with her. "It'll be fun."

Having never set foot behind the velvet partition myself, I mocked her ruthlessly and refused to go. *Tough love*, I thought, being twenty-three to her mere twenty-two. Kathryn never worried a charlatan might take her money. Her charm and confidence always led her into good jobs, with cash to spare on playful things. She insisted it was worth it for the thrill.

One medium, though, turned out not to be a lark. Kathryn glided into that woman's chair with a breezy smile and said, "I don't want to know anything bad."

When the reading began, the medium grew quiet for a long time. She kept closing her eyes, looking as if she were about to speak but then pressing her lips together. The woman's obvious struggle to parse the vision into something she could reveal scared Kathryn into changing her mind. "Please," she said. "Tell me what you see."

"You're going to live a long life and experience incredible love." The medium then predicted intense pain, extended time in hospital, and the loss of a child. Kathryn called me after the session, distraught, knowing she could count on me to blow it off. I was happy to oblige.

Year after year, what was foretold has come true for Kathryn: in the form of miscarriage, in the form of cancer . . . and on April 3, 2015, when a Winnipeg city bus crashed into the front end of Kathryn's Acura— breaking her neck and shattering her pelvis in three places. Kathryn felt herself floating into the greatest sense of peace she had ever known, then heard Ben, her five-year-old son, crying, "Mommy," from the back seat. His voice called her back. Kathryn held on to life.

I asked her, weeks later, while she was still in the rehab hospital with a "cage on her head" (as she endearingly called her halo brace), if she ever thought back to the medium's prediction.

"Of course," she said softly. "I remembered it almost while the accident was happening. It's how I knew I wasn't going to die."

———

Beads clack softly as I loop an old necklace of Auntie Mary's around my wrist, forming a many-stranded bracelet that ends a couple inches below my LET IT BE tattoo. I'm wearing Sean's favorite T-shirt, a soft gray slub cotton with QUEEN'S P.E.C. in red lettering, one of the few spared items when I purged his belongings from our bedroom. Overtop everything, I pull on an enormous dark gray cable-knit sweater. This cozy perma-hug was a gift from Kathryn when she came out for Sean's funeral. I tug the cuffs down, deliberately hiding the former possessions of Mary and Sean, as I prepare to visit a medium for the first time.

The medium's home is a short drive from mine, and when she greets me at the door, I think *spinach dip and bridge club*, not crystal balls and tarot. She leads me down greige-carpeted stairs to a room that smells like sandalwood oil. Ethereal music plays in the background. We sit opposite each other in upholstered chairs, and she takes some deep breaths and appears to go into a meditative state.

She extends her hand in invitation. Her skin is warmer and better moisturized than mine. She traces her thumb across the lines of my palm, then looks into my eyes. "Who is R?"

Sean's brother's name starts with *R*, but none of my dead peeps do. Besides, *R* is the *first* letter they give you on *Wheel of Fortune*. I shake my head.

She says, "I see a mantel." The natural evolution of funeral flowers, memorial candles, and framed photos into altars for the dead, in the living room above the fireplace, makes me frown. *Not mine.* The two mantels in our house are both bare, save for a thin film of dust.

When she looks at my unadorned left hand and says, "I see a ring," I see my money flying out the window. She tells me my grandmother is there, and if that's so, then I'm a real dick to Grandma, because I'm not even listening anymore, lost in a flush of shame for having tried to believe. I wait out the next forty-five minutes, socially bound to politeness. The woman takes payment at a table laden with angel cards and crystals for sale. I scowl at those items as I zip my wallet shut.

From $200, there's enough change for a cookie-dough Blizzard and I steer myself through the DQ drive-through on the way home. The cold hits my tongue like an ice pack on an injury. The sweet, milky chocolate coats my disappointment and I swallow it down.

GRIEF DOESN'T GIVE
A SHIT ABOUT STATUS

Taking solace in ice cream turns out to be like losing my sobriety. After over a year of sugar-free green juices and protein shakes, rivers of M&M's carry me through the next several weeks. My brain is foggier and my jeans don't fit as nicely. I spend too much time on Facebook. *Who cares?* Social media time and grief time run oddly parallel, with blurry edges and no discernible stopping point. I like being online because it feels like having friends without having to actually be sociable.

The day I see a post from Martha Beck, I brighten up. Her memoir, *Expecting Adam*, told the story of finding out, while doing her PhD at Harvard, that the baby she'd been carrying for six months had Down syndrome. Not only was Martha scrutinized—by colleagues indentured to the idea that intellect is everything—but also she experienced psychic ability throughout the pregnancy, which she attributed to the baby. I read her memoir in the nineties and it's stayed with me ever since. I've even called on it since Sean died, at times when my altered perceptions made me wonder if I might be going mad.

Martha's post announces an online course cotaught with Elizabeth Gilbert, author of the enormously successful, *Eat, Pray, Love*. The three-part class spans six months and will focus on writing as a tool to heal ourselves, to uplift ourselves, and to express ourselves. The price tag is over $1,000, which makes me flinch, but Dash has just chosen to move to our neighborhood school when he starts grade six, which means that funds earmarked for his tuition could go toward mine. I sign up. Those two women have written their way out of some crazy shit. Maybe I can, too.

About eleven hundred people are in the course, a daunting number for my first-ever teleconference class, but the live calls feel surprisingly intimate, just me in an armchair with a blanket over my lap, a notebook, and cup of tea beside me, Martha and cocreator Rowan Mangan on the other end of the line. Occasionally one of the classmates will unmute to ask a question. Over time, I begin to understand why this big cohort doesn't feel intimidating: we're all here because we share the sense of a crossroads, the high stakes of our historical moment, a common purpose toward greater connection.

The preliminary section of the course draws upon Dante's *Inferno*, and over a five-week span, it takes us into the dark underworld of *Purgatorio*. "Abandon all hope, ye who enter here" is a legit warning, but we charge in anyway, to the depths of our personal hells. We come to understand one another's darkest moments, via the online forums and the Sunday-night video chats, when Martha reads some of the group's best work aloud. We come out the other side as comrades in arms, bonded by our collective journey, and by the deeply personal stories we've shared through writing.

The unexpected boon—I make new friends. Social media feels thin, in place of my real-life friendships, but the opposite is true with my new writing crew. Over the coming months, the online connection lets me stay in close contact with people I've come to care for and trust. Even better, none of them has ever known me as part of a couple with Sean.

It's this group who comfort me when I receive the blistering rejection of my application to go back to university. The academic rebuff notifies me of my place (#176) on the wait list. My whole future had hinged on getting a master's degree. My writing friends suggest this derailment may not be the dead end it feels like.

Bolstered, I join the newly formed Facebook group Hot Young Widows Club (as soon as I've ascertained that being young and hot are not strict requirements.) It's led by Nora McInerny, and like her podcast, *Terrible, Thanks for Asking*, the group is amazingly raw and tender. There, I become better acquainted with the great widow-maker of our time: the opioid crisis. Hearing stories of partners lost to accidental or deliberate overdose clarifies an understanding I had after my dad died. Society metes out compassion in tiers, based in part on how the person died. Cancer and accidental deaths are high status (except lung cancer . . . "Did they smoke?"). Suicide and overdose dwell together on the lowest rung.

I remember after my dad's death, the weird cold smell of the Safeway freezer, my sister and I (both in our midtwenties) staring at colorful packages of chicken strips and pierogies. Neither of us seemed able to reach forward and choose something to feed the family. "This is why people bring casseroles," I said. Or maybe I just thought it. Lasagna had always seemed a paltry token, before I understood the life-giving gesture of bringing food to the bereaved. In Hot Young Widows Club, I try to lend extra warmth to people who've been stigmatized and judged when they ought to have been comforted and supported. Sadly, this could be a full-time occupation, and some days it is.

———

Grief doesn't give a shit about status. That's why I'm relieved Dash is transferring to our local school for grade six. When we moved back to Calgary, only a private school offered the same Elementary International Baccalaureate (IB) program Dash had begun in Singapore, so we enrolled him there. The school is great. I couldn't have asked for a better or more supportive environment, especially in the wake of our loss. Their rural campus grows a memorial forest, the Forever Woods, honoring seven students killed in an avalanche in 2003. I know Dash spends time in the forest, contemplating and remembering. It's a beautiful and sustaining place.

However, even though the teachers, students, and facilities are all first-rate, the school's Latin motto—*Nil nisi optimum*, "nothing but our best"—gets me down. The expectation of excellence. The constant striving to make excellent even better. I can't muster it, and I fear its unintended consequences. After a recent Sports Day race, I went to congratulate Dash on his second-place finish. He was doubled over, wheezing. At first I thought he was recovering after the hard run, but it turned out he was hyperventilating from the anxiety of having been defeated by another runner. He's ten years old.

The unrelenting pressure of perfectionism feels like malware, something akin to what drove Sean past the point of good health and happiness. When glossy mailers invite me to the school's fundraising gala, I'm like, "*Nil nisi nope.*" I don't care about excellence, I don't care about IB, I just want Dash to be able to walk to school and hang with friends on the playground afterward. He's down for that, too, and has been expanding his range in the neighborhood. He prints off Google Maps and sets out with *The Heroes of Olympus* in his backpack to explore undiscovered swing sets, trees to read under, and sneak-routes to 7-Eleven. What our new educational plan lacks in ambition, it makes up for in the wholesome beauty of small adventures.

ENDLESS STORIES

Not long after the writing course finishes, Sean's brother Riley celebrates a milestone birthday. His wife, Erin, invites the family to gather in the plush confines of a restaurant's private dining room. The tables are arranged in a square so all fourteen guests can see and hear one another comfortably. After a delicious dinner of osso buco with free-flowing wine, Riley stands and tells us how proud he is of his three grown children, and how thankful he is for the values instilled by his parents, Jack and Pat. The whole room softens, hearing those names.

Riley says, "My own family started with a snowball fight at Queen's," and he looks, dewy-eyed, at Erin, who glances downward while a rosy tinge takes over her complexion.

The rest of us perk up our ears. In twenty years of being related to them, I've never heard a word of this story, never seen a burst of sentimentality like this from Riley.

"Our end-of-term exams had just finished, and we were heading into the Christmas break. Snow was blanketing the campus." Riley's fingertips flutter, snowflakes falling thick and heavy. "A melee broke out in front of Clark Hall. Snowballs flying every which way." He dodges and throws, small gestures painting a 360-degree panorama of snowball action. "Afterwards, everyone filed into the pub . . . and there was Erin."

We can feel the flush on their cheeks, coming in from the cold, young and giddy and primed to fall in love. Riley's story weaves an intimate magic over the room.

Ty speaks next. A New Year's Eve party, canceled due to a terrible snowstorm; Jenn "not getting the memo" and braving the weather, arriving at Ty's door as the party's only guest. Jenn chimes in with her version, where the "alleged" party was an elaborate ruse to get her there. Everyone's in stitches.

Round the room we go, everyone adding brushstrokes to the history of love. Between stories, I think about what I'm going to say.

I'll tell about El Mustacho, the Mexican restaurant in Japan where Sean and I first met, and how it was still the same, nineteen years later, when we took Dash there as a special stop on our way home from Singapore. Sean recalled an old trick, dripping the green hot sauce onto a ten-yen coin, showing Dash how to make it shiny and new. When everyone else at the party has shared, and I'm the only one left, I look down at the table, gathering my courage to speak.

The dining room door bursts open. Three servers bustle in. The guy in the middle holds a '57-Chevy-topped yellow cake, and the two female servers wave sparklers, leading us in "Happy Birthday." I join the singing, watching the fizzly light shoot out in all directions.

This cake just saved my feelings. I don't know how I know this, but the conversational momentum was about to move on, without anyone asking me to share my love story with Sean. Not because the family doesn't care; just the opposite. They love me. They miss Sean. His absence is palpable to everyone in this room. But my telling would be tearful and hard to witness. No one wants to make things awkward or ruin the vibe of a party.

I push the dessert fork through the yellow buttercream. The cake is moist and delicious, but after the first taste I can't eat any more. My stomach is strangled with the idea that if Sean's own family didn't ask about our love story, then no one ever will again.

Driving home, I'm caught in the crazy paradox: People want to be remembered when they're gone, yet everyone's afraid to talk about the dead. The fastest way to forget someone is to stop saying their name. I bet bereaved people feel excluded like this all the time.

Back in my writing class, sharing my assignments turned out to be a solvent, gently eroding my shell of isolation. That process felt life-affirming and necessary. How could other people like me be invited to share their stories without the structure of a class? Most young widows aren't rolling in disposable income, so the venture couldn't cost anything to use, and the stories would be tender, so the space would need to feel like a calm shelter. I search online to find a grief space for sharing stories. Nothing turns up but books and links to counseling services. I envision a quiet corner of the internet, designed to feel like the unexpected but much-needed hug from the desk clerk at Camp Widow.

Over the next several months, with the help of friends and professionals, I create a website for people to share memories of a loved one who has died. When I'm not working on the site, I'm exploring various healing modalities I've heard about from my writing friends: Somatic Experiencing™, The Embodied Present Process™, Compassionate Inquiry, Narrative Therapy, and many more. My goal is to figure out what works so I can help guide others, and if something really takes, maybe it will lead to my next career.

After my website launches, one friend aptly describes it as "the PostSecret of Grief," but the site's existence is unintentionally secret in its own right. The conundrum: paying to advertise doesn't make sense because I don't want to monetize, but somehow I need to spread the word. At my book club meeting, a friend asks if I've heard of Sarah Kerr, organizer of Calgary's Holistic Death Network.

I attend a few monthly Death Network meetings. Sarah is around my age, maybe a few years older, but her hair is completely white and cut into a stylish bob. She seems down-to-earth, smart, and funny. Her engaging style commands the attention of everyone gathered in a dance hall that seats about two hundred people. Clearly, she's esteemed by the people in this community. Each month, a new guest speaker addresses us about a wide range of topics from green burial to Medical Assistance in Dying to Threshold Choirs, who sing at the bedsides of the dying. If I told Sarah my story, might she help me invite grieving people to write and share their own stories? I book an appointment to see her.

DEATH DOULAS

Sarah Kerr refers to herself as a death doula and ritual healing practitioner. Even after watching her online videos and hearing her speak at the Death Network evenings, I'm not entirely sure what that means, so I feel a little antsy as I walk up the steps toward her lapis-blue stucco house.

When I ring the bell, a black-and-white cat jumps down from a window ledge onto the porch and heads toward a neighbor's shrub, tail up and twitching. Sarah answers the door with a warm smile. She's wearing a gorgeous silver necklace with an eagle pendant. I step into her home, full of rich jewel tones and vibrant artwork. Sarah guides me into the living room, and I settle into a deep red armchair. On the coffee table are several beaded stones, like Fabergé eggs, but less ornate. If gemstones and flowers and Arabian carpets could breed, they'd cross-pollinate over generations into something like these beaded stones. The largest one is just a little bigger than the palm of my hand and so enchanting that I long to pick it up. Also on the table is a full box of Kleenex, and a coaster, upon which Sarah sets a mug of spiced tea.

I sip warm cinnamon and cardamom and cloves. Sarah sits down. She's wearing a jean jacket and a white T-shirt with a long dark skirt.

She says, "Before we begin, I want to tell you, I knew Sean. We grew up together in Elbow Park."

I glance toward my shoes in the entryway. Black slip-ons without laces. I could be out the door in two seconds, flat.

How can I tell this woman my story when she *knew Sean*? She probably knows Ty and Megan, too, maybe even the whole family.

Then, another panic: *How does Sarah know him?*

Bumping into Sean's old girlfriends—everywhere—was a running joke. Scott used to offer a jocular warning to their younger friends: "If Sean ever asks your mother's maiden name, don't tell him."

I can't tell if alarm is registering on my face. I look down, to the stones on the coffee table. One has a starburst design at its center, circling around a vivid blue bead. I look back at Sarah. Her eyes have that same vibrant depth. Her demeanor is open and kind. She doesn't seem to be hiding any secrets.

I gesture toward the decorated stones. "These are beautiful."

"Thank you." Sarah smiles.

"Do you mind if I ask where you got them?"

"Not at all. I gathered them over time. Mostly from around here, near the Bow River, and some from near our family cabin in BC."

"Wait, you *made* these? You came up with these designs yourself?"

Sarah picks up the largest one. "In a sense. Sometimes, when I hold a stone, I can feel its energetic pattern. Adding the beads makes that invisible pattern visible." She holds out the glittering oval, offering it to me for a closer look.

The stone feels heavy and surprisingly smooth in my palm. I trace a contour of green weaving into a design that's both geometric and freeform. It's mesmerizing.

"Lots of people have held that stone. We pass it around, like a talking stick. It helps people get to the heart of what they want to say."

Whatever Sarah's past relationship with Sean, she's not making things awkward for me. Quite the opposite. I cradle the stone in both hands, and it dawns on me: if they grew up together, then Sarah knows—without my having to explain it—that Sean wasn't a monster.

He wasn't only a liar and a cheater and a betrayer. He was a good son who loved and honored his parents. He was a loving father to Dash. He was respected by his colleagues. Once, in a managerial survey, Sean was the highest-ranked person in a corporation of thousands. The HR person who debriefed the results with him commented on how rare it is for someone to score equally well across all three levels: managers, peers, and direct reports. Everyone liked and trusted and admired Sean.

If Sarah knew him as a child, then she has a context for Sean that goes beyond even what I know. She knew the *Star Wars*–loving tween who fled from the mustachioed man in the mental hospital. And if Sean and Sarah did hook up, way back when, then she cared for him, even if only fleetingly, at some point. No stranger will ever start out on such an even footing.

I spill the beans. Every single one.

Sarah takes it all in. When I'm done, she says, "Wow, that's a lot."

I agree, blowing my nose into one of the many tissues I've taken from the box. I've used over an hour of our ninety-minute session just to get the story out.

"So anyway"—I clap my hands together and let them rest in my lap— "I built a website for grieving people, and I'm trying to figure out—"

"Whoa, whoa, whoa." Sarah holds up her hands. "We haven't addressed any of the things you've already brought in. Let's slow down and make room for what's here."

She takes out a piece of paper and asks if she can draw me a map. "It's an archetypal cycle that might help give context to your situation." She draws a circle on a piece of paper. "The top half of this circle is life as we know it. When Sean died, you were here." She draws a notch at the top of the circle, the high-noon position. "You had a young family, Sean's career was on the upswing, you'd just moved back to Calgary and were building your new life here. Do you remember the morning of the day Sean died? Waking up thinking it would be just an ordinary day?"

I remember it exactly. I'd gotten up before 6:00 a.m. to put a second coat of paint on a section of wall I'd patched and sanded the night before. The drywall had been torn by a supposedly removable adhesive I'd used to hang spooky artwork for Halloween. The morning of November 4, I'd rubbed my bleary eyes in disbelief. The patch had dried a shade darker than the rest of the wall. My biggest worry was whether Sean, who'd meticulously sanded and painted the wall himself, might be annoyed I'd used the wrong-color paint.

I nod. "I was pretty wrapped up in ordinary things."

"And then, without warning, someone told you . . . Sean has died . . . and the bottom fell out and the whole world became different." Sarah's cadence isn't exactly slow, but her patient, unrushed delivery brings an immediacy to the moment. When she says *Sean has died*, the words land as if I'm hearing this news for the first time. My hands and feet turn cold, and a weight presses into my chest, an anvil dulling the thrum of my heart.

Getting this news in person, from someone who knew Sean, simultaneously pulls out a splinter and makes me hyperaware of the old sore: the disembodied voice on the phone, the cold pine bench, the deafening roar in my ears. Waterworks rise behind my eyes. I shake them off with a deep sigh.

Sarah continues, referring to the map, "Okay, so you'd been trundling along in your daily life when, without warning, you were dropped from up here at the top of the circle"—Sarah draws a vertical line with her finger to the six o'clock position—"to way down here at the bottom, where everything is unfamiliar. It's chaos and darkness. Nothing gradual about it. A complete shock to the system. You found yourself dismembered, your life was torn apart, and you were no longer part of your community. Is this resonating for you? Have you noticed a change in your social relationships?"

I drop my head into my palms.

Sarah waits.

"I have lots of good friends and I love them all. But . . ."

I summarize the change in my social life as succinctly as I can: My mom warned me I'd become a threat after six months; my sister-in-law's joke struck me in the heart; I withdrew voluntarily rather than risk being excommunicated by my friends. I couldn't bear to be the subject of gossip or scorn, so now, by my own doing, I see almost no one regularly.

"Beyond all that, though"—I gesture back to Sarah's map on the table—"when people invite me for dinner, or to parties, I know they're actually inviting her." I tap the twelve o'clock spot. "Not me. Not the Jess who's down here, in the darkness. I don't know how to be the old friend they think they're inviting. It's too exhausting."

Orienting myself to the map, this strikes me as a compound problem. Every time I discovered one of Sean's betrayals, I spun off into a new journey around the circle. I'm in many parts of the deep dark woods, all at once, like when multiple files download to my computer at the same time.

Looking at it that way explains a lot. I feel tired because so much processing is still going on in the background. In some ways, it parallels how each of my friend Kathryn's injuries healed at different rates after her car accident. The slowest-healing part has been her nervous system. Three years on, she's still recovering function in her formerly paralyzed arm. Healing takes time.

Sarah was right to put the brakes on the website conversation for now. I'm like Bambi on ice with this, especially the weirder stuff. There seems such a hard line between "all-in" believers and those who ridicule them. Not with Sarah, though. She was neither fazed nor fanatical about the paranormal things I shared. We didn't venture down that conversational road, but as we skirted it, she'd said, "There are many ways the dead communicate with the living. Dreams, visions, animal visitations, flickering lights . . . There's lots we could dive into on that subject."

I want to know more. We make plans for me to come back again.

COLD GIN JAM

The summer we moved back from Singapore, Sean and I planted a cherry tree in our front yard. Four years later, it's laden with fruit. Dash and I picked a bowlful of sour cherries this morning, daring each other to try them, laughing at each other's puckered expressions. He's gone out to play with a friend, and I'm about to make cherry jam. For company, I put on some upbeat music, a playlist from the HBO series *Entourage*.

I stand in front of the stovetop, grooving along to the music, squeezing out cherry pits and discarding them into a white melamine bowl. I drop the cherries into a black saucepan, over a low burner. A song catches my attention with the line "How do I do it and not get caught?" and I tune in more carefully. The dude is singing about cheating on his girlfriend.

I pivot to the sink, turn on the faucet with my elbow, and wash the cherry juice from my hands. A tap on my screen reveals the title, "Weekend Jumpoff," by Kevin Michael. I restart the song and set it to play on repeat so I can catch all the words. The song begins with a guy swapping cars with a friend. They're colluding to deceive their women.

It makes me wonder how many of my friends helped Sean get away with things. Probably not many—he kept things close to the vest—but also, not none. Anger roils in my belly, knowing I was on the wrong side of a bogus bro code that has baffled me since I was a kid watching *The Flintstones*. I remember the episode where the Water Buffalos sent a plumber to pose as a doctor, diagnosing Fred and Barney with a fake disease, "dipsy-doodle-itis," so they could get away for the weekend. *Why did they lie to Wilma and Betty?* I'd wondered as a little girl, unaware that wives were oppressive and husbands required emancipation.

That's what the guy in this song thinks. He should be able to do whatever the hell he wants. Every weekend, he lies to "Baby," ditches her for someone he picks up at the club, takes that chick to a remote hotel and pays cash, then shows up back home with gifts to make up for it.

Sean brought back earrings from a trip to Australia, once. Small pendants in a gorgeous opaline blue. He usually brought souvenirs for Dash, but not for me, and the change in behavior made me ask, "What's this for?"

"No reason. Just missed you a lot, and the blue stones made me think of your eyes."

I'm really mangling the cherries now. Juice has splattered onto the backsplash tile and drips down in red streaks.

I tried so hard to be a good partner, to build something deep and real, better than any shitty cliché. Maybe Betty and Wilma did, too, off camera in the imaginary world where they had goals and personalities of their own. Decades of social infrastructure were in place to make it easy for Sean to hide things: from the implicit expectation of his friends' cooperation, to technology designed to aid in the cover-up, to my own politeness making me too uncomfortable to say, "Is this a bribe?" when my husband came home with jewelry.

Cherry juice runs down my wrists, stinging a scrape I didn't know I had. The song gets even more aggravating at the chorus, when the weekend's over and the guy is on his way home, planning his excuses: "I'ma tell my baby I'm sorry . . ."

"Baby" will be expected to forgive and forget, move on, get over it.

I said I was sorry. What do you want from me? But forgive and forget is bullshit. I tried so hard to forgive after Sean's initial encounter with Rebekah, but how was I supposed to forget when they still worked together and I saw her at company parties?

Apologies are worthless if the person doesn't actually change their behavior, a point the song drills into me over a soulful hip hop groove. *Ditch the douchebag!* I shout at Baby. But I know where her asshole boyfriend is, and she doesn't. No one takes Baby's side. They just help hide the cheating and blame her for being blind.

That's my inclination, too, and I've been her. *I wasn't even on my own side.* The thought catches my breath, and the music stops, midchorus.

"Goddamn fucking iTunes!" I wheel around to see what's gone wrong with the music player. It's supposed to be transmitting from my phone to the whole-home sound system, but my hands are too sticky to touch the screen. I wash with soap, and when the noise of the faucet stops, I hear the soft plucking of an acoustic guitar. The song is familiar, but it's not from the *Entourage* soundtrack. I can't place it until the words start.

"Love of mine, someday you will die . . ."

Oh my God. My heart is still pounding in an angry froth of adrenaline over the last song. I feel off-kilter, and slightly nauseous. I lean my backside against the countertop and stare into the speaker in the ceiling. The song is "I Will Follow You into the Dark," a ballad about eternal love across the veil of death.

In the early aughts, I subscribed to *Paste* magazine and got a CD sampler of new music every month. That's where I first heard of the band Death Cab for Cutie. Before Dash was born, I played this song for Sean and told him it was how I felt about my love for him. He told me he felt the same way. I whisper along to the last line of the chorus, "If there's no one beside you when your soul embarks, then I'll follow you into the dark."

Something in Ben Gibbard's voice, and in the music, softens my outrage. I fold my fingers together, holding my own hands. This song is about leaving the world together, and crossing into the darkness of whatever comes. It's about death and a commitment that defies any boundary of time and space.

But my storm of outrage lends another meaning to the lyrics. The dark can be mystery, it can be uncertainty, it can be despair. I don't know for sure if Sean still exists somewhere or if he doesn't. But if he could see me now, trying to make a simple batch of jam, being waylaid by the pain I still suffer, would he follow me into the darkness of my mind, so I wasn't alone?

If he joined me there, maybe it wouldn't matter how much Sean was to blame, or how much of the problem I created by being blind, or whether the Flintstones were culpable in any way.

The thought of Sean being here—with me in the darkness and willing to share the pain—levels me. I rush into the powder room and blow my nose, then step back into the entryway so I can hear the song, still playing on the kitchen speaker.

"You and me have seen everything to see, from Bangkok to Calgary." *Holy shit.* On my left, three art deco prints by Billy Ma hang over the basement stairs: Bangkok, Shanghai, and Hong Kong. Just around the corner, above the stairwell landing, a Kelli Pollock print says MEANWHILE IN CALGARY.

Bangkok to Calgary.

It's so specific: the placement of these artworks in my home; the way they interweave with the music and my memories of our life together. *And who the hell even sings about Calgary?* I'm not sobbing anymore, just baffled and weeping softly. I wipe my tears and go back to the kitchen.

The song is over. The only sound is the soft burble of cherries in the pot. I pour sugar over the pulpy red mass and stir, about to add lemon juice, when I remember what Sarah Kerr taught me about responding when something feels like a sign.

"It's like developing a language," she said. "If you do something to show you've received the message, that strengthens the connection. Pay attention, and notice what happens next."

Most of the time, over the course of our twenty-year life together, Sean *got* me. Not only did he make me laugh in impossibly dire situations, but he came through for me, time and time again. I felt stronger because he was in my corner.

If I'm fair, the only reason I'm making jam right now is because Sean provided for us, from planting the cherry tree, to covering the life insurance so I could stay home with Dash for a few more years. Part of me always believed we'd be together again, somehow, after we died—until his betrayal felt so unforgivable it made me never want to see him again. Not in heaven, not in hell, not in my dreams. Nowhere. Hearing these two songs together feels like a reckoning, an owning up, some balance between us restored.

A song I sang, decades ago, on a train platform in Japan, gave Sean the courage to ask me out. I was the only girl he knew who could sing "Cold Gin" by KISS. I search the back of the freezer, then wrap my fingers around the smooth, icy neck of a bottle. As I unscrew the cap, I can almost hear Gene Simmons growl, "It's cold gin time again." I pour a healthy glug over the cherries. The mixture bubbles up, steamy, red, and vigorous as though gin is the only thing that keeps it together.

When the skins have all broken down and the cherries are a dark red sauce, I stir in a dollop of mulled-wine caramel. The spoon comes out coated with a deep-red residue and I pop it into my mouth. It's warm, sour, and cinnamon sweet. I track the sweetness all the way down to my belly.

I've heard forgiveness means giving up all hope of having had a better past. God knows I've imagined waystations where I could have jumped off the Sean train and given myself a different life. Back in Osaka, on the "Cold Gin" night, when Sean said, "The problem is you," I could have said, "Not a problem," patted his riding ducky on the head, and walked away. My friendship with Sean would have collapsed into a singularity, a moment in time.

In another timeline, I could have married Sean, enjoyed all the excitement and adventure of our early years, become part of the Waite family, and given birth to Dash. When things started smelling of Rebekah, I could have cut and run. Loads of divorced people find their way to friendship down the line.

And, if there's a multiverse with infinite possibilities, then there's one where I take Sean to the hospital in Montana after he runs away from us at the auto-body shop. A doctor gets him through the crisis, and when we get home, he finds treatment and support. He comes clean about his struggles. He doesn't die at forty-seven. Slavo offers him a great job in Calgary, and maybe he takes it, or maybe he slows down and teaches Dash to play baseball. *This*. This is the best thing that could have happened.

But it's not what did happen. And sitting here in my cinnamon-cherry-smelling kitchen, I can finally see the ways Sean was right about my life being better now. I have greater trust—both in myself and in the great mystery of life—than I've ever had; I'm taking better care of myself; and I've broken out of the trap of keeping family secrets.

Dash will turn twelve soon, and not long ago he found Sean's weed stash in the back garage. He brought me three lunch-size Tupperware containers full and showed me the secret compartment Sean had built into the workbench to hide them. My heart melted. That kid would have been set for teenagehood if he'd kept those discoveries to himself, but he came to me and we talked about it. Over the years we've talked about most of Sean's struggles. My willingness to be honest with Dash has laid a foundation I hope we can lean on through his teenage years. Adolescence will be tricky without a father. That's inescapable. But Dash still has good memories of his dad, and context for the tough stuff, and the best of Sean's example to draw from.

YELLOW ROSE

Three on the windowsill are faceless, huddled together in elegant robes. Dozens are ceramic, glazed in opalescent pinks and pastel blues; hands drawn in prayer, hands offering flowers, hands extended for little birds to perch upon. Carved wood, cut glass. The largest has alabaster wings arced high above her shoulders, feathers layered like dragon scales. More angels than could dance on the head of a pin. I feel cloistered, unsettled by the sheer number.

"They're all gifts from clients," Margaret says in her British accent, sweeping an upturned palm toward them. I follow the line of her hand to an angel made of crystal and wire, hanging in front of the window, breaking sunlight into tiny rainbows. From the tilt of her halo and her open-handed gesture, I recognize the angel as somebody's mother. Someone was moved to select this one specifically, to wrap it and bring it to Margaret in gratitude. The figurines aren't a testament to the marketing power of the Franklin Mint, or the answer to the perennial question of what to get mom for her birthday. Each of these angels is a departed member of someone's family. They represent the same enduring connections as the stories people send in to my website. In aggregate, they must constitute a life's work.

The friend who referred me to Margaret used to work as a medic. She

told me Margaret worked quietly with the Calgary Police Service, helping them crack murder cases and find dead bodies. My friend suggested
this appointment after I told her the story of "Bangkok to Calgary." I
trusted her enough to book this session.

There's been more to Margaret's work than solving crime. Her walls
hold signed photos of celebrity clients I recognize. "I had one hundred
and seventeen clients from the film and television industry," she says. "I
read for Frank Sinatra when he was alive."

A framed picture, developed from a film camera before the days of
Photoshop, shows Margaret glowing in front of a red rock wall. A perim-
eter of luminescence surrounds her. "That was my light in Sedona," she
says. "We were making a television special. Seven thousand people called
the station in California to say they could see my aura."

I see the light and am appropriately humbled. Looking back at the
bookshelf, I spy a tiny angel, smooth and swaddled in its pearlescent glaze.
I look back at Margaret, who has taken a seat across the table from me.

She tells me she's seventy-nine years old and came into this work after
many years as a palliative nurse. Her father, an English doctor, recommended the shift to midwifery after Margaret discovered herself unable
to bear children. She adopted two children she'd helped deliver into the
world, a daughter and a son. During a recent five-month span Margaret
lost seven loved ones, including her beloved daughter, so now her family
is just her son and herself.

In the living room, I'd seen a portrait of a beautiful woman in her
forties, holding a silky terrier. That must have been Margaret's daughter.
The dog, Teddy, had greeted me at the door. I'm sorry for her spate of
losses, but before I can say so, Margaret opens the reading.

"There are thirty-two cards in the deck. Nothing below a seven."
Margaret lays out three piles. "Which of these represents your past?"

I point to the pile on my right.

She turns each pile face up. "Past, present, and future. Remember at
all times that the cards are just a tool." Margaret studies the cards. "You're

going to come into some money but it won't be until the end of October
or beginning of November."

I'm expecting an IRS refund for the overpayment of taxes on Sean's
estate. The accountant told me a few days ago that the check won't be
issued until the fourth quarter. As Margaret continues, I'm struck by the
specificity of topics she raises and the way they track with verifiable aspects of my life. She tells me my twelve-year-old van will get me through
another couple winters. I've been worrying about whether to trade it in.

"Now, there is a soul who wants to come in first. It's a gentleman who
cradled you as a baby."

"My dad?"

Margaret nods, then tells me my father is concerned. "You have more
support coming from the heavenly plateau than you do from the earthly
plateau. He's come to ask if you've forgiven him for something. He says,
'By forgiving me I can help you more. I want to help you more, but I
haven't got my full set of wings.'"

That doesn't sound like Dad. Granted, he died in 1998 and may have
picked up an otherworldly accent after twenty years on the other side,
but I'd be more convinced if he spoke like Tom Dunne and not Clarence
Odbody, the second-class angel from *It's a Wonderful Life*.

The idea of my dad being limited by my failure to forgive gets my
back up. I've forgiven him already. The pain of his addiction and absence
is not my dominant problem. I love my dad. Shouldn't he have clued in
to that?

"I forgive him," I say, though my heart's in a panic. What if Margaret
and my dad are using some kind of telepathy to register something I
don't see about myself?

"He's not here to upset you or disturb you. He wants to help you
write your story."

I blink, twice. Our family's unspoken motto? *Let no one mention this
again.* For my dad to support writing my story—which necessarily includes a deeply shameful part of his own story—is astonishing to consider.

"He knows, when you share it, people will see that you've come through your adversity and they can come through theirs. It's a way of healing."

Teddy barks from the stairwell, like he did when I rang the doorbell, and I wonder if Margaret's next client is already here. She carries on, undistracted.

"Now, children have first right, so I always bring them in first, but I made an exception today, for your father. There is a child here who was lost very early in life."

I shake my head. *No such child.* Margaret looks at me with the patient expectancy of a teacher who's given a tough problem to a capable student. "Through miscarriage, or abortion, or stillbirth . . ."

I stare at the corner of her glasses, where the rim meets the arm. My fisted hands press into the tops of my quads through the ripstop fabric of my capri pants. "It was, um . . ."

"An early loss," Margaret says.

I close my eyes, remembering.

Irregular bloodwork. Foothills Hospital. "*The tissue will be reabsorbed.*"

"My pregnancy with my son started as twins."

We were in the first trimester and hadn't told anyone. I couldn't bear to think about a dead baby in the womb with my growing baby. Sean held my hand the whole way home. We didn't talk about it in the car, or the next day, or ever again. When we announced our pregnancy, we never mentioned how it had begun.

"It was a girl." My eyes widen. "And I know it's hard to accept what I say, but I hope you will. I have seen them since I was seven—spirits of children. My father had me tested by two psychologists and a psychiatrist, and in the end they said to my dad, as a doctor, 'Don't test her anymore, she's told us exactly who lost a baby in our family.' Now that I'm older I understand: God allowed me to see them because I was not able to have a child of my own. So, I can see them, and yours is a little girl, and she's growing in the spirit world."

My mind is swirling. I press my palms against my face, then rest my hands on the table, almost brushing Margaret's fingertips. The room feels too hot.

"She wants to grow closer to you. If, after this reading, you feel that you can trust me, I'd like you to do something for yourself, not for me. Get any color rose you'd like, to represent her. Take it home and put it in a glass of water with no powder. The powder gives it false life."

On my kitchen table at home is a cut-glass vase with a single white rose in it. Jolene, the massage therapist and energy healer, gave me the flower when I saw her yesterday. Several powder packets are under my kitchen sink, but I forgot to put any in the water.

"After two or three hours, the rose will have acclimatized to the temperature in your room. Hold the rose in the water and keep it very simple. Say, 'I know you're here and I love you very much and this is the name I'm going to give you.'"

I swallow. Sean and I chose our boy's and girl's names when we first started trying to conceive, and over the many years it took for Dash to come along, the names never changed. I already know her name, and her father knew it, too.

I bow my head, close my eyes, and take a deep breath. My phone has been recording for almost an hour. This session has been astonishing. But still, I'd hoped—

"I have a man here who died quite young, and there were many question marks: How he died? What took place? What happened? He told me to bring him in at the end because you'd start crying and wouldn't listen to the other things you needed to hear. He wants to know if you have seen or felt his presence because he's trying to reach you. He's flashing your lights. He's been trying to come to you in your sleep but he can't get in, so he's flashing your lights and what he wants to tell you is, don't worry. Everything will be all right. It's a matter of time. I love you. I love you. I love you."

The corners of my mouth turn down in a grimace and I hold back a torrent of tears. She's saying the right words, but I don't feel it. Everyone's lights flicker sometimes. Everyone wants to hear that they're loved and things are going to work out okay.

"How did he die?" Margaret asks. "I have a sense of it, but there's a reason I'm asking you to tell me."

I hesitate. The more information I furnish, the more I'll second-guess everything later. "The coroner said"—I shake my head, quashing the inclination to insert my own opinion—"a massive heart attack."

"He says it wasn't suicide, but it was, in some ways, a form of suicide because he neglected himself."

Self-neglect adds up. Both his feeling we'd be better off without him, and the autoimmune condition that attacked his heart. "He was under so much stress. He wasn't sleeping enough and wasn't eating properly." My voice is getting pitchy. I take a breath. "Yeah, it took its toll."

When the session ends, I thank Margaret and dip into my purse.

"You will not pay for this reading. You are a single mother and have more important things to do with your money."

"I brought a thank-you note." I hold up a card. I'm planning to add cash, but Margaret's rate wasn't posted anywhere. The first medium I saw charged almost $200 for a disappointing barrage of platitudes. Margaret's reading felt powerfully healing. Under the table, I count out twenty-dollar bills by feel.

"I will not accept money from you, and please do me the courtesy of respecting my wishes and not trying to trick me or force upon me something that I do not wish."

My stomach jumps. I let the money rest in my lap. Then I tuck the cash back into my purse and brush the hair off my forehead. It's damp with sweat.

Paying with money would have been easier than receiving Margaret's generosity. In just over an hour, she's given me lines of connection to my daughter, my father, and a message of love from Sean that—while I couldn't absorb it—is something I've been seeking for years. I feel like I owe her a huge debt.

Heat blasts my face, and the permanent wet-dog smell in my van nearly bowls me over. I lower the windows, trying to collect myself before driving home from Margaret's. Questions swim in my mind: *What's true? What's not? What does it all mean? What should I do now?*

For twelve years, I've had a child with no name: A baby I didn't mention, didn't grieve, didn't even think about. And, yes, it's not *for sure* that Margaret is right about that baby being a daughter. The fetus died before an ultrasound could have determined the sex. But there were so many details that Margaret couldn't have known, even if she googled me before the reading. At any rate, there's this pressure in my belly.

"I'm sorry, baby," I whisper. "I didn't know I was allowed to name you."

By some wondrous coincidence, my friend Tricia Elliott is already on her way from Anchorage to stay with me overnight, on her way through to Banff. A mother of two daughters, who lives in a yurt and tracks animals in the Alaskan wilderness, Tricia is a trained physician, who left conventional medicine and became a poet. Our writing foursome (with Liz Wiltzen and Kate Godin) has been meeting online for a little over a year. Tricia has worked in palliative care. She practices shamanic journeying, and her gentle way of being is attuned with the rhythms of the natural world. There's no one with a more perfect skill set to help with a baby-naming ceremony.

The image of a yellow rose pops into my mind. The flower Jolene gave me might not be the right one. I drive to a flower shop a few blocks away, where I find a small, tightly budded yellow rose. I take it home and put it into the vase with the white one.

That night, by candlelight, with Tricia Elliott holding space, I follow Margaret's guidance and say into the center of the buttery-yellow petals: "Welcome, baby girl. Your name is Julianne."

A GIFT OUTSIDE OF TIME

"Okay, close your eyes!"

I close them and wait in the kitchen, listening to Dash's footfalls as he comes up the stairs. For my first birthday without Sean, a friend took Dash out shopping to get me earrings and a birthday card. Today is my third, and I've just turned forty-seven, the same age Sean was when he died. Whatever Dash has made or bought to celebrate this occasion was entirely his doing. I have no idea what it's going to be.

There's a plastic clatter of something falling onto the tile floor. I feel like my gift may involve some cleanup, on my end, after the fact.

"Um, just a minute. Keep closing them." There's a scuffling sound as he fixes whatever went wrong. "Happy birthday to you," Dash sings, increasing the pace of the song until he gets to "Happy birthday, dear Mo-om—now open your eyes!"

I look at Dash first. He's twelve and has a shadow of peach fuzz over his smile. His eyebrows have turned from their feathery blond to a coarser brown, and he's almost as tall as I am. His expression is proud, and he's looking at the table, where he's just set a LEGO model of a living room with a telescope; a whiteboard full of mathematical calculations; a giant replica of a double helix. There's a sofa and a chair with five mini-figures gathered around a coffee table, eating Chinese takeout. Sheldon Cooper is in his spot, with Penny and Leonard beside him. Dash has built the set of *The Big Bang Theory*.

"You made this?"

He nods.

"Where did you even find it?"

"It was in the back of a cupboard downstairs. Look, it even has Cinnamon!" He points to Raj's little Yorkie on the floor beside the chair.

I remember shoving this LEGO kit out of sight on my forty-third birthday. That morning, foisted into a gift bag by Sean on his way out the door, it was an embarrassment to both of us. For years, it sat as a shameful remnant of our tattered relationship. Now, Dash has built it into a representation of joy and laughter coming back into our dinnertime routine. In some ways, it encapsulates this whole phase of our lives. It's a treasure, an instant heirloom. And still, at its origin, it's the present Sean gave me.

A gift outside of time.

DEFRAGMENTING
WITH DECLUTTERERS

Y ou got a dumpster." Liz Wiltzen grins as she slides her bright blue
Patagonia jacket onto a hanger. Her eyes, the same brilliant blue,
sparkle like she's already proud of me. "We're gonna kick ass today."

"Yeah." I emit a nervous laugh. I'm smiling, but tempted to hide in
the closet behind Liz's puffy blue coat. I bend down and pet Lily, the
golden retriever who's come with Liz from Banff, affording the possibility of her sleeping over if we don't finish today. I'm glad Lily's joined the
canine support squad. This feels like a three-dog job.

Earlier this year, Liz spent over a hundred hours decluttering her own
home, working with Peggy Fitzsimmons, a professional declutter coach
and author of the book *Release*. Peggy's not just an organizational expert,
but also a trained psychologist who helps guide people through the deep-
seated emotion that comes with letting things go, or—as in my case—
even looking at them. Liz is a professional life coach, and I've hired her
to help me get free of the bogeyman in my basement.

When Liz and I discussed this job on the phone, I mentioned the
porn-filled computers so she wouldn't be caught off guard. Still, it's
humiliating. Not only Sean's jam-packed and highly compartmental-
ized hoard, but my own helter-skelter living pattern. All the times I've

stashed kitchen-table miscellany in the laundry room "to put away later."

It's going to take ages to go through all that random stuff. I'm afraid I'll get overwhelmed and fade out when Liz has come all this way to support me. I'm scared I'll waste a bunch of money by stopping to cry or dithering over tins of shoe polish and bags of elastic bands. My stomach was too unsettled to eat breakfast; I can't remember why I thought this was a good idea.

I show Liz downstairs to the laundry room. Its walls are a soft, cheerful orange and the floor tiles are bright orange, lime green, and periwinkle blue. Sean and I chose the wild color scheme to make the space inviting for craft projects. Every flat surface is heaped with small boxes and bags. I hold up a sample bag and show Liz what she's dealing with: scissors, tape, ribbon, scraps of gift wrap, an unopened statement from my cell-phone provider, Nerf bullets, my dogs' rabies tags, and a travel-size bottle of hand lotion.

"Give me a head start," Liz says, so I retreat upstairs and drink a protein shake, hoping for some stamina. Liz is fit and feisty. She's an expert mountain biker who rides year-round, and she and Lily are a trained avalanche-rescue team. If I collapse under the mountain of detritus, at least they'll find me.

Liz calls me downstairs and gestures to a spot on the basement sofa. "We start by defragmenting. You only have to decide on one kind of thing at a time." She brings me a tray. Four pairs of scissors are lined up along the top edge, three upside down along the bottom, blades lined up like piano keys. I blink. *I had seven pairs of scissors?*

Home-organizing shows on television are all about "the reveal." Episodes hinge on the dramatic difference between the unlivable mess and the tidily ever after, where Prince Charming takes the form of cute storage boxes with stenciled labels. The homeowner cries. The audience gets vicarious satisfaction, plus an appetite for cute storage boxes, sold by the show's sponsors.

I've approached decluttering the TV-friendly way several times before, forcing myself into the ruthless mindset of purge, purge, purge and treating the room to a new tablecloth or vase of flowers when I'm done.

Liz's method feels different. I remember stomping around, looking for the damn scissors, thinking they'd been lost, buying new ones. Seeing all seven sets of blades lined up at once, it's clear that having too many scissors is as problematic as not having any. Also, messier. I keep two excellent pairs. One is obvious junk. The other four slide off the tray and into the donation box. I already know that I won't be tempted to buy new scissors next time I'm at a store.

We work, kind-of-thing by kind-of-thing, until 11:00 p.m. I'm bone weary when Liz leashes up Lily, and I clip up both my dogs. We head out all together for a bedtime walk. All day, a rudish question has batted around my brain like a moth. Under cover of the night sky, I let it go.

"Liz, after your first day working with Peggy, you understood the process, right?"

"Yeah."

"So, how come you kept working with her for *a hundred hours*?" It's partly the price tag that makes me ask. It seems counterintuitive to pay money to get rid of things you paid to buy. But with ten hours under my belt, what I'm really wondering is, Once you learn to ride a bike, why hang on to the training wheels?

Liz's expression turns bemused, like she doesn't want to embarrass me with the obvious answer. "Because I couldn't do it by myself."

I stare. Liz is an award-winning artist, a fearless mountain biker, and a successful coach. I'm pretty sure she can do anything.

"Jess, clutter is frozen fear. No one should have to face that on their own."

Back at it first thing in the morning, Liz hands me a tray of papers with a postcard from Peggy's Cove on top. I remember the day in 2007 when Sean mailed it, on a family holiday to Nova Scotia. He was wearing a blue windbreaker and carrying one-year-old Dash on his back. When he zipped into the famous lighthouse to use the post office, I'd thought Sean was sending a postcard to his mom, but a week later this photo card— two adorable puffins standing on a large gray rock—showed up in the mail. I remember his inscription, and tears are forming before I've even flipped it over: "I love you, honey. Puffins mate <u>for life.</u>"

I hold up the card for Liz to see. She sits down next to me on the sofa, tissues at the ready. I take one. "I wasn't expecting to find anything senti-mental." Liz listens as I describe the trip. We'd rented a car and a house in Hubbards. We'd hiked with Dash in a backpack carrier and cycled along an old railway line behind the property every sunny day.

"But one day was gloomy with rain and fog. We spent hours play-ing this Agatha Christie mystery game on Sean's laptop." It was at-mospheric: An isolated house on a stormy coast, teaming up to solve a murder. But by late afternoon the game got glitchy and frustrating. Sean's mood turned as dark as the day. "He was in a funk the whole rest of the night. The next day, we went to Peggy's Cove and he sent me this."

When the postcard showed up in my Calgary mailbox, I delighted in the surprise: a celebration of our immense good fortune to be partners in life's adventure. Now, I wonder: Did Sean write this line as an apol-ogy? Was it a pep talk to himself, white-knuckling his way back onto the marital road he was trying to choose, even way back then? Holding the card, I feel so uncertain. "Part of me wants to keep this because I threw away so many love letters from Sean."

Liz nods, her face solemn and gentle.

"But the feeling that I get reading these words . . . It makes my stom-ach churn."

"Do you want to work with the feeling?"

I shake my head. I just want to let it go. I turn the card message-side-down and drop it into the recycle bin. Goodbye, cute little puffins. Goodbye, collectible postmark from Peggy's Cove lighthouse. Goodbye, tender-yet-cryptic message from Sean. When the emotional wave has receded, we carry on. If Liz weren't here, I'd definitely have bounced out of this task, but her steady presence keeps us on track.

The finish line for the laundry room comes into sight before noon. "We've made great progress," I say. "I don't think we need to do the mechanical room."

Liz is on her way up the stairs with a box of paper. "Let's decide over lunch."

Microwaved minestrone soup and multigrain buns, the same quick lunch I served yesterday. For fun, I watch Lily watch Liz eat. Only a golden retriever could be so fascinated by such humdrum food. Liz opens a small tub of chocolate almonds and offers it to me. I pop one into my mouth.

"So, what if we just crack open the door to the mechanical room and see what it looks like in there?"

Dark chocolate melts on my tongue. It's possible I'm being plied with treats. Or the nourishment of the magical cocoa bean is giving me a boost. Perhaps both. I shrug and nod.

Apart from places where I've disrupted Sean's organizational system, the mechanical room doesn't look cluttered—just well organized and maxed out for storage capacity. An L-shaped commercial-grade desk spans two walls. Sean set up multiple workstations for his various hobbies with pegboard walls holding neatly arranged tools and supplies. There are bins below the desktop, and bins on the shelving above. On the other two walls are floor-to-ceiling IKEA shelves stacked with bins. Each bin approximates an aisle at Home Depot. There's no home repair job for which Sean wasn't prepared and fully stocked.

This room shows me how many things can go wrong in my home. The only person who knew where to find just the right doodad is three years gone. If I throw out the wrong thing, what breaks will be broken forever.

"Round up the dogs and get ready to run. I'm throwing a match in there."

"It won't catch." Liz smiles. "Not enough air."

We go through it. Kind-of-thing by kind-of-fucking-thing. Liz and Lily spend another night. On the third day, I stop Liz from opening the boxes in the last corner. I know what's in them: Tamiya models, toy soldiers, Dinky toys. Childhood treasures and stashed eBay purchases. Something tells me not to get rid of it all right now.

On the first day she was here, Liz took the porn-filled computers to a tech shop to have their hard drives wiped. Her own computer needed service, so she offered to bring them with her, as though it were an errand and not the epic journey to Mount Doom it seemed to me. When I handed the hard drives and computers over to her, something passed between us. Liz told me afterward that it was like I was holding the full weight of shame in my hands.

The infrastructure around the computers—the wall-mounted dual-monitor setup, old-school DVD player and VCR—turned the room into a kind of lair; a sanctuary and prison at the same time. When Sean built models, it grounded and relaxed him. He was never happier than when he was making something. Porn cannibalized Sean's other pursuits.

When he stopped "having time" for his hobbies, Sean kept shopping for them. Instead of creating, he was ordering online and organizing his stash of model-related purchases. Same with LEGO. Same with Christmas decorations, for that matter. The hit of sensation from the purchase replaced the satisfaction of deep creative joy. This is a hallmark of addiction. I have compassion for this and I'm sorry I didn't understand the gravity of it sooner.

Once I recognized the dynamic, bins packed with nested containers became structurally identical to file folders and subcategories within the Matrix of Porn. Seeing the same organizational pattern imposed onto something as morally neutral as finishing nails and drywall screws worked like a poultice on the sting of rejection and loneliness I felt for so long.

In three days, Liz and I have faced it all together. We've donated and recycled vanload after vanload after vanload. When I get the invoice for the dumpster, it will show that we threw away eleven hundred pounds of *stuff.*

Liz does a final vacuum and wipe down of the mechanical room and then brings me back in. "How does it feel to be in this space now?"

I let out a whistle of relief, unaware I'd been holding my breath. My whole body is sore from all the toting and carrying. Liz tilts her blond head to the side. If she's as tired as I am, she doesn't look it. Her eyes are curious.

"So much lighter, but I can't stop thinking. If clutter is frozen fear, then Sean was so afr—" My voice quavers and I swallow.

Liz nods.

"You and I just carried every pound of fear up the stairs and out of the house." I can't describe what's going on inside me. My arms are so tired and shaky they feel like they could float away. I rest one hand on the sheet-metal corner of the furnace stack and tuck the other against the small of my back.

"I feel like, somehow, it's freed Sean, too." The words come out in a rush. I had no idea I was going to say that. "His responsibility for the house, all his compulsions, the weight of the burdens . . . he thought I couldn't love him if I knew."

An untrained person would jump in with a comment here, but Liz stays silent and looks at me intently.

"Sean couldn't stand not finishing things. Yet he left this huge mess behind. And it's all done now. We did it, Liz. There's no more unfinished business here."

Liz opens her arms. For a petite woman, she has an impressive wing-span and she draws me into a powerful hug.

When Dash gets home from school, I lead him down to the transformed space. When we step into the mechanical room, he jumps up and down, laughing. Luggage is stacked neatly on the shelves. The furnace area and hot-water heater are clean and swept. The workspace counter is clear and the tinkering workshop we've set up for him looks inviting—a row of small hand tools along the pegboard, scissors, paintbrushes, and paper towels—ready and waiting to engage with his twelve-year-old imagination.

At dinnertime, when we're settling into the TV room to eat, Dash looks at me and says, "You know the basement?"

"Yeah?"

"I feel like I had an ache that I didn't know I had, and now it's gone."

Dash turns toward the TV and presses the remote. The profile of his face is changing; his jawline is becoming more defined and losing its boyish softness. His hair isn't blond anymore, but turning medium brown, like mine. I know what he means, the vague, gnawing discomfort of living with those rooms the way they were. But that Dash felt it, too, floods me with guilt. I forced him to live with an uneasy knot in his stomach. For years. *I am a terrible mother.*

No. Fuck that. I've worked too hard to let guilt bowl me over.

I could have avoided dealing with the basement for the rest of my life. Maybe that's what purgatory actually is: living around the painful, shadowy parts. Giving the ache a permanent home. I couldn't have cleaned out those rooms until I was ready to face the truth. I couldn't have done it without Liz. Liz couldn't have helped me until she'd done her own work. We did it at the first possible opportunity.

When Dash goes to bed, I run a bath, sprinkling a generous cupful of Epsom salts into the tub and watching the crystals dissolve. Water falls from the faucet, creating small eddies that dissipate and swirl away. This water flows up from our mechanical room, just like the forced air that's blowing through the vent, warming my feet as I peel off my woolen socks. The air we breathe and the water we drink runs through a less congested space now. From our clogged mechanical room to the granulomas that built up in the tissues of Sean's heart, I can see a parallel mechanism at work: things become constricted; vitality gets choked out.

As I slip down into the clear hot water, the muscles in my low back and legs release their grip. The sweat and grime of today's effort wash away. For months after Sean died, I watched his funeral video every night, trying to force out my anger and replace it with sadness. Finally, for the first time since finding the box of Sean's secrets, I feel pure mournful longing for the man I love. The whole man.

THE MOST HURTFUL LIE

Brett's name flits onto my computer screen, commanding my full attention. I haven't heard from Rebekah's husband since I called his office to tell him about the affair. When I turn back to Kathryn, life-size in a full-screen FaceTime window, her mascaraed eyes are curious, mirroring my own astonished look.

"Call you right back." I've hung up and opened Brett's email before Kath has completed her puzzled nod.

Hi Jessica,

It's been a few years since we last spoke. A LOT has happened since then . . . but I am glad it seems you've come so far since Sean's passing (and the events around his life which somewhat entwined us).

I just stumbled upon your website—very strange but the 1st link I hit was the "Kevin Costner guy" . . . so much irony in the nice surprise you received in that box :). At the end you mentioned about it never being too late to reach out—I'm taking this as a very clear sign from the Universe that the timing is right for this communique.

I would love to connect for a chat. I fully understand if you've moved on and will most certainly respect your decision should you not wish to meet/talk.

Bottom line is I hope you're at an amazing place in your life.

Warmest regards,

Brett

Whoa. I read Brett's message twice, heart pounding, then call back and read it aloud to Kath.

"Holy shit! Does he want to date you?"

"What? No."

"We're entwined by the Universe's timing." She's lovey-dovey, teasing.

"That's not how he means it." Having engaged with Brett's vulnerable missive for a full two minutes, I'm surprised by my urge to protect its integrity. But Kath's right, at some level Brett will almost certainly have considered scoring with me as the ultimate act of revenge. I'm familiar with the impulse.

"I've already had vicarious sex with Rebekah." The unwashable-cootie feeling crumples my nose into an exaggerated grimace. "No need to complete the quadrangle."

Kath laughs. "So, are you going to meet him?"

"Maybe." *Absolutely.* Kath's earlier caution against indulging my baser instincts makes me embarrassed to admit the truth. I'm dying to know the impact of my revenge plan on Rebekah. I have other smoldering questions, too: Did she ever acknowledge any wrongdoing? Is it true Brett hooked up with another woman in their hot tub? Are Brett and Rebekah still together?

"What's the Kevin Costner thing?"

"It's the title of a video on my website." People have been sharing stories about their dead loved ones, and I've recorded some onto video. In one episode only, I talked about Sean, after a flood led to my discovering an overlooked condolence book. In the video, I explained how finding the condolence messages brought me comfort at a key moment, and how an inside joke was revealed when one of Sean's colleagues (who I assume bore some resemblance to the handsome actor) signed off as "The Kevin Costner Guy."

The entry by "Kevin Costner" read, "Sean had a genuine and irresistible way of connecting with people. It was an honor to meet and spend time with him—a unique and grand individual. Sean's open and insightful and contemplative way of communicating built amazing belief and engagement with everyone—a special and excellent man. His pureness, energy, vision, ideas and creativity will be greatly missed."

It must have sucked, for Brett, to hear *pureness* commended in a guy who'd been a bona fide douchebag to him. And yet, Brett stuck with the video all the way to the end, where I talked about its never being too late to send a remembrance, or to share your part in another person's story. My whole body is vibrating. "Kath, I posted that video more than a year ago, but it led Brett to reach out now."

"Okay, you gotta meet him. But call me after." The tone of Kath's laughter, as she blesses this absurd but pivotal errand, acknowledges the risk. Meeting Brett could be thrilling, could be edifying, or it could boomerang both of us back to the counselor's couch.

———

Brett's late. I fidget with my phone until his text pings in: an urgent call from his son's high school. Fifteen minutes.

Coffee will jangle my already jittery nerves, but I order a latte anyway, eager for the comfort and camouflage of a warm cup in my hands. *Just coffee, no big thing.* I snag the last free table, a tall two-seater, inches from other patrons. Even with ambient jazz and the din of cappuccinos frothing in the background, I can hear every word spoken among the people beside me. Toddler sleep patterns on one side, projected quarterly shortfalls on the other. Trying to imagine a conversation between Brett and me I'd be okay with other people overhearing, I forget my coffee is a decoy and down the contents of the cup.

Brett walks in. I pop up and meet him just inside the door. We've both aged in the eight years since we last saw each other, but he's still young looking in his late forties, his short hair cut into a stylish fade. During our perfunctory hug, my hand rests briefly on a developed trapezius muscle, palpable even through his jacket. He's an athlete who's never let himself go.

I gesture across the crowded café, point out the table I've secured and its lack of conversational privacy. "You wanna get outta here?"

He gives me a quizzical look. I burst out laughing, realizing what I've said. My face is warm and blushing as we move to the parking lot, deciding on a better venue.

We end up in the sunroom of a quiet restaurant. It's the midafternoon lull, and we have the place almost to ourselves. Sunshine pours through the windows. I tuck my jacket in the corner of the booth and settle in. I order a burger and an iced tea. He gets a cranberry soda.

Brett tells me when I called him back in 2015, he and Rebekah were 90 percent down the road to divorce. He hadn't been a perfect husband. She'd been happy to lay all the blame on him. I nod and listen, remembering I'd been privy to some of what he's telling me through tidbits Sean shared in our daily conversations. Rebekah's confiding so closely in Sean had made me suspect them in the first place.

"What you told me ended up being a light at the end of the tunnel," Brett says. It's been a long process, but their divorce will be finalized soon.

When I first met Brett, I typed him as a hockey boy, of a kind with the billeted players who strutted into my high school as preening kings of the hill. Girls swooned, but never me. I felt a natural immunity, or maybe something closer to a natural fidelity to the boyfriend I loved, and to the part of myself who could anticipate heartbreak. I steered clear of those guys. But my heartbreak-avoidance system was flawed. It failed me with Sean, who I'd felt certain shared my dogged sense of loyalty, and it closed me off from getting to know interesting people over the years. I'm sorry I held Brett against an old stereotype. I can see now he's earnest, reckoning with the same big questions as I am.

Brett mentions he's writing a book. Same here. He's had a lot of physical pain and health problems from the stress of all this. Me, too. He's been learning mindfulness practices to heal. The enemy of my enemy is my new best friend. The server checks to see if we want drink refills. We do.

I tell Brett about a three-day trauma-release workshop I recently completed. "There was a dead ringer for Rebekah in that class. I could barely look at her." I glance over Brett's shoulder as the only other patrons in the restaurant take their leave. "She looked exactly like her, but ten years younger."

"Ten years? Coulda been her. You should see what she spends on plastic surgery."

I raise an eyebrow.

"Well, she kinda has to—a lot of people see her naked."

My burst of wicked laughter encourages Brett to keep going.

"She's got these kinks in the bedroom."

You don't say.

"She's pretty much slept with all her bosses."

Bingo! No wonder she panic-replied when I leveled that very accusation into her work email.

Part of me wants to stop him. I feel like an untrained spy, overloaded with state secrets, my giddy schadenfreude at odds with the trust Brett and I have been building. But I can't make myself relent. I hate her. For what she did, and because my willpower failed every time I tried to forgive her. Even all these years later, she still has the upper hand.

One morning a week, I venture into Rebekah's neighborhood to see my yoga therapist. When I get to the stoplight near the hospital, I hold my breath, worried she's in a nearby vehicle, scoffing at me in my thirteen-year-old minivan. After this lunch, I'll never be nervous about bumping into Rebekah again.

Brett says, "Our son suspected her of cheating on me. He confronted her, and she tore a strip off him so deep, she cut him right to the core."

Gulp. I picture their sixteen-year-old in the kitchen, standing in front of their fancy coffee counter, challenging Rebekah about the affair. I can imagine her yelling, eyes narrow with contempt, her finger pointing into his chest; the strapping young man shrinking into himself, gaslit.

When I wanted to cut Rebekah to the core, I wished for her children to find out *what a worthless, selfish, life-destroying coward their mother really was.* A pang of guilt flares in my belly. I take a sip of iced tea.

Our conversation grows weightier. Brett's mom was hospitalized, in a coma, when the news of Sean's death came in. "I was upstairs getting ready for work when the phone rang—" His refilled soda sits untouched on the table, beads of sweat forming on the glass. "There was this horrible shriek." Brett winces and pulls his head back, recoiling from the sound, even in his memory. "I thought an animal was being attacked outside, but then I heard Rebekah sobbing." He gives me a meaningful look. "I thought my mom had died."

"That must have been awful for you."

"Yeah." His face is tormented with the memory. He blinks twice, behind his glasses, then sets his stubbled jaw. "But she never shed a single tear over my mom."

"That's cold."

"Her children's grandmother." Well-worn lines weave across Brett's forehead.

Sean had told me other women didn't like Rebekah. I have my guesses why, but I keep my mouth shut. We've both said all we needed to say. We chitchat for a few more minutes, then settle with the server.

Our hug at the door is warm. Brett says, "I hope this was half as good for you as it was for me."

It was better.

———

In bed that night, though, my stomach hurts. Snippets Brett mentioned in passing bubble back up. Rebekah's father was a problem drinker. Mine, too. A childhood memory of my young mom, tight-lipped, the color draining out of her face. She'd been straightening up our toy box.

Mom was holding a bottle by the neck, like the ones I'd seen lined up in front of fancy mirrored-glass tiles in people's rumpus rooms. *The possibilities with a bottle like that! Potions and wooden ships and messages across the ocean!* But mom wouldn't put it back in the toy box for my sister and me. The bottle wasn't empty.

A little girl clamoring for possession of a stashed bottle of vodka. That could have been Rebekah, too.

How can I hate a girl whose struggles overlap with my own?

When I assaulted Rebekah's worthiness, I was trying to crush her fucking windpipe. I wanted her to die of shame. I wished for her children to see her as a coward because that was the most hurtful thing I could think to say. Now my wish has come true. Her son has seen his mother wearing the coward's ugliest face: the bully. Her pain is being passed to another generation. I didn't cause it—I know this—but even so, the fulfillment of my wish has hurt a child. That's not the kind of person I want to be.

The next day, my body feels achy and drained. Brett follows up with a text, thanking me for meeting. I thank him back. He told Rebekah about our lunch, and she wasn't pleased. It feels icky, knowing he threw me in her face, but this situation has festered for so long, the fetid resurgence is no surprise.

Brett adds, "It appears she feels no remorse towards what she did to you and me." That should piss me off, but it doesn't. I read Brett's text again, trying to spark some outrage. Nothing.

The way Brett's framed it, expecting Rebekah's contrition looks like a baited steel-jawed trap. The same trap I've been setting for myself all this time, even while she's shown, time and again, she doesn't give a shit about me. Her position has never changed. I don't feel outrage because I can see the hazard. I'm not caught.

Despite the admittedly long odds, I've been able to come to terms with Sean partly because I accepted that I'd never hear the man say, "I'm sorry." Yes, I've sought remorse from him everywhere and finally felt it through a song, but Rebekah's alive. She could make amends (the verifiable kind) if she chose. But if Brett and I need that, we're giving her the power to withhold it. What a torture extender.

Brett and I didn't deserve to be betrayed. We didn't deserve to be lied to. But the most hurtful lie of an affair is the romantic whopper nobody ever apologizes for: two people are moved by an overwhelming chemistry—the whole world falls away.

When Rebekah took up with my husband, I was still here. In creating a relationship with Sean, she also created a relationship with me—not as an unfortunate by-product, but as an inevitability. To this day, she tries to ignore it, but her impact on my life was perceptible long before I knew what was causing the change.

Rebekah's instinct is to erase me from her world. How different is that from my attempt to snuff out her life force in a stranglehold of shame? It's not easy to find common ground with someone who wants to banish you from existence. But at lunch yesterday, Brett changed the equation. The animal wail he heard coming from the kitchen? My body emitted the same tortured cry over the loss of the same man.

That kind of pain isn't just common ground; it's a primordial, alchemical life-altering place. We couldn't see each other, but Rebekah and I were in that pain place together. It's undeniable. She loved Sean, and so did I. That love cost her something, just like it cost me. Maybe sorting out the balance sheet isn't mine to do.

When I tell Kathryn about this later, I'll say, "It's like the spider on roller skates, remember? The Riddikulus spell in *Harry Potter*?" Laughing at Rebekah neutralized her as a monster in my mind, and then, when I recognized her pain, my heart softened and forgiveness just leaked in, like melting snow.

Whose love sustained Sean? That matters less to me today than it did when the affair started; less than when I discovered it; less than yesterday. I still don't like Rebekah. I'm still frustrated by the way the culture seems to reward her modus operandi and punish mine. But her lack of remorse does not aggravate me. Whether that's just for today, or I'm free for good, time will tell.

ESCAPE VELOCITY

In the time since cleaning out the mechanical room, I've felt pretty good, like I've come to terms with Sean, and his continued presence in our lives. Several months ago, I joined a group called Community Healers' Council, led by Sarah Kerr, which has daylong gatherings each month. It's a learning laboratory of experiential practices designed to help us strengthen the bonds within ourselves; to one another; and to the place we live. It's what Joanna Macy terms "the work that reconnects," and it's been helping me learn to trust other people again.

The first few times I went, Dash stayed with friends for the day. I didn't want him to spend twelve hours all by himself, but he's past the minimum age for taking the babysitting course, so when he asked to stay home on his own this month, I agreed. When I came home that night, Dash heard the garage door open and met me at the top of the stairs. His fingertips were speckled with fresh paint, as he held up a toy soldier.

"Wow, look at that! Did you paint it?"

Dash led me to the basement. He'd opened the boxes I'd left un-touched below the workbench and made some amazing discoveries. I can't imagine what he must have felt like—finding a bounty of toys, models, and bric-a-brac—knowing it was once his dad's; knowing it was now his to explore. One file box was full of awards, ribbons, and trophies Sean had won in model-painting competitions as a teenager.

Uncle Riley taught Dash to paint model airplanes. Today, Dash referenced Sean's award-winning models to teach himself how to paint figures. The hobby space Sean set up for that very purpose was once again populated with brushes and toothpicks and little pots of paint. Father-son bonding seemed to have happened in my absence.

It does my heart good to see this is possible, and to see Dash using the space to explore and learn on his own. As much as he needed me near when he was younger, he needs freedom to grow now.

———

On a sunny spring evening, William (liker of tofu and Corfu) drives me to the Killarney Community Centre for a presentation called "A Shamanic Perspective on Death." Sarah recommended the event at our last council meeting. William's best friend is in the late stages of cancer. If anything about this gathering offends William's sensibilities as an atheist and an engineer, I hope there may be at least some benefit in helping him support his friend.

The meeting opens with smudging and drumming, and a short catchy song we're invited to sing along with. The presenter is Barbara "Midnight Rose" Brachi, who looks to be in her late fifties, with long reddish hair. She opens by acknowledging the lineage of wisdom from which she learned what she's about to reveal, then tells us about the Flower Warriors of Oaxaca, Mexico, whose overarching philosophy was "die at the zenith of your power."

To die at the zenith of your power, you must *live as if you know* you could die at any given moment. With Death riding on your shoulder, your life is naturally guided toward a set of principles: You don't owe anyone. You don't procrastinate. You don't hold grudges.

"Having debts or lingering resentments creates a drag on the spirit,"

Barbara says, "and when you become aware of that, Death becomes an ally to help you live your best life. Knowing Death is coming soon is the greatest potential refinement of character we will ever have."

What she's saying is fascinating, and the back of my mind calibrates it against Sean's surface life, which was aligned with the Oaxacan philosophy. "Clean as you go" had been one of his mottoes. He washed measuring cups and mixing bowls while sauces simmered on the stove. His workspaces were always meticulous.

Yet inside, there was so much chaos. Sean didn't die at the zenith of his power, he died at the nadir. It's an awful thought, to have reached such great heights in life, yet fucked up so royally that Death could tap you, in the trough, and leave you circling the drain. The phrase *creates a drag on the spirit* makes me wonder about escape velocity, and what it might mean to launch from a valley rather than a peak.

If we don't live out the full consequences of our actions, do they drag us down and prevent us from dying at the zenith of our power?

I can't stop wondering about it throughout the rest of Barbara's talk. When it's over, I spot Sarah across the room and wave. I take William's hand and we meet up with her in front of the coffee counter. I introduce the two of them, wondering for the first time if they might be related. They have the same last name.

"What did you think of the presentation?" Sarah asks William.

"I wasn't sure I'd connect with it, but it made sense, right off the bat."

I relax a little, relieved to hear William thought it was worthwhile. Over the past couple years, instead of moving toward domestic partnership, William and I have become long-term sweethearts. Bringing him to this presentation felt risky, partly because it's outside our easy-breezy dating pattern, but also because it might consolidate William's position in, what he calls, "the Bermuda Love Triangle."

Later, William will tell me this event was an important turning point. Before tonight, he'd seen his friend as fighting cancer. After, he understood the deathward journey was already underway. It helped prepare

William for what was coming and allowed him to better assist his friend in the final days.

"This was great, Sarah," I say. "Can I come see you to debrief it?"

"Of course." She smiles.

———

Sarah sits opposite me in her red armchair. "Look, it's not that I'm responsible for the eternal fate of Sean's soul," I say, not wanting her to think I'm overcome with hubris, or hopelessly codependent. "But 'drag on the spirit' made me think of something my physiotherapist told me about muscle compensations."

"Go on." Some people wouldn't make the leap between "energetic drag" and the physical body, but Sarah's tracking my line of thought. The shared context of Barbara's lecture has given us latitude to play around with the idea.

"I've had back problems since I was seventeen. Thirty years of compensating patterns, where one muscle does the job of another. I always thought, 'Well, at least the active muscles are getting really strong.' But it doesn't work like that. Compensation patterns actually weaken both muscles. Strength comes when a muscle can efficiently do the job it was designed for."

"I'm with you."

"So, what if the same thing might be true at an energetic level? What if Sean's hanging around here, trying to help Dash and me?" As I say this, I picture a movie character after a split, sneaking over in the night, tending the garden of the family home where he doesn't live anymore. "And I'm over here trying to remedy the awfulness of Sean dying in disgrace. What if we could make it clear: I've got earth life. I'll take care of Dash and the house. You go do your spirit thing. Let's not be tangled and inefficient—you know?"

Sarah nods, "And at the same time you don't want to impede the channel of loving connection that you feel you have with Sean now."

"Exactly." I poise my pen to take down her instructions for what to do next.

"So, what are you going to do?"

Gah. She's Dumbledore-ing me. This past year, I've learned a lot from Sarah through her Community Healers' Council. I'm not the same person who first sat in Sarah's red chair, baffled and brokenhearted a year ago.

There's a long, silent pause. "Well, our wedding anniversary is coming up in about six weeks, and I was thinking that would be a good date to do something to . . . dissolve our marriage contract."

"And negotiate new terms?" Sarah smiles.

"Yes. And as part of the ceremony, I want to ask Sean how he would want me to remember him, now that I understand him more fully than I did when he was alive."

"It's an important question, and I'm getting some sense about what you might do. . . ."

A LIGHT IN THE SKY

As I gather materials for the anniversary ceremony, I notice most of the objects were gifts from writing friends. Tricia sent an abalone shell, I have a quartz crystal pendant from Liz, but nothing to represent Kate Godin, whom I've continued to meet with weekly in the same group.

Kate's funny and smart. She shares a delicate, haunting beauty with the actress Jennifer Connelly, and an edgy, poet's heart with the rocker Patti Smith. I'd have loved to pal around with Kate back in our twenties, when she lived in Manhattan and did freelance writing for high-profile clients like Parsons School of Design and the New School. More than that, I hope to someday hang out with her in the woods of western Massachusetts, where she lives now—or anywhere else on the planet—since we've only ever met online.

It's a little weird to ask someone to send you a gift, but I trust Kate to understand I'm inviting her to stand up for me, like a bridesmaid would if this were an actual wedding instead of . . . an unwedding, or across-the-veil arbitration, or whatever it is that will happen on the anniversary date, July 4.

I email Kate and invite her to send something if she feels called to lend support. In my heart of hearts, I hope she'll write a poem. It would be perfect to seal the ceremony with her skillfully crafted words, asking the question, "How shall I remember you?"

With that road in, I'd be open to whatever answer came.

———

Two weeks before our anniversary, an email comes back from Kate. Reading it, I gasp.

Kate had been invited into a healing circle herself, a sweat-lodge ceremony facilitated by Diné wellness mentor Darryl Slim, to take place on a weekend in mid-June. She'd never been part of anything like it, and as the weekend approached, Kate found herself in a spate of anxiety, anticipating that the experience would be intense, and not sure what it would entail. She was also aware of her commitment to me, and time was ticking to deliver on her promise. In the days leading up to the tepee ceremony, Kate wrote her way through those anxious feelings and peppered her journal pages with the question of how to remember Sean.

The tepee ceremony took place in a hidden field, ringed by trees, on a piece of land where spring water ran so clean those gathered could drink right from the earth. The intricate preparations of building the sweat and erecting the tepee took days. The gathering opened Friday evening and closed Sunday evening, with a final circle the following week.

Steeped in gratitude, and with the smoke of the sacred fire still clinging to her hair, Kate asked aloud, "Hey, Sean, how do you want to be remembered?"

Images swirled up, and as she recorded what she saw in her journal, Kate realized a poem was coming in, and she raced to keep up, to help the message take shape. Its emergence was outside her usual writing process, and she didn't feel, afterward, like it was solely the creative work of Kate Godin.

Kate's email says:

Dear Jess,

*An answer to your question for Sean—how shall I remember you?—
formed as I lay in my tent resting between ceremonies last weekend.
With his permission, I read it aloud when the group re-circled last
night. . . . I wanted them to consecrate it with the powerful, mysterious energy we raised and received over the weekend.*

I'm gobsmacked. Not only because what's come through Kate is an *answer* to my question, but that it was attended to with such care, by a
group in Montague, Massachusetts, whom I may never meet.

There have been times, in my grief, when I've felt completely alone
in the world. To receive a message like this, born thousands of miles
away . . . my hands tremble and it takes a few seconds before I can click
to open the document.

Remember Me Easy

The hard part is over.
Now remember me easy
like ringing a bell
or kissing a baby
or gazing at the moon.
When you forget,
just touch and listen.
anything will do:
a stone, a leaf,
a hand, a heart.
Touch your fingers to it.
Let them rest awhile.
Hear the song.
It is me
as I am

singing to you.
Simple
like the bend in a river
or the fall of a feather
or a single sigh.
The hard part is over
and it is just me
in everything
loving you.

I read the poem a few times over, moved by its simple beauty, its generosity, its gentleness. Then I fold down the laptop screen and walk to
the bathroom. My face in the mirror is blotched red from crying, and
my expression is a grimace, two vertical frown lines etched between my
eyebrows. I splash myself with cold water and pat my face dry. New, hot
tears push their way up as hard as I try to force them down.

Kate's poem has surpassed my wildest expectation. It feels, in
many ways, like a miracle of collaboration, and the breath caught
in my throat is partly astonishment over how these words came into
the world.

At the same time, I feel . . . not jealous, precisely, but somehow left
out. It feels as if, while I was setting the table for an elaborate meal, Sean
dropped by and ate dinner with Kate.

Do I even go through with the ceremony, now that I already have an answer?

I don't tell Kate about my mixed feelings. They're petty and small in
the face of what's been delivered. I'm afraid she'll feel like I'm not happy
with the poem, which is the opposite of the truth. This must be how that
woman at Camp Widow felt, when her neighbor Colleen stopped by
with messages from her late husband.

"Thank you" is my sincere response to Kate. But inside I can't help
but feel this residual, echoing question: *What if that's it? What if I do the
ceremony and Sean doesn't show up?*

On July 4, 1998, Sean and I tied the knot. We'd wanted our nuptials to take place in the garden at the Cross House, a historic house in an eclectic neighborhood near the Bow River, but the rainy weather forced our gathering under cover of a big white tent. We'd planned a morning wedding, mostly because of my dad's tenuous sobriety. Without a boozy reception, I hoped Dad would feel more at ease and find himself able to attend, which he did.

Dad walked me down the aisle, along with Mom, and though some people questioned whether my father deserved the honor, I knew who raised me and I knew who gave me life. When my dad died, three months later, I was never sorry we'd linked arms for that short walk in the rain.

Our friend Steve King played acoustic guitar—the *Princess Bride* theme—to accompany our procession. At the end of the aisle, my parents and I were met by Sean and his parents, all smiling and beautiful as they shook our hands and kissed us on the cheeks. Sean Vincent Waite took Jessica Ann Dunne to be his lawful wedded wife just after 11:00 a.m., and afterward we ate a decadent brunch with so many desserts, the cake was redundant.

This July 4, at 11:00 a.m., I slide my wedding ring back on to the finger where it once belonged. There's comfort in the familiar weight of the chunky gold band, and I feel, for a moment, like the person I used to be.

I slide Sean's ring onto my thumb and draw the two rings close together, so they form an infinity symbol. The Japanese characters engraved into the rings were taken from hand-carved marble hankos, Japanese signatory seals we'd stamped onto our wedding invitations. The friend who carved them embellished mine with stalks of wheat and Sean's with a maple leaf. I found the two marble stamps when Liz and I decluttered the basement.

Twelve hours from now, I'll remove the rings, ending the contract of our marriage in a clear and loving stroke, and hope to overwrite the frazzled and traumatic way things ended after Sean died.

Yesterday, I took Dash to Fish Creek, where he found a stone to represent himself, and one for his dad. I chose stones for myself and Julianne. I prepare a small altar and place the four stones upon it. I gather the marble hankos and our wedding album and leave them at the ready.

———————

By 9:45 p.m., what should be a pale gold horizon has been blocked out by thick dark clouds. The temperature has dropped twenty degrees in two hours. From the looks of the sky, this isn't a storm blowing through, but a fully socked-in night.

Dash is on his bed, rereading a Chris Colfer book. Almost thirteen, he's already prone to fits of nostalgia, and *The Land of Stories* takes him back. "You can read as long as you want, but I'll tuck you in now." I cross the room and sit on the edge of his bed. Some nights, I still lie down next to him at bedtime. It's the time of day when whatever's on his mind comes bubbling out, and I'm happy to sponge it in. But, more and more, he's into his own stories at bedtime. Tonight, that suits me well. "I'll be going out for a few minutes around eleven, but not far away and not for very long. If you wake up and I'm not here, don't worry. I'll be back soon."

"Okay." He's not even a little bothered. His expression is the *trying to be patient with the person who interrupted my book* face. I kiss the top of his head and ruffle his brown hair. "'Night, sweetheart. I love you."

There's a candle on my nightstand and I remember to grab it on my way downstairs, to the little room in the basement where I set up the altar. Following Sarah's instructions, I light the candle and lay a striped silk scarf across the floor. Death is a river that must be crossed. The undulating blue, green, and brown stripes stand in for moving water in the tableau I'm creating.

I sit cross-legged on the floor and imagine my in-laws, Jack and Pat, who met and fell in love and had four kids in seven years. Then, in 1967, Valentine's Day rolled around, and all their little pumpkins were tucked into bed and there was a fire and a bearskin rug, and . . . nine months later, Sean was born. I take the stone that represents Sean and place it on the near side of the river, into a space that represents the Village of the Living.

In 1969, as Sean was toddling around Calgary in footie pajamas, there was a day in Weyburn, Saskatchewan, when Bonnie Bell looked out her window and saw the handsome, young Tom Dunne knocking on her neighbor's door. Bonnie asked to be introduced. A couple years later, when Sean was four, I came into the world. I move my stone into the Village of the Living.

In my mind, I run Sean's and my life stories in tandem, moving the stones closer or farther apart as each of us moved between Saskatchewan, Alberta, BC, and Japan. Finally in 1995, when we fell in love, I bring the stones together to touch. When our babies come, I move Julianne's stone slowly over from the Village of the Living and place her, never born, into the Village of the Ancestors.

The stone I chose for her is smooth, with pretty purple and mauve striations, a little smaller than a kidney bean. It looks tiny, but not lonely, on the far side of the river. Then Dash's stone comes into the Village of the Living, and three stones form the happy triad of our family. I move through the next nine years as slowly and thoroughly as I can, until I come to November 4, 2015. Then I move Sean's stone across the River of Death.

To someone watching, I'd look like a woman sitting on the floor, crying, and playing with rocks in slow motion. But inside it's so much more. I can see, in my mind's eye, a father and daughter on one side of the river, mother and son on the other. No one is suffering or angry or abandoned. We are, each of us, in our right place. At 11:00 p.m., I take off our wedding rings and move them across the River of Death, too.

I turn to a blank page in our wedding album and fix the unsigned card "To My Soul Mate" into place, having decided—at last—it was always meant for me.

"Sean"—I place my hand atop the card—"I promise to make the

most I can out of life and raise Dash to the best of my ability. And I will always, always love you. Thank you for the time we had together."

I stamp the card with my hanko, the signatory seal, in commitment. Then it's his turn. I prepare his hanko by dipping it in the red ink.

"Give 'em the old razzle-dazzle," I say, like I used to on mornings he had a big presentation to deliver. I hope Sean will shine in his new role—be it angel, or vibrational frequency, or deputy minister of afterlife tomfoolery.

"Watch out for us however you can, without compromising the ineffable." I sniffle. And I promise, when my time comes to follow him into the dark, "If you come to meet me, I won't punch you in the face." That hasn't always been guaranteed, but it is now. Sean would laugh. He'd sign off on these terms. I press his hanko next to mine. The two red squares, with our customized squiggles, make it official.

After all that, it's late and I'm worn out, but there's one more thing to do.

Go to the spot.

It's the thing I've known to do since before I made the appointment with Sarah to initiate this ceremony. The call I couldn't ignore, even as I squirmed over whether Kate's poem had made this whole endeavor moot.

Even though it's cold and rainy, even though my body is ready for sleep, something in me insists that I go back to the dog park, to the spot I was standing when Sean said, "The best thing that could happen to you is if I died."

———

My Gore-Tex hood amplifies the percussive downbeat of the rain, and I turn my boots sideways, securing each foothold on the way down the steep hillside. At the base, it's an easy crossing to the other side. I climb up until I reach "the spot." Under the poplar branches, the rain quiets to a pitter-patter. Across the park, leaves flutter and twinkle in the light of a streetlamp.

The sky is gray-amber-pink like an edge of cooked salmon; city lights reflecting against a thick ceiling of cloud. I sit down, cross-legged in the wet grass, and look for the moon, or even the glow of it through the clouds, but the sky is too vaporous and the city too bright. The moon will not show itself tonight.

A few months ago, I made a beaded stone, like the ones I'd seen on Sarah Kerr's table. I take it from my pocket and lie back into the grass, resting the stone against my chest. Its pressure steadies my heartbeat. Rain falls cold onto my face, and I trace the pattern of the beads in the stone's mandala design, remembering Kate's poem.

anything will do:
a stone, a leaf,
a hand, a heart.

I lower my hands into the grass. The blades are reedy and tough, like wet straw between my fingers. Soon, my knuckles ache from the chill.

Kneeling now, blowing warmth into my hands, I watch the sky until I realize I'm waiting. I want something big to show up, like an eagle or an apparition, or lightning flashing out my name. It's greedy, in the face of Kate's poem, to hold out for more. I turn my attention back to the raindrops and the dappled poplars. There's no spectacle, just a neighborhood on a rainy summer night.

As I look across the steep hillside, my mind plays memories from another season: Sean gliding down that slope on a toboggan, holding our snowsuit-bundled toddler on his lap, the dogs bounding along in their snowy wake. Whooping and woofing and Dash laughing, "Again! Again!"

I'm gathering myself to leave when a light appears, dawning just over the cinder-block wall that runs along the south side of the hill.

It must be a plane, but it's so low on the horizon, and there's no engine noise at all.

I track the light as I negotiate my way down the wet hillside. The oval orb grows larger in the sky. My boot skids in the slippery grass and I run to catch my balance, keeping my eyes on the light as it grows larger, drawing nearer and nearer until finally a roar breaks through the muffle of wind and rain. I spread my arms wide, like a child, running to meet it.

The plane passes directly over my head, and in that fleeting, perfect moment I am finally certain: there are souls, right there, in the sky above me—and some of them are coming home.

EPILOGUE

Wow. We made it. Thank you for sticking with me!

One astute reader suggested I'd been "a little coy" about my own beliefs vis-à-vis Sean. She's right. For me, it was paramount that readers decide for themselves what to believe. Discernment is an essential skill, something to hone at every opportunity.

Assuming you've already drawn your own conclusions, I'll venture this: for every unusual-seeming encounter I included here, many others were omitted from the page. Jolene was one of three body workers who came back with messages for me. Margaret was one of three intuitive people who foresaw me writing a book. Once, in Scottsdale, Arizona, a maître d' said, "I'm putting you in purgatory," and seated me all alone in a closed section of the restaurant. A few minutes later, Martha Beck and Elizabeth Gilbert walked in (with Rowan Mangan and Liz Dawn). The VIP section had been reserved for them. As I debated going over to introduce myself, I heard a voice say, *You'll sit at that table when you're invited.*

I omitted writing-related stories so as not to invoke a "chosen one" narrative. (Remember what Sean said: "There's no *Great One.*") Luke Skywalker had Leia, Han, and Chewie. Harry Potter had Hermione and Ron. Frodo had Samwise Gamgee to carry him when he couldn't go on.

Heroes never do it alone. Sidekicks are quiet heroes in their own right. The less exceptional anyone thinks I am, the better job I'll have done in relaying this story. Your natural capacity to connect with your loved ones is just as powerful as mine.

That said, I wasn't the only member of the Waite clan whose television turned on by itself, nor the only one whose "normal life" was interrupted by unexplainable phenomena. I won't name names. Each person's experience is theirs to share; hold dear; explain away or forget. But, because what they told me mapped onto my own experience, I have a high degree of confidence that Sean hung around for a while after his death. Also, I believe he helped me tell this story. If you'd been with me every step of the way, I suspect you might agree.

How's everyone doing, five years hence, with a global pandemic in the interim?

A quick update . . .

Dash: It can't have been easy to grow up in a home where this book was being written. However, after teaching himself to play guitar and drums during the COVID lockdown, Dash is thriving. He's a D&D Dungeon Master, a songwriter and musician, with a teenage band called Method to Madness who jokingly self-assess as "good enough to open for Weezer." They practice in our back garage (which reminds me to keep an eye on Sean's secret compartment). They're fine young men, with talent, dedication, and big dreams. I'm proud of them all, especially the tall, handsome drummer with the beautiful heart and the gift for rhyme.

Jenn: We cool.

Ty: Back in Calgary after a three-year stint in Ontario, Ty's in a different job. His heart broke when I told him the title of this book. "More people will see the title than read the book" was his primary concern. As Sean's big brother and longtime protector, I understand Ty's reaction. I'm sorry for the pain of it, and for whatever unwanted attention comes from those who'd be insensitive or judgmental toward his family. Still,

Ty doesn't hold grudges and we love each other. We're getting closer and closer to fine.

(Btw, how can we get everyone who sees the title to read the book? That would solve *everything*, wouldn't it?)

Scott: Jokingly suggested this title. We both think Sean would be okay with it.

William: Still swimming in the Bermuda Love Triangle.

Bonnie: My mom had a heart attack in 2018, and though she bounced back, she never recovered full health. The next several years were riddled with medical crises (between games of golf, canasta, and mah-jongg). Bonnie passed peacefully with Catherine, me, and her grandchildren by her side on May 15, 2022. We miss her.

Woodward: The cleverest and most determined dog I ever knew. As Sean and I drove to pick him up as a puppy, the car radio revealed the identity of Deep Throat (the source who'd led Woodward and Bernstein to break the Watergate story). Sean had read every Watergate book and was effervescent with the news: "Let's name our pup after Bob Woodward!" (Our next dog was meant to be Bernstein, but puppy Panda proved too much of a goofball.) Woodward died in 2020, at age fifteen.

Sean: I have it on good authority that Sean Vincent Waite crossed to the light on September 11, 2022. Perhaps I'll share those details another time. Six months later, I had a finished manuscript, a literary agent, and a signed contract with one of the top publishers in the world. (Bonus, an acquiring editor who's worked with Bob Woodward. Sean would be starry-eyed.)

Me: First, mea culpa. While it would be easy to let Sean's egregious behavior stand in for every problem in our relationship, I need to acknowledge my biggest regret: I wanted Sean to be everything to me. It may sound trite, but he was my closest confidant, my best friend, my strongest advocate, my most hilarious companion, my lover, our breadwinner, our Mr. Fixit, the imaginer and deliverer of our biggest dreams. There's a kind of tyranny in expecting someone to be all those things, for you, all the time. I was lucky to partner with someone who could fulfill so many of those roles, so much of the time. I wish I'd realized this sooner and released some of the pressure Sean must have felt to be a superhuman husband. Also, I wish I'd found ways to give myself more of what I needed rather than waiting for Sean to deliver it. I've learned from those mistakes and don't intend to repeat them.

My drive to put context around Sean's death and heal my broken heart brought me into proximity with some brilliant scientists, physicians, and scholars over the past eight years. In combining that learning, I've developed a mental model of grief that accounts for what I experienced (both the physical changes and the reciprocal nurturing relationship between the living and the dead). An essay I wrote about this won a literary award in 2022. I'll sneak it in here (if Bob Woodward's editor approves).

IN DEFENSE OF GRIEF

Picture the Incredible Hulk, but instead of becoming a muscle-bound green rage machine, a cognitive scientist transforms into an embodiment of agape, the highest form of unconditional love. I saw this happen once, on YouTube.

John Vervaeke, an award-winning professor at the University of Toronto, appears in a two-panel Zoom conversation hosted by psychologist—and lightning rod for the culture wars—Jordan Peterson. Behind Vervaeke are shelves full of philosophical textbooks. When he speaks, it's evident he's read them all.

About forty minutes into their dialogue on the nature of distributed cognition, Peterson puts forth the catalyzing question "What is love to you, John?"

Vervaeke softens and glows. His voice grows warm. He mentions his long-term partner and says that in loving this woman he cultivates a space inside himself for her to inhabit.

"She finds purchase in me whereby she can realize herself. . . ."

He means *realize* in both senses of the word: She *understands* herself, and she *makes herself more fully real*. The kind of real that turns a wooden puppet into a living boy. The kind of real I *think* I am, until I encounter another, who alters my world and allows me to become *more*—just through knowing them. Vervaeke's girlfriend becomes real for me, through the timbre of affection in her lover's voice.

"She can come to trust that this space of realization will always be available to her." There's a mounting passion in Vervaeke's manner, and my heart pounds as I listen. "And she can come to rely on it: a place where she can transcend herself when she needs to." He describes this reciprocal process as vital to his own ability to realize who he is.

"That's the core of what it is to love somebody."

Vervaeke's eyes shine behind his rectangular glasses, and tears well in mine, feeling the profundity of the couple's love. Vervaeke has just shown me how it was that I came to fall in love with my husband, despite our unpromising start, when I compared his body—redolent of thrice-weekly pub nights—with my own, shaped by years of collegiate basketball. Our five-inch height differential tipped in my favor. I would never have agreed to go out with Sean except that we'd forged a friendship over a five-day statutory holiday in Japan, when I was the only other English speaker he knew in the entire country.

We'd spent that whole week together, meeting each day to tackle a new adventure. The day we hiked through the bamboo forest where Thomas Edison had procured the filament used in the first light bulb, Sean speculated on the way history might have changed if Nikola Tesla's vision of free electricity had won out over Edison's for-profit model. We talked it over, sharing bento-box lunches in the visitors' area, until an amateur artist who'd been sketching *en plein air* approached with a drawing he'd made of the two of us. I glanced at the paper, noticing the way my baggy blue sweatshirt rippled into a Jabba the Hutt silhouette, and that Sean's nostrils looked suited to rooting out truffles. I nodded at the artist and forced a smile. Sean opened his wallet and gave the man two thousand yen.

"You just paid twenty bucks for a picture of yourself with a pig snout."

"I like it. It's a good moment."

For seven months before he asked me for a date, Sean had held a picture of us together. He created a space for me within himself, so that when I finally looked in his direction, I saw in him a place for me that only existed because Sean had created it, in his heart, and with his mind.

I modeled Sean inside myself, too. And over our twenty-year life together, I developed a special sensitivity for occasions when stressors pushed things out of balance for his nervous system. "You ground me," Sean said, many times, holding my hand and gazing into my blue eyes, where he found a portal to a more serene version of himself. "I do better when you're near."

When Sean was felled by a heart attack, the Jess space he had created, the home for me inside himself, that place I'd come to trust would always be available . . . vanished in an instant.

The Sean space inside me—forged over decades by my skin cells, my auditory system, my olfactory receptor neurons—was severed from the being who lit it up. My every breath sampled the air for the mix of sweat, cologne, and leather where his jacket collar met the nape of his neck. Every retinal cell scanned for him in public spaces. The tips of my fingers reached for him in those hypnagogic moments before I fully woke up and remembered he was gone. I felt the void of a Sean-shaped avatar, a hole in my neuroanatomy, and the biological imperative to re-encode all those severed synaptic connections.

Listen, I know the difference between medical reattachment of nerve endings and the semimetaphorical ones I've just described. Six months before Sean died, my best friend was hit by a bus. Her injuries were numerous and critical and included a fracture of her cervical spine. Her left arm was paralyzed and eventually required complex neurosurgery—a brachial plexus triple nerve-transfer—to restore function. Because her surgery and follow-up appointments required her to travel to Calgary, where I live, she stayed with me and I took notes at all those medical appointments. Her surgeons and physical therapists emphasized two key determinants to her recovery:

1. Patience: Axons grow about one millimeter per day. Nerve re-
   growth can take over a year.
2. Persistence: The receptor has to remain alive, so that when the
   nerve grows into place, a connection can happen. Mirror imag-
   ing and visualization help keep synapses viable.

My friend has done physiotherapy, five days a week, for more than six
years. She still has pain and residual effects, but she's recovered to the
point that you'd never know she was once paralyzed. As she continues to
improve, she's become a medical marvel and a beacon of hope for those
newly injured.

She's an inspiration to me, too. Following her lead, I toiled in the
wake of Sean's death, trying to recalibrate to my new reality. I did grief
counseling, trauma work, drum circling, art journaling, TRE tremoring, shamanic healing, holotropic breathing, somatic experiencing, yoga
therapy, compassionate inquiry, life coaching . . . I even wrote a book.
Each of those things helped in its own way. The only thing that hasn't
worked is cookie-dough ice cream, but perhaps the thousandth time will
be the charm. At any rate, I feel better and stronger than before, but I still
cry almost every day, and I still feel like a part of me has died. (Because
the part of me that existed within Sean *did*.)

Thanks to the American Psychiatric Association's 2020 revision of
their diagnostic manual (*DSM-5*), I find that I've suddenly contracted a
mental illness: prolonged grief disorder. My lingering symptoms—and
the fact that it's been more than twelve months since my husband's passing—would qualify me, were I to appeal for psychiatric intervention.
The World Health Organization guidelines for this diagnosis include the
occurrence of a "persistent and pervasive grief characterized by longing
for the deceased, or persistent preoccupation with the deceased accom-
panied by intense emotional pain."

Ahem. Try writing a grief memoir without *all of the above.*

I get it; the physicians who approved this update are inundated with suffering people, clamoring for help, every single day. Pain sucks, being functional feels fantastic, and if meds weren't at least sometimes helpful, they'd have fallen out of use by now. But if this diagnosis had existed sooner, and I'd gone straight to a prescription on day 366, I might have missed out on a lot of healing. Remember what those other doctors told my friend: patience and persistence. Keep your receptors alive.

One of the reasons I follow John Vervaeke is that he advocates for a map that includes four different kinds of human knowing, all equally legitimate. My friend and her neurosurgeon are both expert in brachial plexus injury, but *what* they know and *how* they know it differs. Each perspective has incredible value, and each of them has earned their vantage-specific knowledge.

For me to shout, "But wait! Are you sure prolonged grief is really a *disorder?*" to the governing bodies of the WHO and APA feels not only quixotic but also hapless, like I'd be inviting "expert-denial disorder" (an instantaneous epidemic, per societal response to COVID) to be added to their roster.

So let me temper my voice and gently confide: just like my friend goes to physio almost every day, I go to grief. Its saline hydro-jets wash through me. Its enormous weight topples me into the cocoon of my bed. Its hulking power trickle-charges the parts of me that feel as though they'll die without Sean. Based on the careful attention I've paid my own experience, the hypotheses I've batted around with people wiser than me, and the discourse I've studied from subject-matter experts, what heals pain and sorrow is the very thing that keeps our receptors alive: unconditional love. Presence. Agape.

It's not easy to find that safe, nonjudgmental state in my darkest hours. It becomes even harder if I see myself as disordered.

In the early days after Sean's death, my perceptions became altered: food had no taste; activities I used to enjoy held zero appeal; everyday sounds registered as far too loud. These are well-documented symptoms of grief. But I also experienced things that were *not* listed on the grief pamphlets in my counselor's office. And since the APA's got my number anyway, I'd might as well cop to at least some of that.

Six weeks after my husband's heart attack, I felt faint in the stacks at my local library. I crouched down on the industrial carpet, head between my knees, and when I looked up, all the books were blurry except one. I focused on the only thing I could see clearly: a tiny green button in the shape of a heart, embellished onto the spine of a book. I took the book home with me and found that its plot overlaid directly onto my life, in a way that was both uncanny and deeply comforting.

That day, 136,000 books were in circulation. Long odds, but coincidences happen. A few weeks later, though, the same phenomenon happened *again,* and I started asking a lot more questions.

Altered eyesight (not on the grief pamphlet) may not be categorically different from intolerance to loud noises (on the grief pamphlet). But why should the death of another human affect my hearing in the first place? And feeling as though one is being guided toward books that prove to be stepping stones forward in one's life? That's a whole other kind of sea change.

What I've learned, though, is that these guidance-on-the-down-low experiences are *not* rare. Other people have them, too, but stay quiet for fear of judgment and ridicule. People who've witnessed or studied death and grieving outside the dominant North American tradition could rightly be saying "Duh" right now, but I could only know what my culture transmitted, until my lived experience showed me something else.

What if the function of grief—in all its wild and uncomfortable expression—is to guide human beings to a deeper understanding of the nature of life?

Early on, I white-knuckled my way through a series of interminable, meaningless days. I could have continued doing exactly that until the date of my own expiration. But with my perceptions heightened to some phenomena and dimmed to others, I began to grope my way forward.

Grieving allows me to accept that everyone and everything I love is going to die, including me. When I live as if I understand these things, life becomes more vibrant and fulfilling.

Over the long term, grief has helped me find purchase—not just inside the people I love, but within this whole vast and mysterious world—and to realize, as Mary Oliver put it, *my place in the family of things.* I'm pleased to report that I no longer suffer from Happily Ever After Disorder. I hold my medical options carefully, find companionship in mourning, and patiently tend to my ever-breaking heart.

CHERRY GIN JAM

This delicious jelly-jam can be made with any variety of small sour cherries—and you can use as many as you manage to harvest, preferably from your own back yard or that of a friend. Add a shot of gin if you like, or leave it out.

"Why was I making cherry jam in the first place? I'd heard the wonderful Julie Van Rosendaal on the radio. Somehow, she convinced my culinary-averse self that I could make jam with fruit from my own tree.

Here's Julie's inspiring recipe. I added a dollop of mulled wine caramel. This one will be just as delicious without it."

INGREDIENTS

Nanking cherries

water

sugar

lemon juice

pectin

DIRECTIONS

Put as many cherries as you've managed to pick into a large pot, add half a cup to a cup of water (less than a cup if you have under 8 cups of berries; a cup if it's more) and bring to a simmer over medium-high heat. Cook until the cherries soften and start to release their juices, mashing occasionally with a potato masher.

Strain the mixture through a cheesecloth-lined sieve set over a bowl—or use a jelly bag if you have one. Leave it if you want a clear jelly, or swirl a spoon around in the sieve to coax out as much juice as you can. When you get out as much as you can, toss the sludge with all the pits in it, and put the juice back into the pot.

Measure out about as much sugar as you have juice and set it aside. Add about 1 Tbsp lemon juice per 2 cups of juice to the pot, and shake in some packaged pectin, about a package per 8-10 cups of juice, less if you have less, and you don't need to be precise with your measurement. Bring the juice–pectin mixture to a full rolling boil, then stir in the sugar. Bring it back to a full, hard boil for 2 full minutes—this means a rolling boil you can't stir down. Remove from the heat and skim any foam off the surface. Stir in a shot of gin or two—about a shot per 4-5 cups. Ladle into hot, clean jars, seal and cool.

Makes as much as you like.

JULIE VAN ROSENDAAL

writes about food for *The Globe and Mail*, *WestJet Magazine*, *Western Living*, *City Palate*, *Avenue*, and other publications, and the recipes from her weekly *Eyeopener* columns are posted on the *CBC Calgary* website every Tuesday.

ACKNOWLEDGMENTS

In a sense, this whole book is an acknowledgement of the grace I experienced, living and writing this story. I could fill another three hundred pages thanking everyone who helped along the way.

To the Waite family, en masse: Thank you. I love you. Please forgive me. I forgive you.

Betsy Rapoport, without your early and unwavering support this book would not exist. You said you'd say you knew me when. I'm humbled to say I know you at all. Thank you, for everything.

Amar Deol, Adrienne Kerr, Jenny Xu, Justin Stoller, Hannah Frankel, Ifeoma Anyoku, Falon Kirby, Dayna Johnson, Lisa Wray, Cali Platek, and the entire team at Simon & Schuster. It's been incredible to collaborate with you. Thank you for your expertise, diligence, and faith.

Stacey Kondla, what a wild ride! May all your future deals be so dizzyingly fast and joyful.

To my mentors: Gail Anderson-Dargatz, Rona Altrows, Lorri Neilsen Glenn, Naomi K. Lewis, Lauren Carter, and Ali Bryan. Each of you is unsurpassed in skill, generosity, warmth, and talent. Your fingerprints are woven into this story. I'm so glad they're still visible to me.

To my (many) teachers: how amazing you are! I started from scratch with Write Into Light, then found peers and instructors through Alexandra Writers' Centre, Kelly Madrone's *Book Lab*, Rachel Thompson's *Writerly Love*, Omar Mouallem's Pandemic University, Sarah Selecky's Writing School, Marion Roach Smith, *Writing Down the Bones*, Claire Bidwell Smith, Tembi Locke, Writer's Bridge, Jane Friedman, WGA, Sage Hill, and more. Thank you, one and all.

To writing peeps: Rhonda Seiter, Tricia Elliott, Kate Godin, Liz Wiltzen, Lisa Yahne, Brian Pearson, Suzanne Johnston, Allan Cooper, Anne Marie Nakagawa, Deanna da Paoli, Anna Marie Sewell, Linh Huynh, and Ferrukh Faruqui. WIL friends, Naomi's Protegés, and my book club: Renate, Melody, Lilianne, Kathy, Andrea, and Sandie. Your feedback and support made *everything* better.

I'm grateful for the camaraderie and wisdom of Community Healers' Council, Martha Jo Atkins' *D-School*, Bayo Akomolafe's *We Will Dance With Mountains,* Bonnitta Roy's *Pop-Up School*, The Stoa, Rebel Wisdom, and the indomitable 24-Hour Café.

To the fleet of professionals who tended my ouch-y parts with such care, thank you for easing the pain: Chandy, Tracy, Angie, Fiona, Sarah, Margit, Steve, Shellan, Cindy, Susi, Kelli, Bonnie, Brett, Patricia, Jane, Marv, Gabriella, Ariana, Rhonda, Tricia, Claire, Martha, Betsy, Carly, Philip, Allyson, Lynn, Michael, and Jolene.

This book is set in many locations and populated by people from many different cultures. While I'm trying to write in the spirit of respect, relationality, and truth, there will certainly be places where my limited perspective is lacking. For the most part, this story was written in a place traditionally know as Moh'kinsstis, on the territory of the Blackfoot confederacy: Siksika, Kainai, Piikani, as well as the Iyarhe Nakoda and Tsuut'ina nations, and the Métis Nation Region 3. It's a bountiful, beautiful place to call home.

Thank you, Lisa Yahne and Ryan Waite, for putting your incredible talents into creating artwork and animations to represent the visual elements of the story so powerfully.

Thank you Gail Baxter, Nathalie Babineau, and Allison Lane for helping me think creatively about reaching readers. Thank you Shelley Youngblut for bringing world-class storytellers to Calgary. Wordfest's continual inspiration was a lifeline.

Thank you, Leah Pohlman, for being a champion of reading and a library liaison extraordinaire.

To William, the most faithful and diligent proofreader I've ever encountered, I'm not sure how you did it. (Now, read the part about how great Sean was . . .) I'm lucky you're a patient man. Next stop, Corfu.

Without you, Erin Waite, I'd have curled into the fetal position in 2015 and stayed put. Thank you for being there at every stage, and for the countless hours you've volunteered to help ensure this book finds its readers. You're a stalwart friend and inspiration.

Dash, I'm so happy you are my son. Sorry you've had to read this now. These are not things I'd have wanted to know about my parents as a teen. I hope time serves this story well, so that someday, when you're as old as I am, you'll understand how amazing you are and how loved you've been, every millisecond of your life.

FUSW. For you, Sean Waite.

ABOUT THE AUTHOR

Jessica Waite never realized she was a latchkey kid because she lived so close to her small-town library. Now she leads people to heal through writing and mentors incarcerated writers through the Hero's Journey Prison Writing Project. She's an award-winning essayist who lives on Treaty 7 territory, in Calgary, Alberta. You can find her at jessicawaite.work.